Regulating the End of Life

Regulating the End of Life: Death Rights is a collection of cutting-edge chapters on assisted dying and euthanasia, written by leading authors in the field.

Providing an overview of current regulation on assisted dying and euthanasia, both in the UK and internationally, this book also addresses the associated debates on ethical, moral, and rights issues. It considers whether, just as there is a right to life, there should also be a right to death, especially in the context of unbearable human suffering. The unintended consequences of prohibitions on assisted dying and euthanasia are explored, and the argument put forward that knowing one can choose when and how one dies can be life-extending, rather than life-limiting. Key critiques from feminist and disability studies are addressed. The overarching theme of the collection is that death is an embodied right which we should be entitled to exercise, with appropriate safeguards, as and when we choose.

Making a novel contribution to the debate on assisted dying, this interdisciplinary book will appeal to those with relevant interests in law, socio-legal studies, applied ethics, medical ethics, politics, philosophy, and sociology.

Sue Westwood is a Lecturer in Law at York Law School, University of York, UK.

Regulating the End of Life

Death Rights

Edited by
Sue Westwood

Routledge
Taylor & Francis Group
a GlassHouse Book

First published 2022
by Routledge
2 Park Square, Milton Park, Abingdon, Oxon OX14 4RN

and by Routledge
605 Third Avenue, New York, NY 10158

a GlassHouse book

Routledge is an imprint of the Taylor & Francis Group, an informa business

British Library Cataloguing-in-Publication Data
A catalogue record for this book is available from the British Library

Library of Congress Cataloging-in-Publication Data
A catalog record has been requested for this book

ISBN: 9780367333539 (hbk)
ISBN: 9781032073293 (pbk)
ISBN: 9780429329739 (ebk)

DOI: 10.4324/9780429329739

Typeset in Bembo
by codeMantra

For my cousin,

Marion Christmas (née Felton) MBE.

If she sees an injustice, she does something about it, just like her father taught her.

Contents

Contributors

Editor

Sue Westwood is a Lecturer at York Law School, University of York, UK. She is both a social gerontologist and a feminist socio-legal scholar, interested in ageing, diversity, and equality in regulatory contexts. She is particularly concerned with the quality of health and social care provided to older people, people with dementia, and those at the end of life.

Contributors

Isra Black is a Lecturer in Health Law at the UCL Faculty of Laws, specialising in normative jurisprudence, medical treatment decisions, the end of life, and health and human rights. Isra is an Associate Member of the Rotman Institute of Philosophy, Western University. Previously, Isra was a Lecturer in Law at York Law School, University of York and held postdoctoral posts at Karolinska Institutet and Technische Universität München. Isra has been a Visiting Fellow in the Department of Philosophy, Stockholm University and twice a resident researcher at the Fondation Brocher, Switzerland. Isra received his PhD for research on assisted death from the Centre of Medical Law and Ethics and Dickson Poon School of Law, King's College London.

Glenys Caswell is a sociologist whose research interests centre on the social management of dying and death, with a particular interest in the notion of dying alone and the ways in which such deaths transgress social norms. Projects on this topic include the Leverhulme Trust-funded 'Exploring the social management of lone deaths' and publications include 'For some people dying alone is not such a bad thing – here's why', The Conversation, January 2018, https://theconversation.com/for-some-people-dying-alone-is-not-such-a-bad-thing-heres-why-90034.

Katrine Del Villar is a Postdoctoral Research Fellow and member of the Australian Centre for Health Law Research in the Faculty of Business and Law at the Queensland University of Technology, from which she received her PhD in Law in 2020. Her research focusses primarily on end of life legal issues and mental health and capacity law. She has also been employed on a project funded by the Western Australian Department of Health to provide legal training to medical and nurse practitioners on voluntary assisted dying. Katrine is admitted to practice as a Barrister and Solicitor of the Supreme Court of the Australian Capital Territory, and was previously a solicitor in private practice. Prior to working in academia, Katrine also served as associate to Justice Gaudron of the High Court of Australia, and worked for the Commonwealth Parliamentary Research Service.

Ari Gandsman is a cultural and medical anthropologist and Associate Professor in the School of Sociological and Anthropological Studies at the University of Ottawa in Canada. His work examines the intersection of medical, legal, and ethical questions in the context of limit-experience. He has conducted fieldwork on human rights organizations in post-dictatorship Argentina and right to die activism in North America and Australia. His work has been published in a wide range of journals, and as chapters in edited volumes.

Richard Huxtable is a Professor of Medical Ethics and Law and Director of the Centre for Ethics in Medicine, in the Medical School at the University of Bristol, UK. Much of his research concerns end-of-life decision-making, with his books including *Euthanasia, Ethics and the Law: From Conflict to Compromise* (2007, Routledge); *Law, Ethics and Compromise at the Limits of Life: To Treat or Not to Treat?* (2012, Routledge); and *Euthanasia: All That Matters* (2013, Hodder & Stoughton). He is Principal Investigator on a major Wellcome Trust collaborative project, Balancing Best Interests in Health Care, Ethics and Law (BABEL). He tweets at @ProfRHuxtable.

Penney Lewis studied mathematics, law, and philosophy in the US, Canada, and the UK, where she is a Professor of Law and co-Director of the Centre of Medical Law and Ethics, King's College London, UK. Penney is on secondment to the Law Commission as commissioner for criminal law. In the area of medical law, her research focusses on end-of-life issues including advance decision-making, refusal and withdrawal of treatment. She has published widely on assisted dying including her 2007 OUP monograph *Assisted Dying and Legal Change*. She is a member of the Human Tissue Authority and the Clinical Ethics Committee of St Christopher's Hospice, and was a member of the UK Donation Ethics Committee.

Alex Ruck Keene is an experienced barrister, writer, and educator. His practice as a barrister at 39 Essex Chambers is focussed on mental capacity and mental health law. He also writes extensively in the field, editing and contributing to leading textbooks and (among many other publications) the 39 Essex Chambers Mental Capacity Law Report, the 'bible' for solicitors (and others) working in the area. He is the creator of the website http://www.mentalcapacitylawandpolicy.org.uk/, providing resources and expert commentary on some of the most difficult mental capacity issues. Alex is a Wellcome Research Fellow and a Visiting Lecturer at King's College London; a Visiting Senior Lecturer at the Institute of Psychiatry, Psychology and Neuroscience, King's College London; and a Research Affiliate at the Essex Autonomy Project, University of Essex. He spent 2016 on secondment to the Law Commission as a consultant to their Mental Capacity and Deprivation of Liberty Project and throughout 2018 was a legal adviser to the Independent Review of the Mental Health Act 1983. Alex acted for Noel Conway at all stages up to and including the Supreme Court in his challenge to the compatibility of s.2(1) Suicide Act 1961 with the European Convention on Human Rights.

Thomas F. Tierney is a Professor of Sociology at The College of Wooster (Ohio, USA), and has served as a National Endowment for the Humanities Visiting Scholar (Otterbein University) and a Visiting Fellow at the Center for Biomedicine and Society (King's College London). His research focusses on the values that shape technological development, including biotechnological development. He is the author of *The Value of Convenience: A Genealogy of Technical Culture* (SUNY, 1993), and numerous articles that employ social theory to interpret the implications of advanced medical technologies, such as the growing "bioeconomy" of human tissues and the "right to die" movement.

Els van Wijngaarden works as an Associate Professor in Care Ethics at the University of Humanistic Studies, Utrecht, in the Netherlands. With her PhD on 'completed life in old age', she was the first to explore experiences of relatively healthy older people with a strong wish for a self-directed death as they considered their lives no longer worth living. Her study was awarded the prestigious Research Prize 2017 of the Praemium Erasmianum Foundation. With her current line of research, she builds on this pioneering work, focussing on death and dying in old age with a specific interest for the role of choice and control at the end-of-life.

Ben P. White is Professor of End-of-Life Law and Regulation and a member of the Australian Centre for Health Law Research in the Faculty of Business and Law at the Queensland University of Technology. Ben's area of research focus is end-of-life decision-making and his work is interdisciplinary with publications in law, medicine, bioethics and social science journals. He is undertaking a program of research examining law, policy and practice at the end of life through a series of Australian Research Council and National Health and Medical Research Council grants. He is currently undertaking a four-year Australian Research Council Future Fellowship: *Optimal Regulation of Voluntary Assisted Dying.*

Elizabeth Wicks is a Professor of Human Rights Law in Leicester Law School at the University of Leicester. Her research expertise focuses primarily on issues of human rights in healthcare, bodily autonomy and the right to life. Her books include *Human Rights and Healthcare* (Hart, 2007), *The Right to Life and Conflicting Interests* (OUP, 2010) and *The State and the Body: Legal Regulation of Bodily Autonomy* (Hart, 2016). She is currently working on a new book about suicide and the law.

Lindy Willmott is a Professor of Law and member of the Australian Centre for Health Law Research in the Faculty of Business and Law at the Queensland University of Technology. She researches extensively in the health law field, particularly at the end of life. She has co-authored multiple texts as well as the website 'End of Life Law in Australia', and is involved in empirical research projects funded by the Australian Research Council and the National Health and Medical Research Council. Lindy co-leads a project funded by the Commonwealth Department of Health to provide legal training to medical specialists, and projects funded by both the Victorian Department of Health and Human Services and the Western Australian Department of Health to provide legal training to medical practitioners on voluntary assisted dying.

Anthony Wrigley is Professor of Ethics at Keele University, UK. His research interests are primarily on philosophical issues in bioethics, with a particular focus on questions about the margins of life. Much of his work has been in the areas of palliative and end-of-life ethics, as well as the analysis of key concepts within bioethics, including the concept of vulnerability, harm, moral authority, extended decision-making and advance directives, proxy consent and deciding for others, trust, and the nature of hope when dying. He has held a joint research fellowship at Cornell and Notre Dame Universities in the USA on the theme of Hope and Death. His work on palliative and end-of-life ethics has also received widespread attention in the national press.

Sharon Young completed her PhD thesis examining the centrality of human rights discourses to end of life policy and debate in 2017 at Kingston University, whilst working as an hourly paid lecturer and for a Member of the UK Parliament. In May 2018 she was elected as a Councillor for the Royal Borough of Kingston Upon Thames where she launched "Death Cafe Kingston" and shared her research interests through TEDx Kingston (Let's talk about dying and start living | Sharon Young | TEDxKingstonUponThames - Bing video). She currently works with Surrey Safeguarding Children Partnership.

1 Introducing 'Regulating the End of Life: Death Rights'

Sue Westwood

Overview

This edited volume engages with, and advocates for, the 'right to die' in law. The volume is multi-disciplinary, with contributions from authors from a wide range of backgrounds, including law, socio-legal studies, applied ethics, medical ethics, bioethics, embodied rights, human rights, disability rights, gender studies, feminism, gerontology, politics, philosophy, sociology and vulnerability theory. It is a cutting-edge volume, combining the best of recent debates with new and incisive critical contributions, aimed at progressing the assisted dying and euthanasia debate further forward. This introductory chapter places these contributions in context, offers guidance about how the book can be approached, and provides an outline of each of the chapters and related themes.

Context

Although ending one's life is no longer a crime in many parts of the world, including the UK,[1] assisting someone else to do so still is. This is despite growing support among both the general public (Hendry et al., 2013) and the medical professions (Davis, 2018) and a series of poignant legal challenges in recent years, including, in the UK, those made by Diane Pretty,[2] Debbie Purdy,[3] Tony Nicklinson,[4] and, most recently, Noel Conway.[5] Several attempts to introduce new legislation to the UK Parliament have been unsuccessful, for example the Assisted Suicide (Scotland) Bill (2013), Lord Falconer's Assisted Dying Bill (2014) and Rob Marris's Assisted Dying Bill (2015).

The debate about assisted dying and euthanasia (Lewis, 2007) has engaged internationally with many moral and ethical tensions (Huxtable, 2007, 2012), very few of which, however, have questioned *why* death and dying are regulated in the way that they are (Tierney, 2010). Why, for example, should we have to accept passive deaths, rather than deaths in the manner and timing of our choosing? Why do we have a right to life, but not a right to death, even in the face of unbearable suffering? Why do we have embodied reproductive

DOI: 10.4324/9780429329739-1

rights, to control the beginnings of life, but not embodied death rights to control the endings of life?

This edited volume aims to review and engage with the various debates about assisted dying and euthanasia, and offer new and cutting-edge critiques. It is explicitly in favour of legalising assisted dying and euthanasia (with appropriate safeguards) and moreover of establishing a 'right to die' in law (Coggon, 2006), which would be on a par with a 'right to life'.

How this book can be used

This book can be used in several ways.

- Those who are interested in the broad content can do a straightforward 'begin at the beginning' and work their way through.
- Those who are interested in particular themes may wish instead to delve first into specific sections. Part 1 addresses regulatory contexts; Part 2 addresses ethics, morals and values; Part 3 addresses rights; and in Part 4, I take an overview approach, tying all of the chapters together under an overarching claim for the right to die.
- The book includes chapters which take very different approaches. Readers interested in more abstract analyses may be drawn in particular to the chapters by Penney Lewis (Chapter 2), Isra Black (Chapter 7) and Thomas Tierney (Chapter 10). Readers more interested in lived experience may wish to focus on chapters by Alex Ruck Keene (Chapter 3), Ari Gandsman (Chapter 11) and Els van Wijngaarden (Chapter 12) as well as, perhaps, my own final overview chapter (Chapter 14), which asks what an 'outsider' perspective (through the eyes of hypothetical aliens) can offer to the 'right to die' debate. Readers interested in particular countries' regulatory approaches will wish to consider Penney Lewis's overview in Chapter 2; Chapters 3 and 5 for an analysis of the English context; Chapter 4 which relates to Australia; Chapters 10 and 11 which come from the US; Chapter 12 which relates to the Netherlands; and Chapters 9 and 10 which relate to a European context, particularly to the European Convention on Human Rights.
- For those who wish to engage with all authors' approaches to particular sub-topics, the Index will guide them to the relevant sections. Alternatively, readers can just dip in and out according to their needs/interests.

Definition of terms

Assisted dying is an umbrella term that encompasses voluntary euthanasia, physician-assisted suicide and assisted suicide. In voluntary euthanasia, a person's life is ended for them, at their request. This is distinguishable from involuntary euthanasia where a person's life is ended without their consent or wish. Physician-assisted suicide is where a person is helped to end their own lives by a medical practitioner. Assisted suicide is where a person is helped to end their own lives by someone who is not a medical practitioner. Some authors avoid the term suicide for its association with criminalisation. For example, it was unlawful to end one's life in the UK prior to the 1961 Suicide Act, and until then, people who tried to end their lives and failed were liable to criminal prosecution. For those who wish to avoid referring to ending one's life as 'suicide', 'assisted suicide' can also be referred to as 'assisted dying' (whether physician assisted or not).

The nature of the assistance can be passive, that is, to not do things which would keep the person alive (e.g. to not conduct CPR on someone whose heart has stopped) or active, either by stopping doing things which are keeping the person alive (e.g. removing feeding tubes) or by doing something which will actively bring about someone's death (e.g. providing or administering poisons). Very often the lines between all three can become blurred (see Chapter 7 which goes into this in more detail).

Chapter outlines

This volume is clustered around four main themes: legal changes and challenges; ethics, morals and values; rights claims; and transgressions.

Part 1: Legal change and challenges

In Chapter 2, Penney Lewis, a leading UK academic and now a law commissioner (the Law Commission being responsible for reviewing and proposing reforms to the law of England and Wales), reflects on her landmark book, *Assisted Dying and Legal Change* (Lewis, 2007). In that book, she explored how different regulatory systems in different countries inform legal responses to assisted dying. In this chapter, she considers certain legal routes in light of subsequent legal developments and suggests that one jurisdiction's approach may not be simply transferable to another's without taking the wider socio-legal context into account. Lewis first examines constitutionally entrenched human rights (focussing on legal systems in Canada sand Colombia). She then goes on to consider statutory interpretations of both the duty-based defence of necessity (focussing on the Netherlands) and the defence of medical exception (in multiple countries). She then explores legislative approaches, that is, restrictions on assisted dying to those with a terminal illness (focussing on Washington and Oregon in the US) and use of the rationale of unbearable suffering in cases of euthanasia (considering the Belgium context).

Lewis then goes on to examine and re-evaluate both the claims she makes in her 2007 book and newer claims about the significance of the following for each regulatory approach: the patient's request; the patient's condition, whether related to a terminal illness or unbearable suffering; the type of assistance; prospective approval and retrospective assessment; and the identity of the assistor. Lewis's rich, layered analysis gives a remarkable overview of different legal approaches to assisted dying in different parts of the world, and the legal frameworks that shape them. It also, rarely, demonstrates a leading academic revisiting and reviewing their original work and updating it for contemporary applicability, relevance and salience.

Often, debates about assisted dying can involve complex theory and abstract ideas which take us away from the lived experience that is involved. In Chapter 3, Alex Ruck Keene, a leading practicing English barrister, who is also an academic, reflects on his experience of representing Neil Conway's unsuccessful legal claim to be allowed to be helped to die. Neil Conway's is one of the most recent UK cases where an individual has been denied the right to die. Ruck Keene's reflections on the case – written with Neil Conway's express permission – reminds us of the human consequences of being denied the right to die. Such cases have a profound impact on a human being whose life either has become unbearable and/or faces an unwanted manner of dying in the case of a progressive terminal illness. These cases involve the most courageous human beings involved in the most awful tragedies. Not only do they affect the claimants and those who care about and support them, but they also affect the legal teams who are involved, particularly those representing the claimant themselves.

As Ruck Keene's chapter shows, being involved in assisted dying litigation is much more than just doing a day's work, with barristers such as Ruck Keene caring deeply about their clients' plights and about their thwarted attempts to be allowed to die. He considers how the court's ruling in Neil Conway's case is in conflict with core principles in English law, notably embodied autonomy, choice and control; the privileging of medical judgement over self-determination; 'best interests' decision-making (the foundation of English mental capacity law); proportionality, that is, taking the least intrusive measure(s) to achieve legitimate goals; and certain basic human rights principles exemplified in the European Convention on Human Rights. Ruck Keene reflects, in particular, on the UN Convention on the Rights of Persons with Disabilities (CPRD), its vagueness in relation to assisted dying, and therefore its limited applicability when trying to use it to make disability rights claims in relation to assisted dying in the courts. Crucially, Ruck Keene considers not only the social right *to* some things but also 'not to' others. This is of particular significance in the context of unbearable suffering and what he calls the 'untidy compromises' being made in relation to the present English stance on assisted dying.

Comparative international perspectives offer useful insights. In Chapter 4, Lindy Willmott, Katrine Del Villar and Ben White examine recent assisted dying legislation in Victoria, Australia, to consider to what extent and how it lines up with certain core values. The 'values' (or principles) they consider are the importance of life, autonomy, freedom of conscience, equality, the rule of law, the protection of vulnerable people and the minimisation of human suffering. After outlining each, the authors then go on to apply these concepts to key elements of the new legislation, specifically the permitted method of delivery of assisted dying; eligibility criteria for assisted dying; safeguards and restrictions; monitoring and oversight; and medical practitioners and lawful conscientious objections.

Applying the lens of values to these various dimensions of the new legislation highlights its considerable shortcomings. Specifically, in constricting the method of delivery, a person's autonomous rights are constrained; in tightly limited eligibility, the vast majority of people who want the right to be assisted in dying are excluded; in setting fixed timescales, and deliberate delays as safeguards, it can become too late for some eligible people to take up assisted dying, because they have either died already or lost capacity to consent; in protecting the right of medical practitioners to not only refuse to practice assisted dying themselves but also to refuse to refer a patient on to medical practitioners who will, dying patients are denied equal access to the opportunity of being assisted in dying. The authors use their analysis to argue for values-based regulations which would overcome many of the limitations they have identified.

Part 2: Ethics, morals and values

The right to die debate is informed by wide-ranging ethical and moral arguments. In Chapter 5, Richard Huxtable, one of the leading authors in the field, considers the spectrum of viewpoints which are involved. Huxtable outlines the key ethical arguments in support of assisted dying (choice; self-determination; an end to suffering) and those in opposition to it (intrinsic value of life; integrity of the medical professions; and 'slippery slope' discourse). He then goes on to reflect on each arguments and their interconnections, highlighting, in particular, their respective weaknesses and the lack of robust empirical evidence to substantiate the claims made.

Huxtable suggests that perhaps a 'middle-ground' compromise is required, which involves a balancing of the two opposing positions and finding some resolution which satisfies, to a certain extent, the values and principles which underpin them. He considers what such a compromise might look like, citing authors who suggest that in some ways English law is already operating an untidy compromise, with the unlawfulness of assisting someone in dying, tempered by Crown Prosecution guidelines (CPS, 2014) which severely limit who actually is prosecuted. Huxtable considers suggestions for very narrowly restricted access to assisted dying (e.g. only for someone with a terminal illness in the last six months of life, as advocated for by the campaign group Dignity in Dying)[6] or for keeping prosecution as a *possibility* for medics (as with the police) who end a life, but not unless deemed appropriate after formal review. Huxtable finally considers whether rather than making assisted dying permissible, a new offence might be created, for example 'compassionate killing', which would have non-custodial penalties attached. He concludes by arguing that while a middle ground might not please either proponents or opponents of assisted dying it would offer a way through what currently appears to be an intractable debate without any signs of resolution.

In Chapter 6, Anthony Wrigley, a leading UK bioethicist, considers whether, paradoxically, assisted dying and euthanasia may serve to prolong, rather than curtail, life. He draws on the example given by the life of Belgian Paralympic medal-winning athlete Marieke Vervoort who has a chronic and deteriorating health condition which causes her constant, extreme pain. She said that what has helped her to stay alive, and not end her life, was signing up for euthanasia in 2008, not to undergo it at that point, but for it to be a future possibility for her. Wrigley considers the implications of Vervoort's story for other individuals who want to be assured that they do have a final exit point available to them if their circumstances become intolerable. Wrigley suggests that this is an interesting potential response to those opposed to assisted dying/euthanasia on 'sanctity of life' grounds.

Wrigley then goes on to consider the implications of Vervoort's example for wide ethical debates in relation to active voluntary euthanasia (AVE). In particular, he differentiates between absolutist vitalist 'sanctity of life' arguments in relation to life at any cost, and those arguments which engage with qualified quality of life/fullness of life vitalism. He argues, in particular, that individuals who cannot be sure that others will end their lives for them, at a future point where they consider their lives will be no longer worth living, may end their lives sooner than they would otherwise have done. This would confound some elements of the life-protecting vitalist positions. AVE would also empower each individual to determine the sanctity of their own life rather than have that sanctity imposed on them by others, thereby respecting individual autonomy. Life-extension arguments also appeal to traditional beneficence-based objections (i.e. to do good, not harm) to AVE. Wrigley concludes that life-extension arguments have considerable potential for progressing the debate about euthanasia and also (by implication) assisted dying.

Isra Black's contribution in Chapter 7 is a theoretical and logic-based argument which supports the 'pro tanto' (all things being equal) 'moral permissibility' of assisted dying in certain circumstances. He argues that when applying logical reasoning to certain intrinsic values relevant to the end of life, assisted dying in the case of an autonomous capacitous person can be seen to be a moral 'good'. This is situated within (a) a particular 'state of affairs' relating to the person who wants to die, that is, their unique and specific circumstances and (b) 'benchmark comparisons' of the different options and outcomes hypothetically available to that person, weighted according to that person's reasoned evaluation of their circumstances. Black argues that assisted dying is morally permissible when a person has the 'most reason' to be assisted in dying, serving to override the 'normal' moral wrong of killing.

The key intrinsic value which Black applies is 'well-being' or that which is good for an individual. He considers autonomy to be an element of well-being. He argues that not being well in and of itself is not a rationale for assisted dying, because death denies us the opportunity to do well in the future.

To this extent death is a 'bad' thing because of this. However, the badness of death can be outweighed in certain circumstances, Black reasons, if the individual's well-being demands it. It is not that the individual will be 'well' in death, but that they have limited or no possibility of being well in the future; their well-being is immediately compromised and is likely to be increasingly compromised in the future. Under such circumstances, Black argues, assisted dying may be morally permissible.

Part 3: Rights claims

In the third section, the 'right to die' is approached in relation to rights claims. In Chapter 8, Sharon Young engages with the right to die through the lens of rights discourse in general and specifically in relation to personal liberty and human dignity under the European Convention on Human Rights 1950. Young considers how rights are understood in relation to the end of life and various ways in which rights discourses have been deployed in relation to a purported 'right to die'. She first examines foundational or essentialist approaches to rights, that is, that 'individuals are the bearers of human rights solely by virtue of their humanity'. She then considers individual liberty, drawing on the respective works of John Locke and Immanuel Kant, before considering the concept of human dignity. Drawing on a foundational approach to rights which focusses on personal liberty and human dignity, Young argues for and supports the assertion that individuals have the right to determine when and how they die.

Young then goes on to develop this argument by drawing on empirical data from her own research, namely, focus group discussions she held with members of a death café in North London. These discussions engaged with the meaning of dignity (both inherent and bestowed) and the significance of human agency for a right to self-determine one's death. Young connects this with the principle of (autonomous) liberty. However, Young's research participants engaged with rights, not in respect of formal rights (e.g. statute), but inherent rights, that is, as something foundational to life (and death) itself.

Young proceeds to consider 'anti-foundational' approaches, that is, legal positivism and social constructivism approach that grounds and analyses claims to rights through an emphasis on the social rather than legal context. She considers the case of Diane Pretty, diagnosed with motor neurone disease, who wanted to end her life with her husband's help without the fear that he would be prosecuted. She examines Pretty's legal arguments, suggesting that they constituted both a foundational approach to rights (cohering around self-determination, individual liberty and human dignity) and an anti-foundational approach in that they framed rights as fluid and contingent. Young concludes that both foundational and anti-foundational approaches to rights can support 'right to die' claims.

In Chapter 9, Elizabeth Wicks considers the relevance of Article 9 (Freedom of thought, conscience and religion) of the European Convention on Human

Rights (ECHR) or a 'right to die'. She considers, in particular, whether a belief that one should die with dignity and a wish to be able to do so, including through assisted dying, might constitute manifesting a belief and exercising freedom of conscience under Article 9. Wicks acknowledges that even if it does, Article 9 is a qualified right, that is, it can be interfered with by the state under specific circumstances, including the protection of health and morals, and the rights and freedoms of others. However, the main purpose of Wicks's chapter is to determine whether Article 9 is applicable at all.

Wicks goes on to consider the meaning of 'belief' and whether non-religious beliefs are relevant under Article 9. Considering relevant case law, she explains that although a belief does not have to be a religious one, it must have certain qualities in order to be a legally recognised one for the purposes of the ECHR, including high degrees of 'seriousness' and comprehensiveness. Wicks suggests that this means a belief is restricted to "'religion-plus-other-isms' (such as atheism and pacifism)' and not broader belief systems. Moving on to manifesting a belief, Wicks again analyses relevant ECtHR case law to explore what constitutes such a manifestation in law. Drawing, in particular, on the landmark case of Eweida[7] she concludes,

> the proper approach to the question of the manifestation of a belief is a contextual one that considers why the applicant seeks to perform the act in question and assesses only the closeness of the link between the act and the belief

Wicks concludes by considering whether requesting assistance to die constitutes manifesting a belief under Article 9. She determines that a belief in the right to die does not constitute a belief under the ECHR and therefore any expressions of a belief in the right to die, including a request for assisted dying, would also not constitute a manifestation of a belief under Article 9. Wicks suggests that understandings of 'belief' need to be widened by the courts to encompass secular as well as religious belief systems, which would then afford greater protections including for those who hold a belief in the 'right to die'.

In Chapter 10, Thomas Tierney examines the evolution of intellectual and philosophical thought on euthanasia from the sixteenth through the twentieth centuries. Drawing, in particular, on the Foucauldian concepts of biopower, biopolitics and governmentality, Tierney proposes that discussion about euthanasia have shifted from the spiritual (making reference to the work of Thomas More and Francis Bacon) to the medical (e.g. the work of Karl Friedrich Heinrich Marx), and then the 'thanatopolitical', that is, a politics of death. He examines the negative impact of Nazi eugenics on an emergent pro-euthanasia movement, and then, with more recent medical advancements, a re-emergence of support for euthanasia in some quarters, and subsequent partial legalisation in several countries.

Tierney understands these developments from a Foucauldian perspective. He links increased biopower and biopolitics with governmentality and tensions in relation to the disciplining of death and dying. He argues that increased medical technologies have enabled the transgression of bio-times, producing 'manufactured time'. Tierney suggests that the right to die movement affords an opportunity to critically engage with – and in turn also potentially transgress – normative understandings about what it means to both live and die. He links this to the Foucauldian notions of 'technologies of the self' and 'care of the self' and the critiques of medical dominance over individual preferences in relation to when and how one dies.

Part 4: Transgressions

The fourth and final section considers various ways in which the right to die transgresses established norms. In Chapter 11, Ari Gandsman provides a fascinating account of his anthropological study of people who are members of Exit International, a voluntary organisation advocating for assisted suicide which supports its members in finding out how to end their lives if they wish to. Drawing on interviews, conversations and observations, Gandsman describes 'a secret society' of individuals who are committed to the right to die, some of whom have already acquired the means to end their own lives (e.g. a woman with terminal cancer). Gandsman describes the workshops as sites of resistance to state prohibitions on assisted dying. He reports on the work of Philip Nitschke, Exit's founder, who was investigated several times by the Australian police for 'assisting suicides' and sometimes pejoratively referred to as 'Dr Death' in the media. At each workshop – and in a regularly updated handbook members can purchase, Nitschke and his small team provide details about the different ways to end one's life, and how to obtain different materials to do so. He advocates the use of Nembutal – a drug used to euthanise pets – for a peaceful, painless, death. Buying it is illegal and Exit members are told of, and share with one another, various ways to acquire it, and how to avoid the growing number of scams selling fake Nembutal. In this way, Exit, its networks and events are highly transgressive, subverting the passive acceptance of waiting for dying and death.

Gandsman described Exit's meetings as being laughter-filled rather than being grim. He suggests they are sites of commonality and community for the resistance of death norms, whose bonds are perhaps strengthened by secrecy and taboo. Gandsman observes relief among participants about being able to 'speak the unspeakable'. He also suggests they are sites of a reclamation of power from medicalised regimes. He suggests that this reflects 'necrosociality', that is, shared 'death-directed' subjectivities that are positive and self-empowering rather than negative and pathological. Through necrosocialities, Gandsman proposes, 'dying becomes a process over which one can have a sense of control.'

Gandsman tells the story of David Goodall, an Exit member and advocate who, at the age of 104, was assisted by Exit friends to travel from Australia to Dignitas in Switzerland to be assisted to die. He reflects on accounts of Goodall's death, making connections with his own interviews with Exit members who were actively planning for their own deaths. He observed that for all of them, 'dying at the right time' was crucial. However, for some members, because they could not rely on being assisted to die, they anticipated ending their lives sooner rather than later to be certain they were still able to. Even so, the sense of self-agency, being able to determine when and how they died, was paramount. Gandsman concludes by referring to the death of Michèle Causse, 'a well-known French radical lesbian theorist' who was filmed ending her life at Dignitas. The film shows her 'smiling, making jokes, laughing'. He makes links with an Exit member who said, referring to Exit members who have died feeling 'happy that they went out on their own terms.' Gandsman concludes that laughter – long considered essential to 'ageing well' – is also 'an important component of "dying well"' and of resisting traditional culturally imposed norms of death and dying.

Older people are disproportionately affected by choosing when and how one dies and, in turn, by the subject of assisted dying (Castelli Dransart et al., 2021). In Chapter 12, Els van Wijngaarden reports, with compassion and insightfulness, on a Dutch study conducted with older people who expressed a wish to die rather than continue living. She and her team identified many common themes among their research participants, relating to ageing, meaning, purpose and identity, as well as an ambivalence, a reluctance to lose all hope, and an enduring sense of connectedness to life itself. Van Wijngaarden argues that the wishes of older people for their lives to come to an end should not be discounted as depression or something that can be fixed by anti-loneliness strategies. She suggests that there are deeper, existential issues going on. Despite this, she also argues that policies, systems and communities which marginalise older people, including the very old, could do more to make older people feel they have continuing relevance to their personal and social worlds.

Locating her team's research in the wider context, van Wijngaarden raises interesting questions about the social value placed on a life, and the implications that has for ageing lives. With an increasing emphasis on productivity and less productivity in older age (in the Western world, but not, of course, in other parts of the world) a non-productive life loses meaning and value. This is not a new concept in gerontology (Estes, Swan & Gerard, 1982). However, van Wijngaarden argues that postmodern living has exacerbated this, with the older people in her study reflexively questioning not only whether they wish to live but whether they *should* continue to live.

Van Wijngaarden also prompts important questions about whether an individual should be able to determine when their life is 'complete' rather than waiting for their biological bodies to make this determination. This is especially so for older people with dementia, or anticipating dementia, for many of whom quality-of-life issues prevail, and for whom 'rational suicide', that is, choosing a well-reasoned assisted death has considerable salience. The implication, although not articulated as such by van Wijngaarden and her team, is that denial of assisted dying to people who have simply had enough of life might be an inherently ageist and age-discriminatory state strategy in those countries where it is prohibited.

Dying alone is often regarded as a tragedy. For those people who feel obliged to end their lives alone to protect their loved ones from criminalisation, and would have preferred to have their loved ones with them, it is indeed a tragic way to die. However, as Glenys Caswell demonstrates in Chapter 13, dying alone should not be regarded as inherently tragic. She critiques narratives about people who die alone which are told as 'stories of tragedy and blame', arguing that there are other, non-negative ways of framing lone deaths. People who die alone often create their own highly individualised deaths and in doing so do not conform, Caswell argues, with socially constructed and collectively managed processes of dying and death. She suggests that lone deaths threaten a fear-based 'collective need to manage death'. Instead these deaths are indicative of postmodern reflexivity and self-determination which resist and transgress institutional and societal norms.

Caswell suggests that intentional lone deaths constitute 'self-styled' deaths, also reflected by people in the UK who plan and pay in advance for their own funerals, and by advance care planning. She reports on data from a recent pilot study examining perspectives on death and dying among people who live alone, and explores in depth a single case study, considering the reporting on the death of an individual, who died alone at home, and whose body was not found for several weeks. Caswell critiques the tragic spin placed on this death by the media and the coroner when, in fact, it is not known whether the man concerned was happy to die alone and might even have wanted to. She suggests that tragedy narratives serve to warn off other people who may wish to consider having lone deaths themselves and that this impinges on the rights of individuals who may want to die alone.

In Chapter 14, the Conclusion, I make my own contribution to the debate, offering what I intend to be a provocative argument in support of a right to die. I imagine that an alien has come to earth and is confused by how English law regulates the beginnings and endings of life. Specifically, the alien puzzles over five things.

1 While it is lawful for a person to end their life, paradoxically, it is unlawful to be with them while they perform this lawful act, or to assist them in doing so;
2 While women can be lawfully assisted to exercise control over preventing and ending the new life of others through contraception and abortion, but they (and men) cannot be lawfully be assisted to exercise control over their own bodies' endings;

3 While it is lawful and considered a 'good' to end the life of a suffering, dying, animal, it is unlawful and considered 'bad' to help end the life of a suffering, dying, human being who wants to die;
4 The law protects a person from cruel and inhumane treatment, apart from when they are dying;
5 The right to life is enshrined in law but the right to death is not. Each is considered in turn with the aim of advocating for a regulated right to assisted dying, and for a right to die.

I consider each of these conceptual 'paradoxes' in turn, drawing on many of the chapters in this volume. The argument I present is that the law is overly restrictive, unreasonably restricts autonomous choice, and privileges the able-bodied and medical professions. I propose a vision for the future where assisted dying (i.e. assisting a capacitous adult to end their life when it is their choice to do so) is lawful for those with terminal illnesses, debilitating conditions and older people who wish to perform 'rational suicides' (Richards, 2017). I suggest that 'medical practitioners who do not want to provide this service do not have to do so and refer patients to practitioners who are willing to do so and/or services dedicated to the ending of life'. My conclusion is that lawful assisted dying can help people live more meaningful, death-aware lives.

Notes

1 Suicide Act 1961.
2 Pretty v The United Kingdom: ECHR 29 Apr 2002.
3 R (Purdy) v DPP [2009] UKHL 45.
4 R (Nicklinson) v Ministry of Justice; R (on the application of AM) v The Director of Public Prosecutions [2014] UKSC 38.
5 R (Conway) v SSJ [2018] EWCA Civ 1431.
6 *Dignity in Dying*: https://www.dignityindying.org.uk/.
7 Eweida and Others V. the United Kingdom ECtHR 48420/10 36516/10 51671/10.

References

Castelli Dransart, D.A., Lapierre, S., Erlangsen, A., Canetto, S.S., Heisel, M., Draper, B., Lindner, R., Richard-Devantoy, S., Cheung, G., Scocco, P., & Gusmão, R. (2021). A systematic review of older adults' request for or attitude toward euthanasia or assisted-suicide. *Aging & Mental Health*, *25*(3), 420–430.

Coggon, J. (2006). Could the right to die with dignity represent a new right to die in English law? *Medical Law Review*, *14*(2), 219–237.

Crown Prosecution Service (CPS) (2014). *Policy for Prosecutors in Respect of Cases of Encouraging or Assisting Suicide*. Available at: https://www.cps.gov.uk/legal-guidance/suicide-policy-prosecutors-respect-cases-encouraging-or-assisting-suicide (Accessed 2 April 2020).

Davis, J. (2018). Most UK doctors support assisted dying, a new poll shows: the BMA's opposition does not represent members. *BMJ, 360,* k301.

Estes, C.L., Swan, J.H., & Gerard, L.E. (1982). Dominant and competing paradigms in gerontology: Towards a political economy of ageing. *Ageing & Society, 2*(2), 151–164.

Hendry, M., Pasterfield, D., Lewis, R., Carter, B., Hodgson, D., & Wilkinson, C. (2013). Why do we want the right to die? A systematic review of the international literature on the views of patients, carers and the public on assisted dying. *Palliative Medicine, 27*(1), 13–26.

Huxtable, R. (2007). *Euthanasia, Ethics and the Law: From Conflict to Compromise.* Abingdon: Routledge.

Huxtable, R. (2012). *Law, Ethics and Compromise at the Limits of Life: To Treat or Not to Treat?* Abingdon: Routledge.

Lewis, P. (2007). *Assisted Dying and Legal Change.* Oxford: Oxford University Press.

Richards, N. (2017). Old age rational suicide. *Sociology Compass, 11*(3), e12456.

Tierney, T.F. (2010). The governmentality of suicide: Peuchet, Marx, Durkheim, and Foucault. *Journal of Classical Sociology, 10*(4), 357–389.

Part I

Legal changes and challenges

2 Legal change on assisted dying

Penney Lewis

Introduction

Whether assisted dying should be legalised is often treated as an ethical question transcending national boundaries and diverse legal systems. The result is the loss of important context in which jurisdictions make decisions about assisted dying and the significance of the legal methods chosen to carry out those decisions. Work in this field is dominated by partisan exhortation by proponents or opponents of legalisation.

In this chapter, I revisit claims I have made in *Assisted Dying and Legal Change* (Lewis 2007). In that book, I examine the impact on the resulting regulatory regime of the choice of a particular legal route towards legalisation of assisted dying. The routes examined in the book are constitutionally entrenched human rights; the duty-based defence of necessity; the virtue of compassion; and legislative approaches. In this chapter, I will combine the second route, the duty-based defence of necessity with an approach based on the medical exception to the criminal law. These will be grouped together under the route of statutory interpretation. I will also disregard the virtue of compassion, as no attempts have been made to use this route since it was first proposed.

The examination of the impact of these different alternative routes to legalisation suggests that greater caution is needed before relying on the experience of one jurisdiction when discussing proposals for regulation of assisted dying in others, and the possible consequences of such regulation. In order to evaluate the relevance of a particular legal experience to other jurisdictions, one needs therefore to explore the legal environment in which assisted dying is performed or proposed.

In this chapter, I define euthanasia as the termination of life on request (as in the Netherlands), assisted suicide as any act which intentionally helps another person to commit suicide, and assisted dying as including both euthanasia and assisted suicide.

Constitutionally entrenched human rights

A variety of rights have been used or their use proposed to challenge criminal prohibitions on assisting a suicide or homicide offences, including rights

DOI: 10.4324/9780429329739-2

to life, liberty, security of the person, privacy, dignity, equality, freedom of religion/conscience, property, and freedom from inhuman or degrading treatment.

Unsuccessful attempts were made in Canada (*Rodriguez v British Columbia (Attorney General)* 1993), the US (*Vacco v Quill* 1997, *Washington v Glucksberg* 1997), and the UK (*Pretty v United Kingdom* 2002, *Nicklinson and Lamb v United Kingdom* 2015, *R (Conway) v Secretary of State for Justice* 2018, *R ([Omid] T) v Secretary of State for Justice* 2018, *R (Newby) v Secretary of State for Justice* 2019).

Success eventually occurred in Canada in 2015, when the Supreme Court overruled an earlier decision and found the criminal prohibition on assisted suicide violated the applicant's right to life and security of the person, leading to legislative change. In Colombia in 1997, the Constitutional Court upheld patients' rights to dignity and liberty, which led to executive change.

Canada

In 2015, the Supreme Court of Canada struck down the criminal prohibition on assisted suicide found in the federal *Criminal Code* on the grounds that it infringed the rights of competent adult patients with a grievous and irremediable medical condition causing enduring and intolerable suffering who were willing to provide consent to an assisted death (*Carter v Canada (Attorney General)* 2015). The rights in question were found in Section 7 of the *Canadian Charter of Rights and Freedoms* which provides that "Everyone has the right to life, liberty and security of the person and the right not to be deprived thereof except in accordance with the principles of fundamental justice". The Court granted a suspension of the declaration of invalidity to give Parliament the opportunity to craft a regulatory regime.

In 2016, the Parliament of Canada passed an Act partially implementing *Carter (An Act to amend the Criminal Code and to make related amendments to other Acts (medical assistance in dying) 2016)*. The Act permits medical assistance in dying, which is defined as,

> (a) the administering by a medical practitioner or nurse practitioner of a substance to a person, at their request, that causes their death; or (b) the prescribing or providing by a medical practitioner or nurse practitioner of a substance to a person, at their request, so that they may self-administer the substance and in doing so cause their own death.

The person must be a capacitous adult with a grievous and irremediable medical condition who has made a voluntary and informed request for assistance in dying.

There are four requirements for a "grievous and irremediable medical condition". The person must have a serious and incurable illness, disease or disability, and be in an advanced state of irreversible decline in capability. That illness, disease or disability or that state of decline must cause them enduring physical or psychological suffering that is intolerable to them and that cannot be relieved under conditions that they consider acceptable. Finally their natural death must have become reasonably foreseeable, taking into account all of their medical circumstances, without a prognosis necessarily having been made as to the specific length of time that they have remaining. The Act requires an independent consultation, a waiting period, and a written witnessed request. It includes a conscientious objection provision and imposes a reporting requirement.

In March 2021, changes to the legislation came into force, removing the requirement that a person's natural death must be reasonably foreseeable, and creating two levels of safeguards. The lower level will be applied when a person's natural death is reasonably foreseeable, and such a person may also waive the final consent requirement in anticipation of their potential loss of capacity closer to death. The higher level will be applied when a person's natural death is not reasonably foreseeable (*An Act to amend the Criminal Code (medical assistance in dying)* 2021).

Colombia

In 1997, the Colombian Constitutional Court ruled that a physician should not be prosecuted for ending life at the repeated request of a terminally ill patient who is suffering unbearably because the physician's action "is justified". The Court called on Congress to establish a regulatory regime to vindicate the fundamental right to die with dignity (*Sentencia C-239* 1997). Although a number of Bills were introduced, no progress was made in Congress on this issue.

In 2014, the Constitutional Court reviewed the case of a terminally ill patient who had repeatedly and unsuccessfully sought euthanasia. The Court ordered the Ministry of Health to issue a directive to health care providers immediately, requiring them to set up local expert committees to respond to requests for euthanasia (*Sentencia T-970* 2014). A national expert committee collaborated in the writing of the resulting Resolution which came into force in April 2015. The Resolution requires requests for euthanasia to be prospectively approved by a special hospital-based committee which also bears responsibility for ensuring that the assistance in dying is provided within strict time-limits, and for accompanying the patient and their family members. The patient must be terminally ill, and the request free, informed and unequivocal. Requests in advance of incapacity are permitted. A reporting requirement is imposed. (República de Colombia Ministerio de Salud y Protección Social 2015, art 16).

A 2018 Resolution permits euthanasia for children from the age of six at their competent, informed and voluntary request. Below the age of 14, parental consent is required. Between the ages of 6 and 12, a psychiatric evaluation is required to ensure the child has attained (i) exceptional neurocognitive and psychological development, and (ii) the level of understanding of the concept of death (as irreversible and inexorable) expected of adolescents aged 12 and over (República de Colombia Ministerio de Salud y Protección Social 2018).

Statutory interpretation

Duty-based defence of necessity

The common law has resolutely prevented the interpretation of the defence of necessity to permit euthanasia. A variety of common law rules have been developed to ensure this (Lewis 2012b). These include (1) a ban on the defence in all murder cases (*Dudley and Stephens* 1884, *Howe* 1987); (2) or only in euthanasia cases (*Re A (Children) (Conjoined Twins: Surgical Separation)* 2001); (3) a rule that the defendant must not choose who is to die (*Re A (Children) (Conjoined Twins: Surgical Separation)* 2001); or (4) that there must be a net saving of life (*Bourne* 1938, *Re A (Children) (Conjoined Twins: Surgical Separation)* 2001).

The Dutch courts, by contrast, have been considerably more willing to interpret their defence of necessity as permitting euthanasia. In 2001, Dutch laws expressly regulating euthanasia and assisted suicide were enacted. However, the mechanism of the legalisation of euthanasia and assisted suicide in the Netherlands was the duty-based defence of necessity, as developed through judicial interpretation of the provisions governing the criminal offences of taking life on request ("euthanasia" in the Dutch sense) and assisting suicide, and the defence of necessity (Lewis 2007, 76).

The defence is a statutory one. Article 40 of the Dutch Criminal Code provides that "[a] person who commits an offence as the result of a force he could not be expected to resist [*overmacht*] is not criminally liable" (Lewis 2007, 77). A physician can rely on the defence of necessity when faced with conflicting duties, namely, the need to preserve life, and the professional duty to relieve the patient's suffering. If a doctor faced with such a situation chooses to prefer the value that from an objective standpoint is more important, even if in doing so that doctor must do something that in itself is forbidden, the conduct is justifiable. In 1984, the Dutch Supreme Court [*Hoge Raad*] held that the defence of necessity could be invoked by a doctor where a patient was experiencing her suffering as unbearable. The Supreme Court remanded the case in question back to the appeals court to consider the risk of increasing loss of personal dignity and/or the worsening of the patient's (already unbearable) suffering; the risk that had the physician waited, the patient would no longer have been able to die in a dignified manner; and whether, and if so to what extent, there were any remaining ways to relieve the suffering (Lewis 2007, 78–79).

Thus, in Dutch law, the substantive pillars of the defence of necessity in euthanasia cases are that the patient was experiencing unbearable and hopeless suffering and that no reasonable alternative to relieve her suffering existed. The patient's suffering need not be related to a terminal illness. Indeed, the source of the patient's suffering may be either somatic (that is, stemming from a physiological disorder) or non-somatic. The latter can include the prospect of inhuman deterioration and the possibility of dying in an undignified way (Lewis 2007, 79, 126).

The lack of a reasonable alternative to the patient's unbearable and hopeless suffering gives rise to the defendant doctor's conflict of duties once the patient makes a considered and voluntary request for euthanasia or assisted suicide. If consideration of the patient's request leads to the unavoidable conclusion that euthanasia is the only realistic option, the request places the physician into a conflict of duties. Only a doctor can be faced with this conflict of duties; neither nurses nor lay people are considered to have duties that can give rise to such a conflict (Lewis 2007, 80).

Once the conflict of duties exists, and there is no reasonable alternative to relieve the requesting patient's unbearable and hopeless suffering, the doctor will be found to have acted proportionately and the defence of necessity will be available. However, the defence of necessity will only succeed where the physician's act was carried out with due care. Certain procedural requirements were required to be met, including reporting and consultation requirements (Lewis 2007, 81). Thus, over some thirty years, the Dutch courts developed a duty-based defence of necessity in euthanasia cases, placing conditions on the defence, including an express and earnest request; unbearable and hopeless suffering; consultation; careful termination of life; record keeping; and reporting. These conditions became known as the "requirements of due care" or "careful practice" (Lewis and Black 2012, 16).

The Dutch legislature eventually codified the parameters of this necessity defence (*Termination of Life on Request and Assisted Suicide (Review Procedures) Act 2001*). The codified due care criteria are set out in Section 2(1) of the *Dutch Act*. The substantive and procedural requirements are, unfortunately, jumbled together.

> The attending physician must:
>
> a be satisfied that the patient has made a voluntary and carefully considered request;
> b be satisfied that the patient's suffering was unbearable, and that there was no prospect of improvement;
> c have informed the patient about his situation and his prospects;
> d have come to the conclusion, together with the patient, that there is no reasonable alternative in the light of the patient's situation;
> e have consulted at least one other, independent physician, who must have seen the patient and given a written opinion on the due care criteria referred to in a. to d. above; and
> f have terminated the patient's life or provided assistance with suicide with due medical care and attention.
>
> The case must be reported to a regional review committee. If the committee finds that the case meets the due care criteria, then the case will not be reported to the prosecutorial authorities.
>
> Lewis (2007, 82–83)

The medical exception

The medical exception is the term used (particularly although not exclusively at common law) for the defence or exception to the criminal law which exempts medical practice from some or all offences against the person, for example serious assault. Sir James Fitzjames Stephen (1878, 144, art 204, n 1) was unable to find authority for this exception, but pointed out that none was required as "[t]he existence of surgery as a profession assumes [the] truth [of the exception]". In order to qualify for the medical exception, two elements must be present.

First, the patient's consent is required, although some substitute for consent will suffice when the patient is unable to consent. This substitute may take the form of consent from another person in a prescribed relationship to the patient, appointed by a court, or by the patient prior to the loss of capacity. Alternatively it may be entirely separate from consent, taking the form of a justification such as necessity or best interests (*Brown* 1994, 266).

Second, some form of public policy justification is required (Hughes 1963, 237, Lord Riddell 1924–1925, 95, per Atkin LJ). Consensus over the terminology used for the public policy justification, and over its content, is notable by its absence. The different versions of this public policy justification focus variously on the patient, the public, and the medical profession. Patient-focussed justifications mandate that the procedure be intended to benefit the patient or be therapeutic for the patient. Public-focussed justifications vary in specificity, although they are generally broader than a patient-focussed justification, ranging from "just cause or excuse", to "lawful purpose" to the "public interest" (*Attorney General's Reference (No. 6 of 1980)* 1981, 719, *Bravery v Bravery* 1954, 1180, *Crimes Act (N.Z.)* 1961, s 61A). In more recent cases, courts have tended to use professionally focussed justifications including "proper medical treatment" and "reasonable surgical interference" (*Attorney General's Reference (No. 6 of 1980)* 1981, 719, *Brown* 1994, 231, 245, 266, 276). An even more professionally focussed justification simply reflects "good" or "accepted" medical practice (*Brown* 1994, 258–259, Lewis 2012a).

In the euthanasia context, the medical exception was rejected by the Dutch Supreme Court in an early case. The defendant doctor (who was acting as a friend rather than as an attending physician) argued that her actions were justified "since she acted in accordance with the demands of appropriate professional practice". The court held that no medical exception for euthanasia existed, as it was "evident that even in medical circles in the Netherlands there is no general agreement regarding the permissibility of euthanasia and the manner in which, and the conditions under which, it might be carried out"[1] (Bostrom and Lagerwey 1988, *Pols* 1987).

By contrast, in 2009, the Supreme Court of Montana found that a physician who provides aid in dying by prescribing a lethal dose of medication for a competent, terminally ill patient may use the statutory consent defence to homicide. The court further found that the statutory exception to the consent defence for conduct or resulting harm that is "against public policy" did not apply to physician aid in dying (*Baxter v State*).[2] The court did not explicitly address the medical exception but nonetheless effectively crafted one to the homicide statute in limited circumstances, finding that physician aid in dying is not "against public policy". The statutory interpretation of the majority is somewhat unconvincing (Robinson 2010, 16). Attempts to overrule it legislatively have thus far been unsuccessful, but they continue.

In 2013, Vermont state legislators passed a statute very similar to the Oregon Act, which permits the provision of a prescription for lethal medication to be self-administered by the patient provided regulatory requirements are met. (This regime is discussed in detail in the next section.) The Vermont Act originally contained sunset clauses which would have changed the regulatory framework after three years from a regime modelled on Oregon to a professional practice standard. This would have permitted physician-assisted suicide on the basis of a valid request from the physician's patient with a terminal illness, without requirements for consultation with a second physician, psychiatric evaluation, or waiting periods (*An Act Relating to Patient Choice and Control at End of Life 2013*). Effectively it would have be treated like other medical procedures which are covered by the medical exception to the criminal law. In 2015, the Act was amended to remove these clauses. The Oregon-style regime now continues.

Legislative approaches

Restriction to the terminally ill

Many US states allow legislation to be enacted if a majority votes for an initiative placed on the ballot following a petition signed by a minimum number of voters. Following two narrowly unsuccessful attempts to permit physician-assisted suicide by ballot initiative in Washington and California, Oregon voters passed the first Death with Dignity Act in 1994 by a majority of 52%. The Act permits the provision of a prescription for lethal medication to be self-administered by the patient. The patient must be suffering from a terminal disease, defined as "an incurable and irreversible disease that has been medically confirmed and will, within reasonable medical judgment, produce death within six months". The competence, voluntariness and information requirements are set out in some detail. The patient must have "the ability to make and communicate health care decisions to health care providers, including communication through persons familiar with the patient's manner of communicating if those persons are available". Two witnesses must attest that the patient is acting voluntarily and is not being coerced to sign the request. The patient must make an

> informed decision … that is based on an appreciation of the relevant facts and after being fully informed by the attending physician of: (a) his or her medical diagnosis; (b) his or her prognosis; (c) the potential risks associated with taking the medication to be prescribed; (d) the probable result of taking the medication to be prescribed; (e) the feasible alternatives, including, but not limited to, comfort care, hospice care and pain control.

The attending physician must refer the patient to "a consulting physician for medical confirmation of the diagnosis, and for determination that the patient is capable and acting voluntarily". Further, a counselling referral must be made if either the attending or consulting physician suspects that the patient "may be suffering from a psychiatric or psychological disorder, or depression causing impaired judgment". Lethal medication may only be prescribed if the counsellor determines that the patient is *not* suffering from such a condition. The physician must report each prescription written under the Act to the Oregon Department of Human Services (ODHS), and report each death resulting from the ingestion of the prescribed medication. (*Death With Dignity Act ORS 127.800-127.995* 1999).

The Act was controversial from the moment the ballot measure was passed, and there were a number of ultimately unsuccessful legal challenges to it (Lewis 2007, 150–153). Washington state voters passed an almost identical Act in 2008, as did Colorado voters in 2016. In 2013, 2015 and 2016, respectively, Vermont and California state legislators and District of Columbia council members passed statutes very similar to the Oregon Act. The Hawaii, New Jersey, Maine and New Mexico legislatures passed Oregon-model Acts in 2018, 2019 and 2021.

In 2014, the provincial legislature of Québec, Canada, passed *An Act Respecting End of Life Care* which came into force on 10 December 2015 and legalised euthanasia ("medical aid in dying") for patients at the end of life. In 2017, the Victorian state legislature in Australia passed the Voluntary Assisted Dying Act 2017, which came into force in June 2019. The Act is a procedurally complex version of the Oregon-model, although both self- and practitioner-administration are permitted. The state legislature of Western Australia passed a similar Act in December 2019, which is likely to come into force in mid-2021.

Euthanasia for unbearable suffering

Unlike in the Netherlands, there had been few criminal prosecutions in euthanasia cases prior to its legalisation in Belgium, so legal change had to come from outside the judiciary. The 1980s and 1990s witnessed a series of unsuccessful legislative moves to allow euthanasia. After a change of government and intense legislative debate, the Law on Euthanasia was passed in 2002.[3] It allows only doctors to perform euthanasia. Assisted suicide is not explicitly covered, although Belgium's oversight body, the Federal Euthanasia Control and Evaluation Commission (FECEC) has accepted cases of assisted suicide as falling under the law (Commission fédérale de contrôle et d'évaluation de l'euthanasie 2004). In a recent development, the Public Prosecution Service has taken the position that assisting a suicide is not a criminal offence (De Standard 2019).

The Law on Euthanasia and Assisted Suicide came into force in Luxembourg in 2009 after a heated political and public debate. The law is closely based on the Belgian law, although it does specifically permit physician-assisted suicide as well as physician-administered euthanasia, and is limited to the those in a "terminal medical situation" *Loi du 16 mars 2009 sur l'euthanasie et l'assistance au suicide* (2009).

The influence of the legal route on the resulting regulatory regime

In the following sections, I examine the differing contours of the regulation of assisted dying resulting from these mechanisms of legal change. This examination reveals interesting features, and highlights the importance of choice of legal route in shaping regulatory regimes. The features to be considered are the patient's request; the patient's condition, whether related to a terminal illness or unbearable suffering; the type of assistance; prospective approval and retrospective assessment; and the identity of the assistor. I evaluate the claims I made in 2007 in the examination of each feature, and make and evaluate some newer claims.

The patient's request

> Original Claim 1: Regimes resulting from necessity as a mechanism of legal change are not restricted to cases of an autonomous patient request but will include termination of life without request where necessary to relieve suffering.

Applying the defence of necessity in cases of termination of life without request, as in the Netherlands, is often seen as evidence of a slippery slope. The Dutch jurisprudence permitting the use of the defence of necessity in cases where neonates are suffering unbearably (Lewis 2007, 127–133), and the subsequent adoption of a requirement that such cases be reported to a national review committee are one such example (Griffiths, Weyers, and Adams 2008, [6.2.2.5]–[6.2.3]). Instead, it is the grounding in the doctor-centred duty-based defence of necessity which explains Dutch legal acceptance of termination of life without request where it is necessary to relieve the unbearable and hopeless suffering of a patient lacking capacity, and no reasonable alternative is available to relieve that suffering. Rather than evidence of a slippery slope, the inclusion of unbearably suffering incapacitous patients in jurisdictions where the mechanism of legal change is the defence of necessity should be seen as evidence of Claim 1. There is no logical slippery slope from termination of life on request (euthanasia) to termination of life without request (Lewis 2007, 164–169).

> Original Claim 2 (2a): Regimes resulting from rights as the mechanism of legal change require a capacitous request from the patient unless the relevant jurisdiction allows proxies to exercise rights on behalf of individuals lacking capacity, in which case the possibility of dispensing with the requirement of a capacitous request from the individual exists.

Neither of the relevant regimes in Canada or Colombia has permitted such requests from proxies. However, in these jurisdictions, the decision of a proxy is not considered to be the exercise of a right on behalf of the individual.

In some US states, the decision of a proxy *is* considered to be the exercise of a right on behalf of the individual, though no US states have legalised on the basis of constitutionally entrenched human rights. No constitutional challenges have been brought on these grounds, although they were accepted, in principle, by the Ninth Circuit Court of Appeals (*Compassion in Dying v Washington* 1996, 832, n 120). There is therefore neither empirical support for Claim 2a nor evidence contradicting it.

> New Claim 2 (2b): Whether proxy consent suffices for regimes based on the medical exception will depend on the source of the exception.

At common law, proxy consent is likely to suffice since this is one way in which medical treatment can be lawfully provided to those lacking capacity. In contrast, the more limited way in which the medical exception is employed in Montana would not permit proxy consent since the statutory consent defence to homicide requires the "consent of the victim".

Proxy consent is therefore unlikely to be permissible unless the common law medical exception or constitutionally entrenched human rights are the mechanism of legal change, and in the case of the latter mechanism, only if the relevant jurisdiction allows proxies to exercise rights on behalf of individuals lacking capacity.

Patient's condition – terminal illness

> Original Claim 3: A regime resulting from necessity as the mechanism of legal change cannot sustain a terminal illness requirement.

The logic of this claim is that the conflict of duties may be present in cases where the patient does not suffer from a terminal illness. The necessity-based Dutch regime does not include a terminal illness requirement, bearing out this claim. However, the legislatively derivative regimes in Belgium and Luxembourg are inconsistent in this regard, suggesting that the claim should be limited to regimes which result directly from necessity as the mechanism of legal change (i.e. the Netherlands). While the Belgian regime does not include a terminal illness requirement for adults, the regime in Luxembourg does include a requirement that the patient be in a "terminal medical situation".

It should be noted that additional procedural protections could be imposed for non-terminal illness without invalidating this claim. For example in Belgium, if the patient "is clearly not expected to die in the near future", there is a mandatory additional consultation with either a psychiatrist or relevant specialist, and a waiting period of at least one month (*Law on Euthanasia of 28 May 2002*, §3).

> New Claim 4: Whether regimes based on the medical exception can be limited to those suffering from a terminal illness will depend on the focus of the public policy justification and the interpretation of public policy.

Patient-focussed public policy justifications mandate that the procedure be intended to benefit the patient or be therapeutic for the patient. This criterion is likely to be met if the patient is suffering unbearably and hopelessly, whether or not that suffering is caused by a terminal illness. Public-focussed public policy justifications are generally broader than patient-focussed public policy justifications, so would similarly not be limited to terminal illness. Professionally focussed public policy justifications reflect accepted medical practice, often with an additional role for a court in evaluating that practice through the addition of an adjective such as "proper", "reasonable" or "necessary" (Lewis 2012a, 357–364).

As already noted, there is only one example of a regime based on the medical exception; it is consistent with this claim: The more limited way in which the medical exception is employed in Montana is limited to the terminally ill because the public policy criterion was interpreted in light of the Rights of the Terminally Ill Act:

> There is no indication in the Rights of the Terminally Ill Act that physician aid in dying is against public policy. Indeed, the Act reflects legislative respect for the wishes of a patient facing incurable illness. The Act also indicates legislative regard and protection for a physician who honors his legal obligation to the patient. The Act immunizes a physician for following the patient's declaration even if it requires the physician to directly unplug the patient's ventilator or withhold medicine or medical treatment that is keeping the patient alive. Physician aid in dying, on the other hand, does not require such *direct* involvement by a physician. Rather, in physician aid in dying, the final death-causing act lies in the patient's hands. In light of the long-standing, evolving and unequivocal recognition of the terminally ill patient's right to self-determination at the end of life in [the Montana Rights of the Terminally Ill Act,] it would be incongruous to conclude that a physician's indirect aid in dying is contrary to public policy.
>
> *Baxter v State* 2009 (248–249)

> Original Claim 5: Regimes resulting from legal change based on rights may be restricted to those suffering from a terminal illness on the basis that any violation of those rights cannot be justified by the state interest in preserving life in cases of terminal illness, but could be in non-terminal cases.

Regimes resulting from legal change based on the rights to dignity, liberty, privacy, security of the person and even equality may be restricted to those suffering from a terminal illness on the basis that any violation of those rights cannot be justified by the state interest in preserving life in cases of terminal illness, but could be in non-terminal cases. Examples of such reasoning are found in the decisions of the Ninth and Second Circuit Courts of Appeal in the cases that were subsequently joined to reach the US Supreme Court in 1997. In the Ninth Circuit, the court held that in the case of the terminally ill, the individual's liberty interest "in choosing the time and manner of death" outweighed the state's interests in preserving life (*Compassion in Dying v Washington* 1996, 816–817). In the Second Circuit, the court observed when reflecting on the appellants' right to equal protection: "[W]hat interest can the state possibly have in requiring the prolongation of a life that is all but ended? Surely, the state's interest lessens as the potential for life diminishes" (*Quill v Vacco* 1996, 729).

The Colombian Constitutional Court's 1997 decision is also consistent with this claim:

> The state obligation to protect life must therefore be compatible with the constitutionally mandated respect for human dignity and personal autonomy. This is why the Court considers that in the case of terminally ill patients who experience intense suffering, this state obligation gives way to the informed consent of the patient who wishes to die in dignity. In fact, in this case, the state obligation is considerably diminished insofar as, based on medical evidence, it can be established beyond reasonable doubt that death is inevitable within a relatively short period of time.
>
> *Sentencia C-239* 1997, II.C.3 (translated by Michalowski 2009, 194, 205)

The claim is a relatively weak one, namely that a restriction to terminal illness is compatible with this type of rights-based mechanism of legal change. The claim is not that such a restriction is inevitable (unlike, for example, Claim 1). When might such a restriction be resisted? If the court finds the infringing prohibition to be overbroad or disproportionate either (i) even if there were an exception for terminal illness, or (ii) in its application to a class of individuals which is broader than those who are terminally ill. An example of this latter type of reasoning is found in the Supreme Court of Canada decision in *Carter* (*Carter v Canada (Attorney General)* 2015, [85]–[88]),[4] and has succeeded in the most recent challenge to the post-*Carter* federal regime requiring that death be "reasonably foreseeable" and the Québec pre-*Carter* regime requiring that the patient be at the "end of life" (*Truchon et Gladu v Canada (Procureur Général) et Québec (Procureur Général)* 2019). The governments of Canada and Québec decided not to appeal this decision and as noted above, the federal statute has now been amended to remove the requirement that the patient's death be reasonably foreseeable (*An Act to amend the Criminal Code (medical assistance in dying) 2021*).

The exception to this weak claim is that regimes based on the right to equality finding discrimination against those unable to commit suicide unaided cannot be limited to those who are terminally ill (or more accurately, such a limitation would be exceedingly hard to justify). There is no specimen regime to bear out (or not) this claim. It is though consistent with the dissent of Lamer CJC in *Rodriguez*. The Chief Justice of Canada found that the appellant's right to equality under Section 15(1) of the *Charter* was infringed by the criminal prohibition on assisted suicide which prevented those who were "physically unable to end their lives unassisted from choosing suicide when that option is in principle available to other members of the public" (*Rodriguez v British Columbia (Attorney General)* 1993, [167]). The relevant class was therefore those who were unable to end their lives without assistance, which would include some (but not all) terminally ill persons, but also many who would not qualify as terminally ill. The trial judge in *Carter* also found a similar infringement of the right to equality which was similarly not limited to the terminally ill (*Carter v Canada (Attorney General)* 2012, [15]).

Patient's condition – suffering

> Original Claim 6: Regimes resulting from necessity as a mechanism of legal change will always maintain a suffering requirement, which is not necessarily the case with regimes resulting from rights as the mechanism of legal change.

When necessity is the mechanism of legal change, the essential criteria are hopeless and unbearable suffering with no reasonable alternative to relieve it. The duty to prevent suffering is only triggered when suffering is present. The Dutch and its derivative regimes in Belgium and Luxembourg provide empirical support for this claim, although as we have seen in the analysis of Claim 3, this claim is likely to be less convincing in relation to the derivative regimes.

Indeed, one exception to this claim is already found in the Belgian statute, which allows the patient to make an advance request for euthanasia. However, since the triggering condition is irreversible unconsciousness, advance requests will not be applicable to many scenarios of future incompetence, including dementia. This unconsciousness requirement for advance requests, repeated in the Luxembourg Act, is inconsistent with unbearable suffering, and was the product of political compromise (Griffiths, Weyers, and Adams 2008, [9.4.3.6], [9.4.5], Nys 2017, 21–22).

There have been successive, as yet unsuccessful, attempts to amend the Act to allow an individual to execute an advance request to include cases where he "has lost awareness of his person, his mental and physical state, and his social and physical environment", although is not unconscious (Lewis 2009, 127–128, Lewis and Black 2013, 893). Such amendments would still permit euthanasia via an advance request when the patient is not (or no longer) suffering unbearably.

> Original Claim 7: In contrast, if the right to equality is the mechanism of legal change, a suffering requirement cannot be sustained as there is no such requirement imposed on the relevant comparator class.

There is no specimen regime to bear out (or not) this claim. In relation to Claim 5, we considered the approach of Lamer CJC in *Rodriguez*, who found a violation of the right to equality insofar as the criminal prohibition on assisted suicide prevented those who could not end their own lives without assistance from choosing to do so. An alternative approach to the right to equality is found in the decision of the Second Circuit in *Quill v Vacco*. The Court accepted an argument that the appellants' right to equal protection found in the Fourteenth Amendment was infringed by the inequality between terminally ill patients dependent on life-sustaining medical treatment, who may refuse such treatment and thereby end their lives; and terminally ill patients who do not require life-sustaining treatment and therefore are prevented by the criminal prohibition on assisted suicide from deciding to end their lives. (Although this decision was overturned on appeal to the US Supreme Court, its restriction to the terminally ill provides another theoretical example of the weak claim made in Claim 5.)

Under both of these approaches to the right to equality, a suffering-based criterion cannot be sustained. Those who are physically able to commit suicide or those who are terminally ill and choose to refuse life-sustaining treatment need not prove that they are suffering before doing so.

> New Claim 8: A suffering requirement may be sustainable if the rights to life, security of the person or dignity are the mechanisms of legal change, if infringement is based on the imposition of continued suffering by the state or the risk of premature [assisted] suicide to avoid continued suffering.

In *Carter*, the Supreme Court of Canada agreed with the trial judge that

> the prohibition on physician-assisted dying had the effect of forcing some individuals to take their own lives prematurely, for fear that they would be incapable of doing so when they reached the point where suffering was intolerable. On that basis … the right to life was engaged.
>
> *Carter v Canada (Attorney General)* 2015, [57]

The premise is therefore that only those who fear (i) that their suffering will become intolerable, and (ii) that they will become unable to take their own lives will consider premature suicide (and some subset of this group will die by premature suicide).

The court also found that the right to security of the person was engaged: "by leaving people like [the appellant] to endure intolerable suffering, it impinges on their security of the person" (*Carter v Canada (Attorney General)* 2015, [66]). The interpretation of the constitutional right to dignity in the 1997 decision of the Constitutional Court of Colombia similarly includes the right not to be forced to suffer unbearably:

> The Constitution is based on the philosophy of eradicating cruelty, and the prevention of cruelty is also required by respect for human

> dignity. However, according to the majority opinion, nothing can be crueller than to oblige a person to subsist despite experiencing disgraceful suffering.
>
> Michalowski 2009, 192 (paraphrasing *Sentencia C-239* 1997, [II.C.1])

By contrast, in 2007, I claimed that if the rights to autonomy or liberty are used, a suffering requirement cannot be sustained. The only example then available was the decision of the Ninth Circuit in *Compassion in Dying v Washington*, in which the court relied on the liberty interest protected by the Due Process clause of the Fourteenth Amendment. We have already seen that a terminal illness requirement was embedded in the court's analysis, consistent with Claim 5. A suffering requirement was not explicitly included, although the individual's suffering was certainly at the front of the court's mind:

> when a mentally competent adult is terminally ill, and wishes, free of any coercion, to hasten his death because his remaining days are an unmitigated torture, that person's liberty interest is at its height. For such a person, being forced to live is indeed being subjected to "pain … [and] suffering that is too intimate and personal for the State to insist on…"
>
> *Compassion in Dying v Washington* 1996, 834, citing *Planned Parenthood of Southeastern Pennsylvania v Casey* 1992 (852)

While I stand by this claim, it is notable that no court has taken such a route. Perhaps the closest has been the entwining of the rights to liberty and security of the person in *Carter* based on an "underlying … concern for the protection of individual autonomy and dignity"; the latter having a suffering requirement attached (*Carter v Canada (Attorney General)* 2015, [64]–[66]). Autonomy is perhaps not as attractive to litigants and judges as it is to commentators (Lewis 2007, 22–26, 41–42).

Type of assistance: euthanasia (active termination of life) and/or assisted suicide

> Original Claim 9: When necessity is the mechanism of legal change, both assisted suicide and euthanasia are permissible providing that the suffering and no reasonable alternative requirements are met.

The Dutch and derivative regimes support Claim 9; all permit both termination of life on request and assisted suicide. The latter is not explicitly covered by the Belgian statute, although Belgium's oversight body, the Federal Euthanasia Control and Evaluation Commission (FECEC) has accepted cases of assisted suicide as falling under the law (Commission fédérale de contrôle et d'évaluation de l'euthanasie. 2004, 13–14). In a recent development, the Belgian Public Prosecution Service has taken the position that assisting a suicide is not a criminal offence (De Standaard 2019).

> Original Claim 10: If rights are used as the mechanism of legal change, the right to equality could be used to challenge any limitation to assisted suicide if the individual is unable to commit suicide even with assistance.

Under either of the two hypothetical regimes resulting from the right to equality as the mechanism of legal change considered above, assistance in dying cannot be restricted to assisted suicide but must include the possibility of termination of life on request if the individual is unable to commit suicide with assistance. In fact, whichever right is used as the mechanism of legal change, the right to equality could be used in complement with that right. Thus, if the individual is unable to commit suicide with assistance, the right to equality could be used to challenge any limitation to assisted suicide. For example, the majority of the US Ninth Circuit in *Compassion in Dying v. Washington* accepted an argument based on the right to liberty but, nevertheless,

> recognize[d] that in some instances, the patient may be unable to self-administer the drugs and that administration by the physician, or a person acting under his direction or control, may be the only way the patient may be able to receive them.
>
> *Compassion in Dying v Washington* 1996 (832)

Prospective approval

> Original Claim 11: If rights are the mechanism of legal change, prospective approval could be consistent with such regimes, provided that the approval process does not unduly burden or disproportionately infringe the patient's rights.

In 2007, I observed that

> [w]hile prospective approval may be a cautionary approach adopted by judges setting out interim measures which will operate only until the legislature responds to a judicial decision that individuals have a right to assistance in dying, prospective approval is not mandated under such regimes.
>
> Lewis (2007, 147–148)

This is indeed what subsequently occurred in Canada. In February 2016, the Supreme Court of Canada granted a four-month extension to the one year suspension of the declaration of invalidity the Court had originally granted in 2015. At the same time, a majority of the Court created a constitutional exemption for those meeting the 2015 *Carter* criteria. Such persons could "apply to the superior court of their jurisdiction for relief during the extended period of suspension" (*Carter v Canada (Attorney General)* 2016). Eighteen persons made such applications (Lewis 2020).

The Colombian regime is a more permanent example of this claim. The Constitutional Court required prospective approval in order to guarantee that the patient's consent was free, informed and unequivocal (*Sentencia T-970* 2014, [7.2.5]). Requests for euthanasia must be approved by a special three-person multi-disciplinary hospital-based committee comprising a specialist in the patient's condition (not the treating physician), a lawyer, and a psychiatrist or clinical psychologist. Informal data suggests the cumbersome procedure is little used (Nolen 2019). That prospective approval regime may indeed be unduly or disproportionately burdensome at the end of life (Lewis 2020), and could be vulnerable to further constitutional challenge in this respect.

> Original Claim 12: A formal prospective approval requirement is inconsistent with necessity as the mechanism of legal change.

Even if a doctor had not obtained prospective approval, she would still be able to claim retrospectively that she had faced a conflict of duties. While the underlying defence would still be available, doctors could be encouraged to obtain prospective approval if referral to disciplinary and/or prosecutorial authorities were likely without it, or by using a separate lesser offence of failing to obtain prospective approval (along similar lines to the Dutch offence of failing to report an assisted death (*Wetboek van Strafrecht (Criminal Code)* 1881, Art 228(1)) (Lewis 2007, 134–135). No such regimes require prospective approval.

Assistor

> Original Claim 13: Regimes resulting from necessity as the mechanism of legal change will apply only to those who have a professional duty to relieve suffering which may conflict with their duty to preserve life.

Empirical support for this claim is found in the Netherlands and derivative regimes which apply only to doctors, and not to other health care professionals or loved ones. The restriction to doctors has been repeatedly upheld by the Dutch courts, most recently by the Supreme Court in 2019 (*Heringa* 2019, Ost and Mullock 2011, 168–169, discussing Schellekens and the facts of Heringa, The World Federation of Right to Die Societies 21 April 2019).

> Original Claim 14: If rights are the mechanism of legal change, restriction to doctors could be consistent with such regimes.

As with prospective approval requirements, when rights are used as the mechanism of legal change, a rule that only doctors can perform assisted dying *could* be imposed, provided that such a requirement did not unduly or disproportionately burden the exercise of the chosen right. One such example is that the Supreme Court of Canada decision in *Carter* is limited to consideration of restrictions on physician-assisted death.

However, unlike regimes resulting from necessity as the mechanism of legal change which are premised on the doctor's duty to prevent suffering, there is no *necessary* requirement that *only* doctors may provide assisted dying; indeed the subsequent Canadian legislation applies to nurse practitioners as well as doctors.

Legislative approaches

> New Claim 15: Regimes originating with legislation may superficially resemble regimes based on rights (eg Oregon) or necessity (eg Belgium; Luxembourg), but rights-based challenges against limitations embedded within such regimes will be more difficult as the underlying right is not yet established.

Equality-based challenges to legislative regimes may be more likely to be successful than those using other rights, for example by alleging discrimination against those who cannot commit suicide without assistance, or even with assistance. Alternatively, the entire regime could be constitutionally challenged either on division of powers grounds, or through the identification of other constitutional flaws. Examples of division of powers challenges are relatively easy to identify: The federal legislature in Australia repealed the short-lived Northern Territory euthanasia regime[5] (*Euthanasia Laws Act 1997 (Cth.), Sched. 1* 1997); there have been a number of ultimately unsuccessful federal attempts to invalidate or restrict the Oregon regime (Lewis 2007, 151–152, 157); and prior to the decision in *Carter*, the federal government of Canada considered such a challenge to the Québec statute permitting medical aid in dying. There was also an unsuccessful attempt to invalidate the California statute for failing to comply with state constitutional rules on the legislative process (*People ex rel. Becerra v. Superior Court* 2018).

The recent successful challenge to the Québec statute (discussed in Claim 5) can be distinguished as the relevant constitutional rights were established soon after the statute was enacted by the Supreme Court of Canada decision in *Carter* (*An Act Respecting End-of-Life Care 2014, RSQ c S-32.0001* 2014); (*Carter v Canada (Attorney General)* 2015); (*Truchon et Gladu v Canada (Procureur Général) et Québec (Procureur Général)* 2019).

Conclusion

The Northern Territory (Australia) statute which combined elements from both rights- and necessity-based regimes is an example of the greater freedom possessed by legislators in comparison to judges, who may be constrained by the way in which a claim has been brought using constitutionally entrenched human rights, or, in the case of common law judges, the need to develop the substantive law incrementally in a consistent and principled fashion with due regard to precedent. Experience from Canada and Colombia demonstrates that legislatures in jurisdictions with constitutionally entrenched human rights risk expansive regimes if they fail to act, even pro-active legislatures like Québec risk being forced by rights-based challenges to bring their regime into line (*Truchon et Gladu v Canada (Procureur Général) et Québec (Procureur Général)* 2019). The greatest scope for legislative autonomy is pre-emptive, avoiding judicial interpretation of constitutionally entrenched rights and/or statutory or common law defences.

Statute

An Act Relating to Patient Choice and Control at End of Life 2013.
An Act Respecting End-of-Life Care 2014, RSQ c S-32.0001.
An Act to amend the Criminal Code and to make related amendments to other Acts (medical assistance in dying) 2016.
An Act to amend the Criminal Code (medical assistance in dying) 2021.
Attorney General's Reference (No. 6 of 1980) [1981] QB 715 (CA).
Crimes Act (N.Z.) 1961.
Death With Dignity Act ORS 127.800-127.995.
Euthanasia Laws Act 1997 (Cth.), Sched. 1.
Rights of the Terminally Ill Act 1995 (Northern Territory, Australia)
Termination of Life on Request and Assisted Suicide (Review Procedures) Act 2001.
Wetboek van Strafrecht (Criminal Code).

Case law

Baxter v State 354 Mont 234, 224 P3d 1211 (2009) (Montana Supreme Court).
Bourne [1939] 1 KB 687 (Central Criminal Court).
Bravery v Bravery [1954] 1 WLR 1169 (CA).
Brown [1994] 1 AC 212 (HL).
Carter v Canada (Attorney General) [2012] BCSC 886.
Carter v Canada (Attorney General) 2015 SCC 5 (Supreme Court of Canada).
Carter v Canada (Attorney General) 2016 SCC 4 (Supreme Court of Canada).
Compassion in Dying v Washington 79 F3d 790 (1996, 9th Cir (en banc).
Dudley and Stephens (1884) 14 QBD 273.
Heringa Hoge Raad, 16 April 2019, No 598 (18/00573).
Howe [1987] AC 417.
Nicklinson and Lamb v United Kingdom (2015) 61 EHRR SE7 (ECHR).
People ex rel. Becerra v. Superior Court 29 Cal.App.5th 486 (2018).
Planned Parenthood of Southeastern Pennsylvania v Casey 505 US 833 (1992).
Pols Nederlandse Jurisprudentie 1987, no. 607 (Supreme Court).
Pretty v United Kingdom (2002) 25 EHRR 1 (ECHR).
Quill v Vacco 80 F3d 716 (1996, 2nd Cir).
República de Colombia Ministerio de Salud y Protección Social. 2015. Resolución 1216 de 2015 por medio de la cual se da cumplimiento a la orden cuarta de la sentencia T-970 de

2014 de la Honorable Corte Constitucional en relación con las directrices para la organización y funcionamiento de los Comités para hacer efectivo el derecho a morir con dignidad.
República de Colombia Ministerio de Salud y Protección Social. 2018. Resolución 825 de 2018 por medio de la cual se reglamenta el procedimiento para hacer efectivo el derecho a morir con dignidad de los niños, niñas y adolescentes.
R ([Omid] T) v Secretary of State for Justice [2018] EWHC 2615 (Admin).
R (Conway) v Secretary of State for Justice [2018] EWCA Civ 1431.
R (Newby) v Secretary of State for Justice [2019] EWHC 3118 (Admin).
Re A (Children) (Conjoined Twins: Surgical Separation) [2001] Fam 147 (CA).
Rodriguez v British Columbia (Attorney General) [1993] 3 SCR 519 (Supreme Court of Canada).
Sentencia C-239 (1997) (Corte Constitucional, República de Colombia).
Sentencia T-970 (2014) (Corte Constitucional, República de Colombia).
Truchon et Gladu v Canada (Procureur Général) et Québec (Procureur Général) 2019 QCCS 3792.
Vacco v Quill 521 US 793 (1997).
Washington v Glucksberg 521 US 702 (1997) (US Supreme Court).

Notes

1 The medical exception is discussed in Leenen (2001, 126), Welie (1992, 429–432), Griffiths, Bood, and Weyers (1998, 91–97), Weyers (2001, 11, 19), and Adams and Nys (2005, 5, 14, n 21).

2 Although the case had been argued on the basis of the patient's rights under the state constitution, the majority declined to rule on the constitutionality of the statutory provisions as they were able to decide the case without reaching the constitutional questions.

3 For a discussion of the reasons for and process of legal change, see Adams and Nys (2003, 2005), Griffiths, Weyers, and Adams (2008), Jones, Gastmans, and MacKellar (2017), and Nys (2017).

4 See also the concurring opinion of Arango Mejía and Gaviria Díaz in the 1997 decision of the Colombia Constitutional Court (*Sentencia C-239* 1997).

5 In 1995, the Northern Territory of Australia passed the Rights of the Terminally Ill Act, which legalized physician-assisted suicide and physician-performed voluntary active euthanasia (*Rights of the Terminally Ill Act 1995 (Northern Territory, Australia)* 1995, s 3). The Act was overturned by the Australian Parliament in 1997, having been in force for less than a year (*Euthanasia Laws Act 1997 (Cth.), Sched. 1* 1997). The substantive requirements of the Northern Territory statute were similar to those now in force in Oregon: terminal illness and a competent, voluntary request. However, unlike Oregon, there was a suffering requirement. This was coupled with a subjective "no reasonable alternative" constraint. The doctor could not proceed if there were "palliative care options reasonably available to the patient to alleviate the patient's pain and suffering to levels acceptable to the patient". Numerous procedural safeguards were also included (*Rights of the Terminally Ill Act 1995 (Northern Territory, Australia)* 1995, ss 4, 7(1)(b), (c), (d), (h), (i), 8(1)). The Northern Territory experience is discussed by Chesterman (1998, 384–385), Amarasekara (1997), Mendelson (1995), Gillett (1995), Plattner (1997), and Manzione (2002). For information on the use of the law during the brief period of its operation, see Kissane, Street, and Nitschke (1998).

References

Adams, M., & Nys, H. (2003). Comparative reflections on the Belgian Euthanasia Act 2002. *Medical Law Review, 11*, 353–376.

Adams, M., & Nys, H. (2005). Euthanasia in the low countries: Comparative reflections on the Belgian and Dutch Euthanasia Act. In P. Schotsmans and T. Meulenbergs, (eds). *Euthanasia and palliative care in the low countries* (5–35). Leuven, Belgium: Peeters.

Amarasekara, K. (1997). Euthanasia and the quality of legislative safeguards. *Monash University Law Review, 23*(1), 1.

Bostrom, B, & Lagerwey, W. (1988). The high court of the Hague Case No. 79065, October 21, 1986. *Issues in Law and Medicine, 3*, 445.

Chesterman, S. (1998). Last rights: Euthanasia, the sanctity of life, and the law in the Netherlands and the Northern Territory of Australia. *International and Comparative Law Quarterly, 47*, 362.

Commission fédérale de contrôle et d'évaluation de l'euthanasie. (2004). Premier rapport aux chambres legislatives (2002–2003).

De Standaard (2019). Arts niet vervolgd voor hulp bij zelfdoding [Doctor not prosecuted for assistance with suicide] (Online) 26 April 2019. https://www.standaard.be/cnt/dmf20190426_04353439.

Gillett, G. (1995). Ethical aspects of the Northern Territory euthanasia legislation. *Journal of Law and Medicine, 3*, 145–151.

Griffiths, J., Weyers, H., & Adams, M. (2008). *Euthanasia and law in Europe*. Bloomsbury Publishing.

Griffiths, J., Weyers, H., & Bood, A. (1998). *Euthanasia and law in the Netherlands*. Amsterdam: Amsterdam University Press.

Hughes, G. (1963). Two views on consent in the criminal law. *The Modern Law Review, 26*(3), 233–248.

Jones, D. A., Gastmans, C., & MacKellar, C. (Eds.). (2017). *Euthanasia and assisted suicide: lessons from Belgium* (Vol. 42). Cambridge: Cambridge University Press.

Kissane, D. W., Street, A., & Nitschke, P. (1998). Seven deaths in Darwin: Case studies under the Rights of the Terminally III Act, Northern Territory, Australia. *The Lancet, 352*(9134), 1097–1102.

Leenen, H. J. (2001). The development of euthanasia in the Netherlands. *European Journal of Health Law, 8*(2), 125–133.

Lewis, P. (2007). *Assisted dying and legal change*. Oxford: Oxford University Press.

Lewis, P. (2009). Euthanasia in Belgium five years after legalisation. *European Journal of Health Law, 16*(2), 125–138.

Lewis, P. (2012). The medical exception. *Current Legal Problems, 65*(1), 355–376.

Lewis, P. (2021). Should assisted dying require the consent of a high court judge? In B. White and L. Willmott, (eds). *International perspectives on end-of-life reform: Politics, persuasion and persistence*. Cambridge: Cambridge University Press.

Lewis, P. J. (2012b). The failure of the defence of necessity as a mechanism of legal change on assisted dying in the common law world. In D. Baker and J. Horder, (eds). *The Sanctity of Life & the Criminal Law: The Legacy of Glanville Williams*, Cambridge: Cambridge University Press.

Lewis, P. J., & Black, I. (2012). The effectiveness of legal safeguards in jurisdictions that allow assisted dying. Commission on Assisted Dying (Online) January 2012. https://demosuk.wpengine.com/wp-content/uploads/2016/09/Penney-Lewis-briefing-paper.pdf.

Lewis, P., & Black, I. (2013). Adherence to the request criterion in jurisdictions where assisted dying is lawful? A review of the criteria and evidence in the Netherlands, Belgium, Oregon, and Switzerland. *The Journal of Law, Medicine & Ethics, 41*(4), 885–898.

Manzione, L. L. (2001). Is there a right to die: A comparative study of three societies (Australia, Netherlands, United States). *Georgia Journal of International and Comparative Law, 30*, 443.

Mendelson, D. (1995). The Northern Territory's euthanasia legislation in historical perspective. *Journal of Law and Medicine, 3*, 136.

Michalowski, S. (2009). Legalising active voluntary euthanasia through the courts: Some lessons from Colombia. *Medical Law Review, 17*(2), 183–218.

Nolen, S. (2019). Colombia takes medically assisted death into the morally murky world of terminally ill children. *Globe and Mail (Canada)*, 1 March 2019. https://www.theglobeandmail.com/world/article-colombia-takes-medically-assisted-death-into-the-morally-murky-world/ (Accessed 10 July 2019).

Nys, H. (2017). A discussion of the legal rules on euthanasia in Belgium briefly compared with the rules in Luxembourg and the Netherlands. In D. A. Jones, C. Gastmans and C. MacKellar, (eds). *Euthanasia and assisted suicide: Lessons from Belgium* (7–25). Cambridge: Cambridge University Press.

Ost, S., & Mullock, A. (2011). Pushing the boundaries of lawful assisted dying in the Netherlands? Existential suffering and lay assistance. *European Journal of Health Law, 18*(2), 163–189.

Plattner, A. L. (1997). Australia's Northern Territory: The first jurisdiction to legislate voluntary euthanasia, and the first to repeal it. *DePaul Journal of Health Care Law., 1*, 645.

Riddell, L. (1925). The legal responsibility of the surgeon. *Transactions of the Medico-legal Society, 19*(1), 83–100.

Robinson, J. (2010). Baxter and the return of physician-assisted suicide. *Hastings Center Report, 40*(6), 15–17.

Stephen, J. F. (1878). *Digest of the criminal law.* St. Louis: FH Thomas.

The World Federation of Right to Die Societies. (2019). Dutch lawsuit (Heringa) has come to a final end, (online) 21 April, https://www.worldrtd.net/news/dutch-lawsuit-heringa-has-come-final-end.

Welie, J. V. (1992). The medical exception: Physicians, euthanasia and the Dutch criminal law. *Journal of Medicine and Philosophy, 17*(4), 419–437.

Weyers, H. (2001). Euthanasia: The process of legal change in the Netherlands. In A. Klijn, (ed). *Regulating physician-negotiated death* (11–27). Amsterdam: Elsevier.

3 Contesting death rights*

Reflections from the courtroom

Alex Ruck Keene

Introduction[1]

There have been a considerable number of cases brought around the world by individuals seeking to assert a right to be assisted with dying before the courts. At the time of writing, the most recent of these to have reached a conclusion in England and Wales was that brought by Noel Conway to challenge the compatibility of the ban on providing assistance with suicide (or assisted dying, as Mr Conway would prefer it to be called) with the European Convention on Human Rights (ECHR). In this chapter, I reflect on Mr Conway's case and its implications.

The chapter does not represent a full discussion of the case during its complicated life up to the Supreme Court, nor does it provide a critique of the judgments given during its course. Those can be found elsewhere in this volume. Rather, the chapter constitutes personal reflections deriving from the case from the perspective of Counsel instructed in it, as junior Counsel for Mr Conway. It is therefore not a conventional chapter in an academic work, and needs also to come with some caveats.

First, while I have Mr Conway's consent to write it, as well as that of Dignity in Dying,[2] who supported his challenge, it does not address, because it could not, decisions taken as to the strategy deployed to advance the case. Not only are those privileged and confidential matters, but it would be of little wider interest either to hear a justification of decisions taken which worked or defence of those which appear not to have worked. That is a judgment that better falls to others.

Second, as Counsel instructed in the case, my task (as with any barrister or lawyer) was to seek to develop my client's case as effectively as possible, irrespective of what I may have felt on the cause that Mr Conway may have represented. Readers may be able to detect from what follows my own personal feelings about that cause, but they are not, or should not be, a primary consideration.

Third, and most important, litigating a case such as this was undoubtedly uniquely stressful in terms of the issues involved and the depths of emotion

* This chapter was written prior to Mr Conway's death. The statement he made before he asked for his ventilation to be stopped can be found at: https://www.dignityindying.org.uk/news/noel-conways-final-statement/ (accessed 15 June 2021).

DOI: 10.4324/9780429329739-3

that they provoked for all concerned. But whatever I (or the other lawyers – or indeed the judges) may have felt is as nothing compared to what Mr Conway experienced. I would strongly recommend that those who want to understand his perspective read his book *Hard Days' Journey into Night* (Conway, 2019). Whether or not one agrees with the outcome of his challenge, I would defy anyone not to marvel at his grace and courage, as well as that of his family around him.

Background

While this is not a memoir, it may be of assistance to readers to understand something of my background and how I came to be instructed (i.e. appointed to be on the team representing Mr Conway in court). I have been in practice as a barrister in England at 39 Essex Chambers since 2003, increasingly specialising in mental capacity law (broadly defined). For some time prior to being instructed in Mr Conway's case, I also combined my practice with an academic career, in particular as a Wellcome research fellow at King's College London, as well as a visiting lecturer there, teaching on the mental health, ethics and law MSc jointly run by the Law School and the Institute of Psychiatry, Psychology and Neuroscience. I developed a growing interest in end-of-life matters, in part stemming from my involvement as a very junior barrister in Leslie Burke's case.[3] I also had a sideline as a law reformer, including 18 months spent on secondment to the Law Commission working on the Mental Capacity and Deprivation of Liberty project.[4] In the latter guise, I had to think long and hard not only about the demands of the United Nations Convention on the Rights of Persons with Disabilities (of which more later) but also about the gaps between what statutory law may require in any given area and the actual application of that law in practice.

Professional delicacy tends to militate against asking why you may have been instructed on a particular matter (and the cab rank rule requires barristers to accept instructions in matters where they are professionally competent and available).[5] However, it may have been a combination of some or all of the above that led to my instruction by Irwin Mitchell as junior Counsel for Mr Conway, notwithstanding the fact that I had not at that point had any direct experience of matters relating to assisted dying. During the – long – course of the case, I was also heavily involved in developing guidance for the British Medical Association/Royal College of Physicians on decision-making in relation to clinically assisted nutrition and hydration, and was instructed as legal adviser to the independent review of the Mental Health Act 1983. I note both of these because they formed part of the wider context in which the reflections below were developed.

Facts of the case

Mr Conway, aged 67 at the time that the proceedings started, had been a university lecturer, married, with a son, daughter, step-son and grandchild.

In November 2014, having had previously been very fit and active, he was diagnosed with motor neurone disease ('MND'), a degenerative and terminal illness. He wanted, at the point where he had only six months to live, to be permitted to seek medical assistance to end his own life, while he still retained the physical and mental capacity to do so.

It is no longer a criminal offence to end one's life in England and Wales. However, it is unlawful to assist someone to do so. Under s.2(1) Suicide Act 1961 ('SA 1961'), any medical professional who provided Mr Conway with the assistance he sought would be prima facie committing a criminal offence. Mr Conway could therefore not realistically expect to succeed in enlisting such support. By judicial review proceedings initiated in December 2016 against the Secretary of State for Justice, Mr Conway therefore sought a declaration under s.4(2) Human Rights Act 1998 that s.2(1) SA 1961 was incompatible with Article 8(1) European Convention on Human Rights ('ECHR') ('Right to respect for private and family life, home and correspondence'). He argued that it operated so as to prevent him from receiving assistance from any medical professional in securing death at a time of his own choosing, when he retained the ability to undertake the final act(s) required, and when he:

1 Had been diagnosed as terminally ill and given a clinically assessed prognosis of 6 months or less to live;
2 Had the mental capacity to decide whether to receive assistance to die; and
3 Had made a voluntary, clear, settled and informed decision to receive assistance to die.

Mr Conway further put forward proposals for safeguards which included the requirement of a High Court judge to determine and declare whether criteria (1)–(3) were met in individual cases.

Mr Conway's challenge was ultimately unsuccessful, the Supreme Court acknowledging that the issue was of '*transcendent public importance. It touches us all. We all have to experience the death of people about whom we care. We all have to contemplate our own death*'[6] but that, '*not without some reluctance*,'

> The prospects of Mr Conway's succeeding in his claim before this court [were not] sufficient to justify our giving him permission to pursue it, with all that that would entail for him, for his family, for those on all sides of this multi-faceted debate, for the general public and for this court.[7]

Mr Conway has described how he was,

> Particularly disappointed that the Courts have instead listened to the arguments of doctors who have never met me but think they know best about the end of my life. I have no choice over whether I die; my illness

> means I will die anyway. The only option I currently have is to remove my ventilator and effectively suffocate to death under sedation. To me this is not acceptable, and for many other dying people this choice is not available at all.
>
> Quoted in Shropshire Live (2018)

I will leave it to readers to consider how his lawyers may have felt.

Reflections on the case

I acted for Mr Conway from the point of drafting the grounds of challenge to the Suicide Act through the end of his case, working together with three Queen's Counsel at different stages (Richard Gordon QC, Nathalie Lieven QC and David Pannick QC) and another junior barrister, Annabel Lee. As set out in the introduction, the purpose of this chapter is not to undertake an after-action report, but to reflect from a personal perspective on matters that struck me most in the course of acting in the case. There are four that exercised, and continue to exercise me, which may also be of wider importance for readers of a work such as this, and to the wider public debate about these issues. They are (1) the autonomy asymmetry, (2) the irrelevance or insufficiency of mental capacity, (3) the curious case of the UN Convention on the Rights of Persons with Disabilities, and (4) the place of social rights in the debate about whether assisted dying should be lawful. I shall now consider each in turn.

The autonomy asymmetry

Perhaps because of my background and interest in mental capacity matters, in particular at the end-of-life, one thing that struck me with dramatic and increasing force was the extent to which Mr Conway's case challenged some (unspoken) articles of faith in the medical treatment context, and the curious ways in which this was responded to. In particular, I found it difficult to escape the impression that Mr Conway's case was felt by the courts to not only pose the question of *how* the law (whether made by the courts or by Parliament) should respond to a request for assistance with dying but also *whether* it should even recognise his right to make such a request.

While refusing to accept a request and refusing to accept that a request could even be validly made reach the same end point, on a proper analysis the second approach raises deep questions about the extent to which the concept of 'autonomy' actually does or should play the cardinal role that it is said to in medical treatment cases.

Lord Sumption had laid the groundwork for this in *Nicklinson*[8] when questioning whether mental capacity was sufficient, observing (at paragraph 228) that – in essence – '[i]t is one thing to assess some one's mental ability to form a judgment, but another to discover their true reasons for the decision which they have made and to assess the quality of those reasons.' In other words, Lord Sumption appeared to suggest, we might not want even to allow a person to make a request, even if they had capacity, because we were troubled about their reasons for doing so. This is especially if we were troubled about the extent that they might be influenced by 'indirect social pressure' on them 'arising from the low self-esteem of many old or severely ill and dependent people, combined with the spontaneous and negative perceptions of patients about the views of those around them' (paragraph 228).

At least some of the judges who considered Mr Conway's case also shared this view. While expressly disavowing that they were speaking about Mr Conway himself, the first court which looked in detail at his case, the Divisional Court,[9] noted (at paragraph 100) that

> [t]he involvement of the High Court to check capacity and absence of pressure or duress does not meet the real gravamen of the case regarding protection of the weak and vulnerable. Persons with serious debilitating terminal illnesses may be prone to feelings of despair and low self-esteem and consider themselves a burden to others, which make them wish for death. They may be isolated and lonely, particularly if they are old, and that may reinforce such feelings and undermine their resilience. All this may be true while they retain full legal capacity and are not subjected to improper pressure by others.[10]

What struck me forcefully during the course of the case, and what still strikes me is, is how this argument cuts at the foundations of the absolute right to refuse physical health treatment that is so central to the English concept of autonomy.[11] In other words, the pressures that Lord Sumption identifies are, logically, not equally at work where a person is refusing treatment. Indeed, this was recognised by the Supreme Court of Canada in *Carter v Canada*,[12] the Supreme Court in that case noting that

> [114] At trial Canada went into some detail about the risks associated with the legalization of physician-assisted dying. In its view, there are many possible sources of error and many factors that can render a patient "decisionally vulnerable" and thereby give rise to the risk that persons without a rational and considered desire for death will in fact end up dead. It points to cognitive impairment, depression or other mental illness, coercion, undue influence, psychological or emotional manipulation, systemic prejudice (against the elderly or people with disabilities), and the possibility of ambivalence or misdiagnosis as factors that may escape detection or give rise to errors in capacity assessment. Essentially, Canada argues that, given the breadth of this list, there is no reliable way to identify those who are vulnerable and those who are not. As a result, it says, a blanket prohibition is necessary.
>
> [115] The evidence accepted by the trial judge does not support Canada's argument. Based on the evidence regarding assessment processes

> in comparable end-of-life medical decision-making in Canada, the trial judge concluded that vulnerability can be assessed on an individual basis, using the procedures that physicians apply in their assessment of informed consent and decisional capacity in the context of medical decision-making more generally. Concerns about decisional capacity and vulnerability arise in all end-of-life medical decision-making. **Logically speaking, there is no reason to think that the injured, ill, and disabled who have the option to refuse or to request withdrawal of lifesaving or life-sustaining treatment, or who seek palliative sedation, are less vulnerable or less susceptible to biased decision-making than those who might seek more active assistance in dying. The risks that Canada describes are already part and parcel of our medical system.**
>
> Emphasis added

It was also striking that clinical guidance that featured heavily before the court in Mr Conway's case sought to guide clinicians to question the 'true reasons' for the decision that has been made. In guidance drawn up by the Association for Palliative Medicine (2016) addressing ventilator removal at the request of those with motor neurone disease, a section (page 15) on 'validating the decision' directs a senior doctor that they need to ensure that the request is 'a settled decision of a patient with capacity', and, in documenting the decision to proceed with withdrawal and evaluating the decision, suggests that the doctor should record, inter alia,

- That alternative approaches are known and rejected by the patient
- That the patient knows they will die as a consequence of withdrawal
- That there is no coercion, **nor is the decision is driven by mistaken kindness to the family**
- That this [is] a settled view of the patient[.]

Emphasis added

The guidance leaves tantalisingly open what should happen if the doctor takes the view that the decision **is** driven by mistaken kindness to the family. How is this to be squared with the conventional wisdom that an adult with capacity can refuse treatment for any reason, whether good, bad or non-existent?[13] Sadly, this question was left unanswered by the courts in Mr Conway's case.

By way of (strange) irony, these arguments were unfolding at precisely the same time as the independent Review of the Mental Health Act was considering whether the (equally traditional) exclusion from the right to refuse treatment should apply to those detained under the Mental Health Act 1983.[14] In that context, the justification for not accepting such refusals as binding (at least in the context of secure against a risk that the person would otherwise pose to themselves) is ultimately the societal 'hunch' that the person will in some way come to accept and welcome the intervention carried out against their will when they were 'not in their right mind', to use the colloquial phrase.

Not least because of the conjunction of the case and my work on the Review, I must confess that I spent some considerable time wondering whether the intellectually honest answer to Mr Conway's case was, in reality, that **refusals** of treatment simply should not be honoured – in both the mental and physical health zones – where the medical professionals could justify intervention on the basis that they could secure the person's life. In other words, a person's right to say 'no' to medical treatment should not be accepted at any point where a medical professional considered that they could, in fact, save their life.

The insufficiency of capacity?

In English law, a prime determinant of autonomy is the concept of 'mental capacity', defined as a person's ability functionally to understand, retain, use and weigh information (or to communicate a decision).[15] However, while, as noted above, it is always asserted that a person with capacity has the right to refuse even life-sustaining treatment, in reality, it is difficult to avoid the suspicion that the test for mental capacity is sometimes 'bent' in order to achieve the outcome of securing a person's life. In the physical health zone, just as much as in the mental health zone, we therefore may suspect that treatment refusals are only really honoured where there is a reason that the clinicians (or, ultimately, the judge) can understand and respect, even through gritted teeth.[16] Interestingly, this can also be seen even in the case of those lacking capacity to make decisions as to treatment, including life-sustaining treatment. The Court of Protection[17] has increasingly focussed in 'best interests' decision-making[18] on the wishes and feelings of the person concerned even where they lack capacity (Ruck Keene and Auckland, 2015).[19] In deciding whether to consent on behalf of 'P', the person concerned, to treatment, in the face of P's objections, it is possible to see, in different case law, the judges looking to identify whether the refusal reflects a sufficiently clear and consistent expression of their values, honouring it where it does and overruling where it does not. Contrast, for instance:

- *Wye Valley NHS Trust v B* [2015] EWCOP 60, a case in which the Court of Protection declined to hold that a life-saving operation was in the best interests of a man lacking capacity to decide whether to consent to or refuse the procedure. This was on the basis that the judge considered that to allow it to be undertaken would represent an unjustified attack as on his 'fierce independence' (paragraph 43). The judge was clearly influenced by the fact that the man had no fear of death based on his religious beliefs); and
- *East Lancashire Hospitals NHS Trust v PW* [2019] EWCOP 10, a case in which the judge decided that a very similar life-saving operation should

> go ahead in the face of the patient's (incapacitous) opposition. In her decision, the judge was influenced by the fact that the evidence was that man did not wish to die, but had a delusional belief as to mechanisms that could save his life.

This therefore may suggest that courts are not merely looking for capacity but some form of narrative coherence when it comes to refusals of treatment. See for example, the *C* case, in which the court found highly persuasive in its determination that a patient had capacity to refuse dialysis following an overdose the evidence of her adult daughters that this refusal was '*entirely in keeping with both her (unusual) value system and her (unusual) personality.*'[20]

By a side wind Mr Conway's case may therefore shed important light on some of the underpinning, and frequently unexplored, assumptions that go into determinations of capacity in the context of medical treatment. At a minimum, I would suggest that it should make assessors of capacity examine their own beliefs and values before assessing the capacity of a person to make a decision to accept or refuse life-sustaining treatment, to ensure that they are not – inadvertently – either asking too much or too little of the person.[21]

However, all of this leaves unanswered the question of how society is to approach the problem of 'self-imposed coercion' in decision-making about life-sustaining treatment, at least through the conventional prism of mental capacity.

Does it, perhaps, suggest that we need to look more closely at the work of those who, drawing from feminist scholarship, emphasise the extent to which the traditional conception of autonomy enshrined in the law simply does not properly take into account the extent to which individuals do not make decisions in isolation? (Kong, 2017). And/or does it mean that we should be welcoming the recent expansion of the inherent jurisdiction of the High Court to grant whatever relief it considers necessary and proportionate to secure the right to life and the 'higher autonomy' of vulnerable adults even where they have the capacity to choose to make unwise decisions?[22] This expansion, at least in some cases, appears to allow the High Court to direct against that adult to prevent them doing what they are asking to do.[23]

I will look in the last section of this chapter at whether there are alternative ways in which to address some of these dilemmas, but I want to look first at the UN Convention on the Rights of Persons with Disabilities ('CRPD') as a further disruptor to conventional thinking about decision-making in the medical treatment context.

The UN Convention on the Rights of Persons with Disabilities (CPRD)

The CRPD did not appear in any of the judgments of the courts considering Mr Conway's case, even though it featured in arguments put before the courts, both for and against that s.2(1) Suicide Act is incompatible with the ECHR (as a tool for interpreting the ECHR):

- For the argument, on the basis that it supported the proposition that domestic laws should not place hurdles in the face of those who, through physical impairment, are unable to exercise the same right to determine the time and manner of their death as would a person without such physical impairment;
- Against the argument, on the basis that any move towards making assisted dying easier would be to reinforce pressure on those with disabilities to consider their lives of lesser value than those without disability.

I was also heavily engaged in other work relating to the CRPD throughout the course of the case, and was watching with considerable interest how the CRPD fared in one of its first substantive outings before the English court courts. That the courts in Mr Conway's case made no reference to in their judgments reflected, I suspect, their frustration at the difficulty of interpreting it in his case. That gives rise to wider questions as to how arguments relating to the CRPD should be tailored to domestic courts,[24] but for present purposes, I want to look at what the CRPD might tell us about how to navigate some of the turbulent waters thrown up by Mr Conway's case.

The CRPD, concluded in 2006, seeks to bring about a radical change in the approach adopted in the social, political and legal arenas to those with disabilities (and, indeed, to the very concept of disability). Disabled persons' organisations had a significant input into its drafting (although the actual drafting was done by representatives of member states). The CRPD has been very widely ratified, the UK doing so in 2009. The UK also ratified the Optional Protocol, enabling individuals or groups to take complaints to the Committee on the Rights of Persons with Disabilities (the oversight body for the CRPD) ('the CRPD Committee'). The CRPD Committee, the majority of whose members are themselves disabled persons,[25] can request information from and make recommendations to states which are party to the Convention, usually in the form of 'concluding observations' on the reports of those states on their compliance with it; some 94 concluding observations having been issued at the time of writing.

The status of the CRPD in England and Wales has recently been summarised thus:

> While the *UNCRPD* remains currently an undomesticated international instrument, and therefore of no *direct* effect [...], it nonetheless provides a useful framework to address the rights of persons with disabilities. By ratifying the *UNCRPD* (as the UK has done) this jurisdiction has undertaken that, wherever possible, its laws will conform to the norms and values which the *UNCRPD* enshrines [...].[26]

The CPRD therefore represents a set of 'norms and values' agreed on internationally in respect of the approach to be taken to disability.

The CRPD, however, appears to point in interestingly divergent directions when it comes to the question of assistance with dying. On the one hand, autonomy and dignity are central to the CRPD,[27] and much of the work of the CRPD Committee to date has been directed to seeking to ensure that decision-making in relation to medical treatment is undertaken solely on the basis of consent.[28] That would suggest that the CRPD supports the propositions (1) that a person in Mr Conway's position be able to make a request for medical assistance to enable them to fulfil his autonomous desire to determine the time and manner of his death, and (2) it is for a person in Mr Conway's position to determine what they consider to be a dignified manner of death, rather than for society or a court to identify for them what would be dignified.

On the other hand, there is an – understandable – emphasis in the CRPD on ensuring that those with disabilities are not discriminated against either in their enjoyment of the right to life (Article 10) or in their right to the highest attainable standard of health (Article 25). That aspect of the CRPD was relied on by those concerned that any change to s.2(1) Suicide Act would give the message that the lives of those with disabilities are in some way worth less than those without disabilities.

What therefore has the CRPD Committee said, as the source of authoritative guidance on the meaning of the Convention? It has said nothing of direct relevance in any of its general comments or other general guidance documents. In scrutinising the compliance of member states with the CRPD, it has examined Belgium, where not only assistance with dying but also euthanasia is permitted, and made no mention of either in its concluding observations. It has, however, in its examination of Canada in 2017, noted in the context of the right to life enshrined in Article 10[29] that it was,

> 23 [...] concerned about the adoption of legislation that provides for medical assistance in dying [which includes euthanasia], including on the grounds of disability. It is also concerned about the absence of regulations for monitoring medical assistance in dying, the absence of data to assess compliance with the procedural safeguards regarding such assistance, and the lack of sufficient support to facilitate civil society engagement with and monitoring of this practice.

However, the Committee did not then go on to recommend that medical assistance in dying be abolished, but rather that Canada should,

> 24 (a) Ensure persons who seek an assisted death have access to alternative courses of action and to a dignified life made possible with appropriate palliative care, disability support, home care and other social measures that support human flourishing;

(b) Establish regulations pursuant to the law requiring collection and reporting of detailed information about each request and intervention for medical assistance in dying;

(c) Develop a national data standard and an effective and independent mechanism to ensure that compliance with the law and regulations is strictly enforced and that no person with disability is subjected to external pressure.

It therefore appears that the CRPD Committee considers that even euthanasia – that is, going beyond that which was contended for by Mr Conway – is not per se contrary to the CRPD. I suspect that that may come as a surprise, and indeed a source of some alarm, for some disability rights activists opposed to assisted dying and/or euthanasia[30] although not for those in support of it (Shildrick, 2015). It will, in this context, be of interest to see whether the CRPD Committee maintains its 'pro-autonomy' stance with regard to the related question of when life-sustaining treatment can be withdrawn from a person in a prolonged disorder of consciousness, which it is due to consider at the time of writing regarding the case of Vincent Lambert.[31]

It equally appears, however, the apparent tensions between the relevant articles of the CRPD outlined above ultimately resolve in favour of what might be an important, and perhaps so far under-examined, partial solution to the dilemmas raised by Mr Conway's case, namely, the importance of social rights, to which I now turn.

Social rights

I suspect largely because of the other work that I was involved in during the currency of Mr Conway's case, the recommendation of the CRPD Committee outlined above at paragraph 24(a) of its concluding observations resonated strongly with me as I worked on Mr Conway's case. I should emphasise that nothing that I saw of Mr Conway's case led me to think that he was in any way provided with anything other than 'appropriate palliative care, home care and other social measures to support human flourishing',[32] but it is, I think, appropriate to take stock and ask whether this is always the case. If the honest answer is that there are some circumstances under which a request for assistance is made because the person has not been provided with appropriate care, then where would this take us?[33]

It seems to me that this question requires us to acknowledge that exactly the same questions arise in relation to treatment refusal and, again, to grapple with the fact that the law, as it stands in England and Wales, does not, on its face, mandate an exploration of the context within which the right to say 'no' is being exercised. In particular, the law does not require consideration of whether the power of refusal is being exercised out of desperation in the face of the absence of other choices. Jonas-Sébastien Beaudry has written powerfully about this in the Canadian context, highlighting, in particular, the case of Archie Rolland, a Montreal landscape architect who suffered from amyotrophic lateral sclerosis, who chose to stop his ventilator support because of a lack of adequate social support. As Beaudry describes it, both Rolland and his mother made it abundantly clear that he was not ending his life because of his medical condition but because he did not receive adequate care from the state (Beaudry, 2018).

Social rights, in other words those rights which can broadly be characterised as the right 'to' certain things, are traditionally seen as distinct to civil and political rights, which can broadly be characterised as the right not to be subject to certain things. The CRPD combines both sets of rights under one Convention. By placing a focus on social rights – including the right to independent living (Article 19), and the right to the highest attainable standard of health (Article 25) – it seems the CRPD potentially helps think things through in a way which starts further upstream than the debates have focussed on to date. It seems to me that the CRPD, by giving enforceable – positive – rights to high-quality care and social support, would – in at least some situations – means that the person would not be placed in the position where their only option was either to request assistance with dying or (where relevant) to refuse life-sustaining treatment. I note that a similar line of thinking is evolving in the mental health context, with the recognition that the cycle of crisis, compulsion and coercion can only be broken with the provision of adequate support in the community. The deputy chief inspector of hospitals and lead for mental health at the English Care Quality Commission (CQC)[34] has noted,

> [a] significant number of people with a learning disability or autism are admitted to a hospital because the health, care and education system has failed to support them to live fulfilling lives in their own home. Once there, they may become stuck in the hospital because of the absence of any alternative.[35]

For my part, it is a huge pity that the debates about the CRPD in the English context have been side-tracked into (frequently sterile) debates about the precise meaning of supported decision-making, rather than being channelled into these more productive areas. Doing so may well have a series of unanticipated, and interesting, beneficial effects across a whole range of areas going far beyond those of Mr Conway's situation.

Of course, a focus on social rights can only take one so far, and society will always be confronted with the situation where a person with decision-making capacity, provided with all appropriate support (familial, social and health), has, nonetheless, decided that they wish to seek assistance with dying.

Conclusion

The courts decided in Mr Conway's case that whether the law should be changed was ultimately a matter for Parliament as the 'conscience of the nation'.[36] It is for others to argue – in this volume and elsewhere – as to whether that was the right decision. I hope that I will be forgiven, however, for observing that I may not be the only person[37] to have considered it a little rich of Lord Sumption, following his retirement from the Supreme Court bench, to have observed that

> the law should continue to criminalise assistance in suicide and [...] the law should be broken. I think that it should be broken from time to time. We need to have a law against it in order to prevent abuse but it has always been the case that this has been criminal and it has always been the case that courageous relatives and friends have helped people to die, and I think that that is an untidy compromise of the sort that I suspect very few lawyers would adopt, but I don't believe that there is necessarily a moral obligation to obey the law and, ultimately, it is something that each person has to decide within his own conscience.[38]

Lord Sumption might be confident that the police and Crown Prosecution Service (CPS) would respect his judgment call in the event that his conscience led him to break the law. However, it is not immediately apparent, I might suggest, that we can be equally confident that the police and CPS would respect the judgment of someone of less lofty a stature.

Ultimately, it may be necessary to continue to live with such an untidy compromise for a greater good, but in this chapter, I have sought to highlight some of the wider questions which my involvement in the case made me ask myself and, in particular, the extent to which Mr Conway's case throws up a significant number of other untidy – and unacknowledged – compromises with which society is currently living.

Statute

Human Rights Act 1998.
Mental Health Act 1983.
Suicide Act 1961.
United Nations (UN) Convention on the Rights of Persons with Disabilities.

Case law

ACCG v MN [2017] UKSC 22.
Carter v Canada [2015] 1 SCR 331.
CD v London Borough of Croydon [2019] EWHC 2943 (Fam).
East Lancashire Hospitals NHS Trust v PW [2019] EWCOP 10.
JK v A Local Health Board [2019] EWHC 67 (Fam).
Kings College Hospital NHS Foundation Trust v C & Anor [2015] EWCOP 80.
Lambert v France (2015) ECHR 185.
R (Burke) v General Medical Council [2005] EWCA Civ 1003, [2006] QB 273.
R (Conway) v The Secretary of State for Justice & Ors [2018] EWCA Civ 1431.
R (Nicklinson) and another v Ministry of Justice (CNK Alliance Ltd and another intervening) [2014] UKSC 38; [2015] 1 AC 657.

Re A (Capacity: Social Media and Internet Use: Best Interests) [2019] EWCOP 2.
Re B [2002] 2 All ER 449.
Re T (Adult: Refusal of Medical Treatment) [1992] 4 All ER 649.
Southend-On-Sea Borough Council v Meyers [2019] EWHC 399 (Fam).
Wye Valley NHS Trust v B [2015] EWCOP 60.

Notes

1 Parts of this chapter draw (in a different form) on a chapter co-written with Dr Zoë Fritz – Refusing and Demanding Treatment in Intensive Care in Danbury, C., Newdick, C., Waldmann, C., & Ruck Keene, A. (eds) *Law and Ethics in Intensive Care* (2nd edition OUP, 2020).
2 Dignity in Dying is a UK campaigning organisation, whose aim is to legalise assisted dying for terminally ill, mentally competent adults: see https://www.dignityindying.org.uk/ (accessed 12 October 2019).
3 Leslie Burke was a man with a progressive condition, who was very concerned that doctors following guidance issued by the General Medical Council would withdraw clinically assisted nutrition and hydration at a point when he had capacity to make decisions about his medical treatment and still wished it to continue. See *R (Burke) v General Medical Council* [2005] EWCA Civ 1003, [2006] QB 273.
4 Law Commission's Mental Capacity and Deprivation of Liberty project: https://www.lawcom.gov.uk/project/mental-capacity-and-deprivation-of-liberty/.
5 A professional rule requiring barristers to accept instructions from professional clients (including solicitors) under certain conditions, irrespective, inter alia, of the nature of the case to which the instructions relate; whether the client is paying privately or is publicly funded; and any belief or opinion which you may have formed as to the cause of the client.
6 Order of the Supreme Court and accompanying reasons, 27 November 2018: https://www.supremecourt.uk/news/permission-to-appeal-determination-on-r-on-the-application-of-conway-v-secretary-of-state-for-justice.html (accessed 5 June 2019).
7 Order of the Supreme Court and accompanying reasons, 27 November 2018: https://www.supremecourt.uk/news/permission-to-appeal-determination-on-r-on-the-application-of-conway-v-secretary-of-state-for-justice.html (accessed 5 June 2019).
8 *R (Nicklinson) and another v Ministry of Justice (CNK Alliance Ltd and another intervening)* [2014] UKSC 38; [2015] 1 AC 657.
9 In particularly complex or significant cases, the High Court can sit with two judges to hear judicial review challenges, one of whom will be a Court of Appeal judge. When two judges sit like this, the High Court is known as the Divisional Court.
10 See also the discussion in the judgment of the Court of Appeal: [2018] EWCA Civ 1431 at paragraphs 161–163.
11 Putting aside the (large) exception of the position in relation to mental health treatment for those detained under the Mental Health Act 1983.
12 *Carter v Canada* [2015] 1 SCR 331.
13 *Re T (Adult: Refusal of Medical Treatment)* [1992] 4 All ER 649.
14 The final report being available at https://www.gov.uk/government/publications/modernising-the-mental-health-act-final-report-from-the-independent-review (accessed 5 June 2019).
15 s1 Mental Capacity Act (MCA) 2005.

16 The classic example of acceptance through gritted teeth (on the basis that the patient had capacity) being that of *Re B* [2002] 2 All ER 449.
17 A specialist court empowered to make decisions as to capacity and best interests in relation to (inter alia) medical treatment. For more details about the court and its decision-making in relation to mental capacity, see Ruck Keene et al. (2019).
18 A fundamental principle of the MCA is the 'best interests' principle, which is that any decision made on behalf of a person who lacks mental capacity must be made in that person's best interests.
19 This was also a key feature of the British Medical Association/Royal College of Physicians guidance on decision-making in relation to clinically assisted nutrition and hydration on which I was working at the time: www.bma.org.uk/canh (accessed 5 June 2019).
20 *Kings College Hospital NHS Foundation Trust v C & Anor* [2015] EWCOP 80 at paragraph 63, see also paragraph 97.
21 On this, see also: Ruck Keene (2019); Kong and Ruck Keene (2015); and the work being undertaken by the Mental Health and Justice Project on complex capacity assessments: www.mhj.org.uk (accessed 5 June 2019).
22 See, in particular, *Southend-On-Sea Borough Council v Meyers* [2019] EWHC 399 (Fam); see also Herring (2016).
23 See for discussion of the dilemmas here, *JK v A Local Health Board* [2019] EWHC 67 (Fam) and *CD v London Borough of Croydon* [2019] EWHC 2943 (Fam).
24 This is not the only case in which I have been in which similar frustration was experienced, giving rise to no substantive reference to the Convention before the courts – it also had an equally fruitless outing before the Supreme Court in *ACCG v MN* [2017] UKSC 22 where it was deployed in argument but did not appear in the judgment.
25 Note, the CRPD and much of the international community refer to 'persons with disabilities', but the preferred term in England and Wales is 'disabled person'.
26 *Re A (Capacity: Social Media and Internet Use: Best Interests)* [2019] EWCOP 2 at paragraph 3.
27 Among other references, the preamble recognises at (n) '*the importance for persons with disabilities of their individual autonomy and independence, including the freedom to make their own choices*'; Article 1 provides that the purpose of the CRPD the promotion of the 'respect for the [...] inherent dignity' of all persons with disabilities; and Article 3(a) provides that the first general principle of the Convention is '*[r]espect for inherent dignity, individual autonomy including the freedom to make one's own choices, and independence of persons.*'
28 See in particular Committee on the Rights of Persons with Disabilities, 'General Comment on Article 12: Equal Recognition before the law' (CRPD/C/GC/1, adopted 11 April 2014).
29 CRPD/C/CAN/CO/1 (8 May 2017), available at https://tbinternet.ohchr.org/_layouts/treatybodyexternal/Download.aspx?symbolno=CRPD%2fC%2fCAN%2fCO%2f1&Lang=en (accessed 5 June 2019).
30 See, for instance, campaign groups such as 'Not Dead Yet' in the UK: http://notdeadyetuk.org/.
31 In an individual complaint against France. Previously, in *Lambert v France* (2015) ECHR 185, the Grand Chamber of the European Court of Human Rights held that withdrawal of life-sustaining treatment from such a person does not automatically breach the right to life contained in Article 2 ECHR, and endorsed a model of decision-making that bears considerable resemblance to that contained in the MCA 2005. See further in this regard Ruck Keene and Lee (2019).
32 To use the language from the concluding observations of the CRPD Committee on Canada.

33 See, in this context, Westwood (2017).
34 The Care Quality Commission: https://www.cqc.org.uk/.
35 Restraint, seclusion and segregation in hospitals and care homes: an update on our work from Dr Paul Lelliott, Deputy Chief Inspector of Hospitals and lead for mental health: https://medium.com/@CareQualityComm/dr-paul-lelliotts-blog-4ed9f3c853a9 (accessed 5 June 2019).
36 *R (Conway) v The Secretary of State for Justice & Ors* [2018] EWCA Civ 1431 at paragraph 63.
37 I am not: see the observations of the former Court of Appeal judge, Sir Stephen Sedley, in a review of the printed version of lectures in the London Review of Books (Vol 41 Number 17, 12 September 2019), observing this was a 'remarkable stance for anyone, let alone [for] a judge' to take.
38 In an answer given to a question posed at the end of his first 2019 Reith Lecture for BBC Radio 4: http://downloads.bbc.co.uk/radio4/reith2019/Reith_2019_Sumption_lecture_1.pdf, accessed 5 June 2019.

References

Association for Palliative Medicine of Great Britain and Ireland (2016). *Withdrawal of Assisted Ventilation at the Request of a Patient with Motor Neurone Disease: Guidance for Professionals.* London: APM, http://apmonline.org/wp-content/uploads/2016/03/Guidance-with-logos-updated-210316.pdf.

Beaudry, J-S. (2018). The Way Forward for Medical Aid in Dying: Protecting Deliberative Autonomy Is Not Enough. *Supreme Court Law Review, Second Series, Volume 85.* https://papers.ssrn.com/sol3/papers.cfm?abstract_id=3189417

Conway, N. (2019). *Hard Days' Journey into Night.* London: Garmston Publishing.

Herring, J. (2016). *Vulnerable Adults and the Law.* Oxford: Oxford University Press.

Keene, A. R., & Lee, A. (2019). Withdrawing Life-Sustaining Treatment: A Stock-Take of the Legal and Ethical Position. *Journal of Medical Ethics, 45*(12), 794–799.

Kong, C. (2017). *Mental Capacity in Relationship: Decision-Making, Dialogue, and Autonomy.* Cambridge: Cambridge University Press.

Kong, C., & Keene, A. R. (2018). *Overcoming Challenges in the Mental Capacity Act 2005: Practical Guidance for Working with Complex Issues.* London: Jessica Kingsley Publishers.

Ruck Keene, A. R. (2019). Is Mental Capacity in the Eye of the Beholder? *Advances in Mental Health and Intellectual Disabilities, 11*(2), 30–39.

Ruck Keene, A. R., & Auckland, C. (2015). More Presumptions Please? Wishes, Feelings and Best Interests Decision-Making. *Elder Law Journal, 5*, 293–301.

Ruck Keene, A. R., Kane, N. B., Kim, S. Y., & Owen, G. S. (2019). Taking Capacity Seriously? Ten Years of Mental Capacity Disputes before England's Court of Protection. *International Journal of Law and Psychiatry, 62*, 56–76.

Shildrick, M. (2015). XI. Death, Debility and Disability. *Feminism & Psychology, 25*(1), 155–160.

Shropshire Live (2018). Supreme Court Rejects Noel Conway Assisted Dying Case Appeal. *Shropshire Live (Online)*, 27 November, https://www.shropshirelive.com/news/2018/11/27/supreme-court-rejects-noel-conway-assisted-dying-case-appeal/ (Accessed 5 June 2019).

Westwood, S. (2017). Older Lesbians, Gay Men and the 'Right to Die' Debate: 'I Always Keep a Lethal Dose of Something, Because I Don't Want to Become an Elderly Isolated Person'. *Social & Legal Studies, 26*(5), 606–628.

4 Voluntary assisted dying in Victoria, Australia

A values-based critique

Lindy Willmott, Katrine Del Villar and Ben P. White

Introduction

In debates about whether voluntary assisted dying (VAD) should be legalised, we are all too familiar with the arguments for and against reform. Neither proponents nor opponents convince the other side of the legitimacy of their argument, nor expect to do so. Consensus is never reached. In this chapter, we offer an alternative lens through which to consider whether legislation should be enacted and, if so, the nature of that regulation. That lens is through an articulation and consideration of the values that we argue should underpin regulation of decision-making as individuals approach the end of their lives. While this approach will not result in others necessarily agreeing with our conclusions about whether or not VAD should be lawful, or the nature of any regulation, it does provide transparency and justification for our proposed stance.

We identify seven core values for this purpose: the importance of life, autonomy, freedom of conscience, equality, the rule of law, the protection of vulnerable people, and the minimisation of human suffering. These values are fundamental principles which are embedded in the Australian legal system, and are derived from case law and international human rights norms. They are protected by the common law and legislation across a range of legal areas, particularly the criminal law. To illustrate, the criminal law recognises the fundamental importance of human life by criminalising murder and assisting suicide. At the same time, our legal system also recognises the principle of autonomy by requiring doctors to comply with an advance directive that refuses life-sustaining treatment, even if that will result in a person's death. The other values are embedded in our legal systems in equivalent ways. Given the universality of these values, they would also resonate in other legal systems so may provide a useful framework for grappling with this issue in other jurisdictions.

In this chapter, we use this values-based approach to critique the *Voluntary Assisted Dying Act 2017* ('the VAD Act') which commenced operation in the Australian State of Victoria in June 2019. The VAD Act represents a very conservative, highly prescriptive model of VAD. It has been described by the

DOI: 10.4324/9780429329739-4

Victorian Premier as the 'safest, and most conservative model in the world' (Andrews 2017).

The purpose of this chapter is to use our values framework to critique the VAD Act. The stated aim of the Victorian parliament was to design a legislative framework that is 'safe and compassionate' (Victorian Government 2017, 5). Its explicit aim was to balance respect for human life and the protection of vulnerable people against respect for the autonomous choices of those who are suffering from terminal conditions, and the compassionate alleviation of the suffering of those people (ibid., 44). However, in this chapter, we explore whether the legislation is successful in promoting these values, or whether amendments to the VAD Act are needed.

In the next section, we articulate the values that we argue should underpin legislation on this topic, and explain the implications of each value for the design of a legislative framework. The subsequent section then critiques the Victorian legislation against those values and conclusions are drawn about whether the legislation successfully promotes them.

Values that should underpin voluntary assisted dying law reform

As noted above, seven core values have been identified as relevant to developing and evaluating any model of access to VAD. These values are explored in more detail elsewhere (Willmott & White 2017), but each will be outlined briefly below.

The importance of life

The Australian legal system, like many other legal systems worldwide, recognises the fundamental importance of human life. The value of life is protected through the criminal law, which prohibits homicide in most circumstances, and makes assisting suicide unlawful. It is also explicitly recognised in common law cases on the withholding or withdrawal of potentially life-sustaining treatment.[1] However, the value of life is not absolute, and decisions can be made by or on behalf of a person to refuse life-sustaining medical treatment in certain circumstances (Willmott, White & Then 2018). For example, in some circumstances the burdens of treatment may outweigh the benefits so that treatment is not regarded as being in the person's best interests and can be withdrawn. This recognises that the value of human life is not unqualified, but may be outweighed in some circumstances by the disvalue of suffering.

In the context of VAD, it is commonly argued that the value of life can be protected through *prohibiting* VAD. However, it can also be argued that *permitting* VAD may advance the value of life. The Supreme Court of Canada in *Carter v Canada (Attorney General)* [2015] 1 SCR 331, paras. 57–58, noted that where ending one's own life is legally permitted but VAD is not, some individuals may feel constrained to end their life in advance of an anticipated decline in physical capacity, to avoid being unable to legally choose to die at a later time when their condition has deteriorated. A legal system which allows for VAD under controlled circumstances would avoid this pre-emptive loss of life (see Chapter 6, this volume).

Autonomy

The principle of respect for autonomy is recognised as a fundamental value underpinning the Australian common law. This is reflected in its role as a core value in health law which upholds a competent individual's right to determine what treatment he or she receives or does not receive. The law prioritises autonomy over the State's interest in the value of life when a competent adult decides to refuse medical treatment.[2] However, in all states and territories in Australia the law currently prohibits a competent adult from exercising autonomy to seek assistance to end his or her life, except in the limited circumstances where VAD is now lawful in some states. In this respect, the law currently protects a narrow interpretation of autonomy as the 'right to prevent physical interference with one's bodily integrity' (Willmott & White 2017, 491), rather than a broader interpretation of autonomy as a right to self-determination (Skene 2004).

When considering laws relating to VAD, the principle of autonomy is frequently proffered to argue that the law should promote the broader value of autonomy as self-determination, that is, having one's will respected and acted on so that one could request assistance to die in certain circumstances. This reflects the contemporary Australian community's understanding of autonomy, and is consistent with the approach adopted by the Victorian Legislative Council Legal and Social Issues Committee when articulating the core values that they believed should underpin end-of-life care (LSIC 2016, xxi). It should be recognised, however, that like other values, respect for autonomy is not absolute and must be balanced against other competing values such as the importance of life. In other words, it would be justifiable to put some limits on the exercise of autonomy, for example by designing eligibility requirements to have access to assistance to die.

Freedom of conscience

Freedom of conscience is a freedom often combined with freedom of thought, religion and belief, and refers to the right not to be coerced or restrained in a way that limits that freedom.[3] It is a value derived from international human rights instruments (e.g. International Covenant on Civil and Political Rights, Article 18).[4] It is recognised explicitly in legislation in those Australian jurisdictions with domestic human rights laws. Australian law already respects the conscience of health professionals in relation to abortion by not requiring them to participate in termination procedures if that would be contrary to their conscience, and peak medical bodies endorse the ability of medical practitioners and nurses to practise medicine in accordance with their conscientiously held beliefs (AMA 2019; ANMF 2015; MBA 2014).

The value of conscience suggests that health professionals should not be required to participate in VAD where doing so is contrary to their conscience. However, the right to act according to conscience is not absolute, and can be overridden where competing values require. For example, where a competent adult refuses potentially life-sustaining treatment, a medical practitioner must respect this choice notwithstanding his or her own conscientious beliefs. In the context of VAD, a health professional's right to freedom of conscience may conflict with an individual's right to access a lawful health service (VAD). Whether the Victorian legislation satisfactorily balances these competing interests is considered in more detail later in the article.

Equality

Equality is another core value of the Australian legal system. Unlike other Western countries, in Australia there is no general constitutional guarantee of equality, and the High Court has rejected attempts to imply it from the text and structure of the Constitution (Simpson 2018). However, the rule of law requires that the law treat people equally (Law Council of Australia 2011, 2). The *Convention on the Rights of Persons with Disabilities* (CRPD), which Australia has ratified, and human rights and anti-discrimination laws in the various Australian jurisdictions, all 'endorse equality and reject discrimination, including discrimination on the basis of disability' (Willmott & White 2017, 493). In Victoria, section 8(3) of the *Charter of Human Rights and Responsibilities Act 2006* (Vic) affirms that '[e]very person is equal before the law and is entitled to the equal protection of the law without discrimination …'.

Australian law adopts both formal and substantive concepts of equality, depending on the context. In the specific context of Victoria's *Charter of Human Rights and Responsibilities*, the value of 'equality before the law' has been held to require formal equality of treatment only.[5] By contrast, 'equal protection of the law without discrimination' imports substantive notions of equality: that is, equality of opportunity, including the adoption of positive measures to ameliorate conditions which may discriminate on the ground of disability.[6] The value of equality requires that laws conferring rights and duties should generally apply to all individuals, rather than privileging some and excluding others. Australian law does recognise, however, that some discrimination or differential treatment may be lawful when its purpose is to afford equal opportunity or equality of outcome to certain groups which have experienced disadvantage.[7] When critiquing VAD laws, the value of equality, in the sense of equal treatment and non-discrimination, must be considered in two respects. First, the mode of assisted death should not be limited to self-administration, because this would discriminate against those whose disability prevents them self-administering medication. Second, having a disability should not of itself prevent a person from accessing VAD, if the person satisfies other legislative criteria.

Rule of law

The Australian legal system is built on the rule of law (Bailey 2009, 242–253; Toohey 1993, 168–169), a concept of ancient origin which incorporates fundamental principles such as the separation of powers, the equal application of laws, and procedural requirements such as access to a fair hearing (Bingham 2010; Tamanaha 2004, 33). Two important components of the rule of law are that the law must be 'certain and clear' and 'should be applied to all people equally and should not discriminate between people on arbitrary or irrational grounds' (Law Council of Australia 2011, 2).

In the context of VAD, the values of clarity and certainty require that any regulatory regime should have clearly expressed legal parameters so that health professionals and individuals wishing to access VAD can know how the regime applies and can act according to the law. In particular, offence provisions should be unambiguous, and key terms should be defined. There should also be certainty in the application of the law, which can be achieved through appropriate legislative safeguards to ensure that only those defined as eligible under the law have access to VAD, and robust oversight systems to ensure regulatory compliance with the scheme.

The second component of the rule of law – that 'law should be applied to all people equally and should not discriminate between people on arbitrary or irrational grounds' (Law Council of Australia 2011, 2) – is relevant to two aspects of VAD legislation. First, eligibility criteria to receive assistance under the legislation should have 'a demonstrable and rational basis' (Law Council of Australia 2011, 2) and should not arbitrarily or discriminatorily exclude a person or group of people. Second, safeguards and oversight mechanisms should be incorporated into the law to ensure that 'all people should be held to account for a breach of law, regardless of rank or station' (Law Council of Australia 2011, 2).

Protecting vulnerable people

Protecting vulnerable people within the community is at the heart of many branches of Anglo-Australian law (Herring 2016), including the law of torts (Stapleton 2003), equitable doctrines of undue influence and unconscionability (Hall 2012; Moore 2018), adult guardianship law (White, Willmott & Then 2018), and most especially criminal law (Lanham 2006). For example, Australian criminal law imposes duties on responsible caregivers to provide the 'necessaries of life' to vulnerable persons in their care (Willmott & White 2017, 496), and protects vulnerable people from being encouraged or coerced to take their own life by criminalising assisting a suicide (Otlowski 2000, 88).

Because this value is central to our legal system, it is essential that any legal response to VAD protects vulnerable people (LSIC 2017, xxi). But who is classified as vulnerable is a contested concept (Hall 2019, 7; Mayo & Gunderson 2002, 17–20), and may differ depending on the context. In the context of VAD, the Victorian Ministerial Advisory Panel on Voluntary Assisted Dying identified four specific groups of people as potentially vulnerable: the elderly, children, people with disabilities, and those with mental illness (Victorian Government 2017, 53–54, 82, 84, 88–90, 91). Other authors have eschewed any identification of certain 'populations' (Fineman 2008, 8) as inherently vulnerable, preferring instead situational or relational definitions of vulnerability (Brown, Ecclestone & Emmel 2017; Hall 2012, 31; Mackenzie, Rogers & Dodds 2014) or descriptions of universal vulnerability (Fineman 2008, 8).

In the context of VAD, every person seeking access to VAD may be described as situationally and relationally vulnerable by virtue of the fact that they are terminally or chronically ill, suffering and wishing to die. Therefore, it is undeniably important that the law provides safeguards to protect all people requesting VAD from the risk of coercion or undue influence arising from personal relationships or relationships with treating health professionals or care institutions. This can be achieved through eligibility criteria and procedural safeguards to ensure that a request for assistance to die is autonomous, voluntary and free from external pressure or coercion. It is also important that VAD laws do not exclude certain groups by labelling them as essentially or inherently 'vulnerable'. Care must be taken to ensure that people are not excluded from a system permitting VAD in a way which is discriminatory or disrespectful of their autonomous choices, simply because they fall within the category of those considered to be 'vulnerable' (Silvers 1998).

Reducing human suffering

A final value, found only in the end-of-life context rather than in the wider Australian legal system, is the value of reducing human suffering. This value is discerned chiefly from the common law doctrine of double effect. The doctrine of double effect legally protects a health professional who administers medication that may incidentally hasten death when a person is at the end of life and the professional's intention is to relieve pain and suffering rather than cause the person's death (White & Willmott 2018b). In this way, the law recognises that the value of life may be subordinated to the value of reducing human suffering in some circumstances. If VAD is legalised, this enables suffering to be addressed in a wider range of cases where an individual satisfies the eligibility requirements.

Critique of the Victorian legislation against the above values

Having identified and explained the values that we consider should guide law-making in the context of VAD, this section critiques the VAD Act against these values. Given the word constraints of this chapter, we place particular emphasis on those parts of the Act where these values are not promoted.

Method of providing voluntary assisted dying

Overview of the law

The primary method of VAD permitted by the VAD Act is 'self-administration'. This involves a medical practitioner prescribing lethal medication which the patient then takes themselves (VAD Act, ss.45, 47). Administration of the medication by a practitioner (referred to in the Act as 'practitioner administration') is only authorised if the person seeking assistance to die has a disability which renders them 'physically incapable of the self-administration or digestion' of the medication (s.48(3)(a)). This narrow model of VAD contrasts with the majority of legislative models which were proposed but not enacted in Australia, which would have authorised the patient to choose the method of administration (Willmott et al. 2016, 27). Further, under the recently enacted *Voluntary Assisted Dying Act 2019* (WA) (s.56) and *End-of-Life Choices (Voluntary Assisted Dying) Act 2021* (Tas) (s.86(5)), greater choice is available to the patient to determine the method of administration.

Consistency with values

The Victorian decision to establish self-administration as the method of VAD except where this is a physical impossibility for the person appears to have been based primarily on the value of protecting vulnerable people. Deliberate self-administration of a lethal medication is a strong indication that a person's wish to die is autonomous, voluntary and enduring (Victorian Government 2017, 141). The inclusion of an exception, allowing practitioner administration where self-administration is not physically possible, ensures that the VAD Act does not discriminate on the basis of disability, which furthers the value of equality (p. 141).

However, the VAD Act restricts the choice of administration for the majority of people who are eligible and capable of self-administration, but have a preference for the medical practitioner to administer the lethal medication. If a person is physically able to swallow and ingest a lethal medication, the VAD Act does not allow for a practitioner to administer the medication. This restriction fails to respect the value of autonomy. Some people who are physically able to swallow and ingest a lethal medication may consider self-administration to be an unacceptable, or overly burdensome, option. In international jurisdictions where both methods are lawful, there is an overwhelming preference for practitioner administration over self-administration (Emanuel et al. 2016, 85). Further, some evidence suggests that the rate of complications and technical problems is twice as high when the lethal medication is self-administered, compared to when it is administered by a qualified medical practitioner (Groenewoud et al. 2000). Given these factors, individual autonomy would be better respected by permitting all persons eligible for VAD to choose between self-administration or practitioner administration. Allowing individual choice between these methods would conform with models proposed in other Australian States, as well as international regimes such as Canada, the Netherlands, Belgium and Luxembourg (Emanuel et al. 2016, 79).

While self-administration as a default under the legislation may offer protection for vulnerable people by ensuring decisions to request VAD are voluntary and enduring, there are other ways to ensure these fundamental requirements are met. Limiting practitioner administration to those who are physically unable to administer the medication is inconsistent with the core value of respecting autonomy, by preventing people requesting VAD having access to choice as to the manner of their death, as well as prohibiting access to the safer option.

Eligibility

Overview of the law

There are five main eligibility requirements to receive VAD under the VAD Act: decision-making capacity; age; a terminal medical condition; suffering; and residency (VAD Act, s.9(1)). Access to VAD is limited to an adult who is an Australian citizen or permanent resident, and has been resident in Victoria for at least 12 months. The person must have an incurable disease, illness or medical condition that is advanced, progressive and is expected to cause death within six months (or 12 months in the case of a neurodegenerative condition [VAD Act, s.9(4)]), and is causing suffering that cannot be relieved in a manner that the person considers tolerable. The request for VAD must be made voluntarily and without coercion by a person who has decision-making capacity (VAD Act, s.9). Disability and mental illness alone are not grounds to request VAD, but a person with a disability or mental illness who is suffering from a terminal medical condition as described above and meets the other eligibility criteria is not precluded from accessing VAD.

Consistency with values

The VAD Act's eligibility criteria reflect a balancing of several of the core values: autonomy; the importance of life; reducing human suffering; and protecting vulnerable people. The decision to allow access to VAD advances the values of respecting autonomous choice and the compassionate alleviation of suffering. Further, the restriction of VAD to those with a terminal condition prioritises the values of respecting human life and safeguarding vulnerable people, by ensuring that only those who are already dying may request assistance to die. However, some of the eligibility requirements in the VAD Act (such as the inclusion of a temporal limit on eligibility for VAD and the differential timeframe for neurodegenerative diseases [12 months] compared to other terminal conditions [six months]) have concerning implications for the values of equality and the rule of law.

CONSISTENCY WITH VALUES: DECISION-MAKING CAPACITY

The VAD Act is restricted to people with decision-making capacity. It does not permit decisions made by a substitute decision-maker, or decisions made in advance of anticipated loss of decision-making capacity via an advance directive, as occurs, although rarely, in the Netherlands and Belgium (Chambaere et al. 2015; Rurup et al. 2012). The capacity criterion promotes the value of autonomy, by ensuring that a request for assistance to die is made by a person with an ability to understand, retain and weigh that information in coming to their decision. This could also arguably provide a safeguard for vulnerable adults without decision-making capacity. The framework would not enable a substitute decision-maker to request assistance to die on their behalf.

CONSISTENCY WITH VALUES: AGE

The core value of autonomy is also consistent with the requirement that a person must be an adult to access VAD (Willmott & White 2017, 501). Adults are presumed to have decision-making capacity, and although minors may have capacity to make decisions concerning medical treatment including, in some cases, refusing life-sustaining medical treatment, they are often not considered to have sufficient maturity to make difficult decisions concerning death and dying (Victorian Government 2017, 54, 215). A prohibition on children accessing VAD is consistent with the Australian law which limits the ability of minors to request withdrawal of life-saving medical treatment in some cases, and with the consensus in the majority of overseas jurisdictions that access to VAD be limited to adults (Victorian Government 2017, 53). Only Belgium and the Netherlands permit requests for VAD to be made by children under the age of 18, and this occurs in practice only in very rare cases (CFCEE 2018, 11; Rietjens et al. 2014).

CONSISTENCY WITH VALUES: MEDICAL CONDITION

Three key values – the importance of life, autonomy and protecting vulnerable people – are engaged in determining what medical conditions meet the eligibility criteria for VAD. The VAD Act, like the majority of Australian Bills concerning VAD to date (Willmott et al. 2016, 34), and like VAD laws in US states, adopts narrow eligibility criteria, restricting access to VAD to people with a terminal illness, that is, people whose death is already inevitable and impending. The VAD Act also requires the disease that will cause that death to be incurable, advanced and progressive.

The requirement that the medical condition will cause the death of the patient recognises the intrinsic value of human life and constrains the values of autonomous choice and the alleviation of suffering, and the subjective value of life to the individual. It prevents people with unbearable suffering that they consider makes their life not worth living, but whose conditions are not progressively leading to death (or death within a specified timeframe), from exercising autonomous choices and seeking relief from their suffering through VAD. Some other jurisdictions such as Belgium and the Netherlands have chosen to resolve this tension more in favour of autonomous choice and the alleviation of suffering. These regimes allow individuals to access VAD if they suffer from a medical condition (in Belgium, the condition must be 'futile') which renders a person's quality of life intolerable for the person, even where the condition might not be terminal, and death not immediately foreseeable. Similar broader medical eligibility criteria have been proposed in several Australian Bills which failed to pass (Willmott et al. 2016, 34).

While the requirement that the medical condition causes the death of the person can be justified through a process of balancing relevant values (Willmott & White 2017, 502–503), particular problems arise by the inclusion of a temporal requirement that death is anticipated to occur within six months. Although this appears to respect the value of human life by restricting VAD to those already close to the end of life, there are significant difficulties accurately predicting when death is likely to occur, even in advanced terminal conditions (Chevlen 1996; Downar et al. 2017; Glare et al. 2008; Lynn et al. 1996). This means that some people whose death is imminent will be excluded by incorrect prognoses, thus failing to respect the core value of compassionate alleviation of suffering. In contrast, others who may have had years to live will be incorrectly predicted to die within six months (Lynn et al. 1996, 321–322), making them eligible for VAD, contrary to the policy goal of valuing human life. A temporal requirement that is unable to be estimated with precision will result in inconsistent application of the legislative criteria, 'with unjustified variations across diseases, across physicians, and across regions' (Lynn et al. 1996, 334). This results in uncertainty and arbitrariness in the application of the law, which is contrary to fundamental components of the rule of law.

Uniquely, the VAD Act contains two separate temporal limitations on eligibility – that death is expected within six months for most medical conditions, but is expected to occur within 12 months for people with neurodegenerative conditions. This differential timeframe has not been adequately explained by Parliament. It appears to have been motivated by a concern that people with neurodegenerative conditions might lose capacity and become ineligible to access VAD, although evidence supporting this was not provided. It is discriminatory and contrary to the value of equality to allow people with neurodegenerative conditions to access VAD earlier than people with other terminal conditions. It clearly values the lives of those with neurodegenerative conditions differently than those with other conditions, as well as placing different value on the suffering experienced by each group. This distinction also infringes two foundational principles of the rule of law: namely, that laws apply equally to all, and that laws should not discriminate on 'arbitrary or irrational grounds' (Law Council of Australia 2011, 2).

CONSISTENCY WITH VALUES: NATURE OF SUFFERING

The VAD Act adopts a relatively broad approach in relation to suffering. First, it does not require physical pain, which some other Australian Bills have (Willmott et al. 2016, 35–36). Second, the Act makes clear that suffering is a subjective determination as to when it is not tolerable for the person based on the methods for alleviating suffering the person considers are acceptable. This promotes the twin values of reducing human suffering and respect for individual autonomy, by allowing the individual who is directly affected by the illness to determine the point at which the suffering outweighs the value of life for that individual (Willmott & White 2017, 504).

Safeguards

Overview of the law

The VAD Act contains numerous safeguards designed to ensure the accuracy of diagnosis and prognosis; and that patient requests for VAD are well-informed, competent and voluntary. The VAD Act prescribes a very detailed request and assessment process, requiring three separate requests by the person over a period of at least nine days (although this period can be reduced if the medical practitioners believe the person is likely to die during this period). One of these requests must be in writing, and signed by two independent witnesses who attest that the person is competent, acting voluntarily and understands the implications of their request (VAD Act, ss.34–36). Where VAD will be administered by a medical practitioner, the patient must make a fourth request immediately before administration to confirm the patient wants to proceed (s.64).

To be judged eligible to receive VAD, a person must undergo two independent medical assessments (VAD Act, Part 3, Divs 3 and 4) by suitably qualified and experienced medical practitioners (s 10). The medical assessments evaluate the person's diagnosis and prognosis, as well as capacity and voluntariness of the request for VAD (s.20(1)(b)). A medical practitioner must apply for and receive a permit from the relevant government department prior to VAD being provided (ss.47–48).

A unique feature of the legislation is that it specifically prohibits all registered health practitioners (including medical practitioners, nurses and allied health professionals) from directly or indirectly initiating a discussion about

VAD, or suggesting it as a treatment option (s.8). The legislation also contains numerous administrative safeguards, including detailed requirements to provide information to patients (ss.19, 28, 57, 58), designed to safeguard the autonomy and voluntariness of the patient's decision. There are also medication management procedures to protect the community by ensuring the secure storage and disposal of any lethal medication held by a patient at home (ss.61, 62). This safeguard is designed to ensure that the substance is used only by the person who has been assessed as eligible for VAD.

Consistency with values

Although the careful and prescriptive process for accessing VAD is designed to safeguard vulnerable people while respecting the autonomy of those with capacity to request assistance to die, there is a risk that the very detailed nature of these safeguards may compromise the VAD Act's ability to adequately promote autonomy, and may contribute to, rather than reduce, human suffering at the end of life, as is explained below.

CONSISTENCY WITH VALUES: REQUEST AND ASSESSMENT PROCESS

The multi-stage request and assessment process for VAD is designed to be rigorous in excluding those who are not eligible, and to ensure requests for VAD are voluntary decisions made by competent individuals. The requirement for at least one independent second medical opinion, confirming diagnosis, prognosis and capacity, is a feature common to all the Bills drafted in Australia and also international regimes. The need for repeated requests and other safeguards including the confirmation by (at least) a second medical practitioner arguably reaches a satisfactory balancing of values of the rule of law (compliance with the legislation) and promotion of autonomy (ensuring access by competent adults with an enduring request) with the value of life and protecting vulnerable people.

CONSISTENCY WITH VALUES: ENSURING THE REQUEST IS AN ENDURING ONE

An important safeguard in the VAD Act is a requirement that the request for assistance be an enduring one. One component of this safeguard is the need for a nine day period between the first and final request. A cooling off period of between 10 and 15 days is common in most international legislative regimes. Of note though is that this requirement, which is designed to foster autonomy, may paradoxically risk compromising this value, as there is a risk that the patient may lose capacity during this time (possibly because of pain-relieving medication), rendering the person ineligible for VAD (Downie 2017, 139; Willmott & White 2017, 507).

CONSISTENCY WITH VALUES: PROHIBITION ON INITIATING DISCUSSIONS

The prohibition on health practitioners initiating conversations about VAD is unique to Victoria. It is not a feature of any international legislative framework, and has been described as 'paternalistic' (Johnston & Cameron 2018, 456). The policy intent was to ensure that a 'person is not coerced or unduly influenced into accessing voluntary assisted dying and ... the request for voluntary assisted dying is the person's own voluntary decision' (Victorian Government 2017, 91). However, preventing medical practitioners from raising VAD as a possible option (unless information about VAD is requested) compromises patients' ability to exercise fully autonomous choice between options available at the end of life (Willmott et al. 2020, 109). It may also obstruct the equal, non-discriminatory implementation of the VAD Act, by limiting access to more educated patients who are independently aware of their options, and excluding less informed patients who rely on their medical practitioners for information about treatment options (Johnston & Cameron 2018, 458–459).

Oversight

Overview of the law

The VAD Act contains a suite of mechanisms for monitoring the provision of VAD and ensuring compliance with the legislative regime. There are too many to consider in this chapter, so the focus here is on two main oversight mechanisms.

The first is the establishment of a new independent statutory body, the VAD Review Board ('Board') which has oversight of the scheme as a whole (VAD Act, s.92). The Board receives mandatory reports from medical practitioners and dispensing pharmacists at each step in the process of request and assessment of eligibility for VAD (ss.21, 30, 41, 49, 60, 63, 66). These reports enable the Board to ensure the legal requirements have been complied with in each individual case, and to evaluate overall patterns and trends in the administration of VAD, such as instances of 'doctor shopping' (Victorian Government 2017, 168).

The second oversight mechanism is the prior authorisation which must be obtained from the relevant government department before a medical practitioner can provide a patient with access to VAD. This application is made by the medical practitioner on completion of the required assessments, following the waiting period and after the third request from the patient.

Consistency with values

A rigorous oversight mechanism which ensures that the legislation operates as intended by parliament will promote all of the articulated values, but in particular the rule of law. This is promoted by the Board having oversight over individual cases, and the system as a whole. Oversight also promotes the value of life and protecting vulnerable people by ensuring that only those who are eligible for VAD have access to it. Reporting all cases of VAD will safeguard the quality of the process (Smets et al. 2010), and therefore safeguard vulnerable individuals from abuse or coercion. Also, the value of autonomy is promoted by ensuring those who satisfy the eligibility requirements are able to have access to VAD.

The second main oversight mechanism, the requirement of pre-authorisation, is unusual internationally and warrants further examination. As this form of oversight occurs before VAD is administered, it is arguably a more effective safeguard for the value of human life than regimes which review processes after the death has occurred. However, this safeguard also requires more onerous processes and will delay a person's access to VAD, thereby potentially frustrating other values, such as autonomy and reducing human suffering. It is also unclear what degree of scrutiny will be undertaken by the government department before issuing a permit. The process itself may become a barrier to access, as medical practitioners may perceive the requirements to be unduly onerous or time-consuming. It must be questioned whether the processes and delay inherent in pre-authorisation, particularly if there is not detailed scrutiny of the individual case, achieve the correct balance between the competing values.

Role of conscience

Overview of the law

In Victoria, as in other jurisdictions, medical practitioners (and indeed all health practitioners) are not obliged to participate in VAD. Those who have a conscientious objection to assisting patients to die can choose not to be involved in the request and assessment process, in the administration of VAD or at any other stage (VAD Act, s.7). They are also not required by the VAD Act to refer the patient to another practitioner who does not hold a conscientious objection.

Consistency with values

The value of freedom of conscience is protected by the provisions in the VAD Act enabling health and medical practitioners to refuse to provide information about or participate in VAD. However, there being no duty on a conscientiously objecting practitioner to refer a patient may impede access to a lawful health service and so compromise respect for autonomous choices and compassion for intolerable suffering for some patients. There may also be issues with equality and discrimination, particularly for a patient living in a rural or remote area where the only available medical practitioner has a conscientious objection to participating in VAD. How the legislation is implemented in practice will be critical to the VAD Act's ability to successfully balance these values.

Conclusion

Values held by individuals influence their views on what is right to do, or to allow to be done. In a similar way, parliamentarians who are charged with governing our countries support or oppose legislation on important social issues informed by their own set of values. This values-based exercise comes into sharp focus when members of parliament debate whether VAD should be permitted and, if it should be, the nature of the framework regulating its practice.

The values held by Victorian politicians led them to a collective decision to design a 'safe and compassionate' framework that permits and regulates VAD (Victorian Government 2017, 5). We would argue, however, that an appropriately drafted legislative regime should do more to promote the values articulated in this chapter, namely, the importance of life, autonomy, freedom of conscience, equality, the rule of law, the protection of vulnerable people, and the minimisation of human suffering.

As the critique in this chapter illustrates, the VAD Act promotes all of these core values, to varying degrees in different contexts. The enactment of legislation permitting VAD demonstrates respect for people's autonomous choices, and a desire to alleviate suffering at the end of life. However, in this chapter, we argue that future legislation should depart from the Victorian model in some significant ways to better promote the articulated values.

The dozens of unsuccessful attempts to pass legislation in Australian States and Territories over the past decades demonstrate the political challenges confronting parliaments that attempt reform in this field. The Victorian government is therefore to be commended for enacting legislation to permit VAD. However, as more jurisdictions in Australia and elsewhere consider reform (White & Willmott 2018a), we urge a shift in some critical aspects of the Victorian regulation, as articulated in this chapter, to better reflect the values that we consider should underpin such a regime.

Acknowledgments

The authors would like to thank Rebecca Meehan and Emily Bartels for their formatting and editing assistance.

Legislation

Charter of Human Rights and Responsibilities Act 2006 (Vic).
Disability Discrimination Act 1992 (Cth).
End-of-Life Choices (Voluntary Assisted Dying) Act 2021 (Tas).
Voluntary Assisted Dying Act 2017 (Vic).

Voluntary Assisted Dying Act 2019 (WA).
UN Convention on the Rights of Persons with Disabilities (CRPD).
UN International Covenant on Civil and Political Rights (ICCPR).

Cases

Brightwater Care Group (Inc) v Rossiter (2009) 40 WAR 84.
Carter v Canada (Attorney General) [2015] 1 SCR 331.
Director of Public Transport v XFJ [2010] VSC 319.
H Ltd v Anor (2010) 107 SASR 352.
Hunter and New England Area Health Service v A (2009) 74 NSWLR 88.
Kuyken v Chief Commissioner of Police [2015] VSC 204.
Matsoukatidou v Yarra Ranges Council [2017] VSC 61.
Re JS [2014] NSWSC 302.

Notes

1 See, for example, *Brightwater Care Group (Inc) v Rossiter* (2009) 40 WAR 84 and *Hunter and New England Area Health Service v A* (2009) 74 NSWLR 88.
2 See, for example, *Brightwater Care Group (Inc) v Rossiter* (2009) 40 WAR 84, *H Ltd v Anor* (2010) 107 SASR 352 and *Re JS* [2014] NSWSC 302.
3 See, for example, *Charter of Human Rights and Responsibilities Act 2006* (Vic) s.14.
4 International Covenant on Civil and Political Rights, Article 18: (1) Everyone shall have the right to freedom of thought, conscience and religion. This right shall include freedom to have or to adopt a religion or belief of his choice, and freedom, either individually or in community with others and in public or private, to manifest his religion or belief in worship, observance, practice and teaching. (2) No one shall be subject to coercion which would impair his freedom to have or to adopt a religion or belief of his choice. (3) Freedom to manifest one's religion or beliefs may be subject only to such limitations as are prescribed by law and are necessary to protect public safety, order, health, or morals or the fundamental rights and freedoms of others. (4) The States Parties to the present Covenant undertake to have respect for the liberty of parents and, when applicable, legal guardians to ensure the religious and moral education of their children in conformity with their own convictions.
5 *Kuyken v Chief Commissioner of Police* [2015] VSC 204, [33] (Garde J); *Matsoukatidou v Yarra Ranges Council* [2017] VSC 61, [50] (Bell J).
6 *Matsoukatidou v Yarra Ranges Council* [2017] VSC 61, [50] (Bell J); *Director of Public Transport v XFJ* [2010] VSC 319.
7 For example, the *Charter of Human Rights and Responsibilities Act 2006* (Vic) s 8(4) states that 'measures taken for the purpose of assisting or advancing *persons* or groups of *persons* disadvantaged because of *discrimination* do not constitute *discrimination*'. See also *Disability Discrimination Act 1992* (Cth) s 45.

References

Andrews, D. (2017). *Media Release: Voluntary Assisted Dying Model Established Ahead of Vote in Parliament* (25 July). Available at: https://www.premier.vic.gov.au/voluntary-assisted-dying-model-established-ahead-of-vote-in-parliament [Accessed 2 March 2019]

Australian Medical Association (AMA) (2019). *Position Statement on Conscientious Objection*, Available at: https://ama.com.au/position-statement/conscientious-objection-2019 [Accessed 5 March 2019]

Australian Nursing and Midwifery Federation (ANMF) (2015). *Policy on Conscientious Objection*. Available at: http://anmf.org.au/documents/policies/P_Conscientious_Objection.pdf [Accessed 5 March 2019]

Bailey, P. (2009). *The Human Rights Enterprise in Australia and Internationally*. Sydney: LexisNexis.

Bingham, T. (2010). *The Rule of Law*. London: Penguin.

Brown, K., Ecclestone, K., & Emmel, N. (2017). The Many Faces of Vulnerability. *Social Policy and Society*, *16*(3), 497–510.

Chambaere, K., Vander Stichele, R., Mortier, F., Cohen, J., & Deliens, L. (2015). Recent Trends in Euthanasia and Other End-of-Life Practices in Belgium. *New England Journal of Medicine*, *372*(12), 1179–1181.

Chevlen, E. (1996). The Limits of Prognostication. *Duquesne Law Review*, *35*(1), 337–354.

Commission fédérale de Contrôle et d'Évaluation de l'Euthanasie (CFCEE) (2018). *Huitième rapport aux Chambres législatives années 2016–2017*. Available at: https://organesdeconcertation.sante.belgique.be/sites/default/files/documents/8_rapport-euthanasie_2016-2017-fr.pdf [Accessed 8 March 2019]

Downar, J., Goldman, R., Pinto, R., Englesakis, M., & Adhikari, N. K. (2017). The "Surprise Question" for Predicting Death in Seriously Ill Patients: A Systematic Review and Meta-analysis. *CMAJ*, *189*(13), E484–E493.

Downie, J. (2017). Medical Assistance in Dying: Lessons for Australia from Canada. *QUT Law Review*, *17*(1), 127–146.

Emanuel, E. J., Onwuteaka-Philipsen, B. D., Urwin, J. W., & Cohen, J. (2016). Attitudes and Practices of Euthanasia and Physician-Assisted Suicide in the United States, Canada, and Europe. *JAMA*, *316*(1), 79–90.

Fineman, M. A. (2008). The Vulnerable Subject: Anchoring Equality in the Human Condition. *Yale Journal of Law and Feminism*, *20*(1), 1–23.

Foster, C. (2015). Suicide Tourism may Change Attitudes to Assisted Suicide, but Not Through the Courts. *Journal of Medical Ethics*, *41*(8), 620–620.

Gauthier, S., Mausbach, J., Reisch, T., & Bartsch, C. (2015). Suicide Tourism: A Pilot Study on the Swiss Phenomenon. *Journal of Medical Ethics*, *41*(8), 611–617.

Glare, P., Sinclair, C., Downing, M., Stone, P., Maltoni, M., & Vigano, A. (2008). Predicting Survival in Patients with Advanced Disease. *European Journal of Cancer*, *44*(8), 1146–1156.

Groenewoud, J. H., van der Heide, A., Onwuteaka-Philipsen, B. D., Willems, D. L., van der Maas, P. J., & van der Wal, G. (2000). Clinical Problems with the Performance of Euthanasia and Physician-Assisted Suicide in the Netherlands. *New England Journal of Medicine*, *342*(8), 551–556.

Hall, M. I. (2012). Mental Capacity in the (Civil) Law: Capacity, Autonomy, and Vulnerability. *McGill Law Journal*, *58*(1), 1–35.

Hall, M. I. (2019). Relational Autonomy, Vulnerability Theory, Older Adults and the Law: Making It Real. *Elder Law Review*, *11*, 1–22.

Herring, J. (2016). *Vulnerable Adults and the Law*. Oxford: Oxford University Press.

Johnston, C., & Cameron, J. (2018). Discussing Voluntary Assisted Dying. *Journal of Law and Medicine*, *26*, 454–463.

Lanham, D. (2006). The Purposes of Criminal Law. In D. Lanham, B. Bartal, D. Evans, & R. Wood (eds.), *Criminal Laws in Australia*, 1–15. Annandale: Federation Press.

Law Council of Australia (2011). *Policy Statement: Rule of Law Principles*. Available at: https://www.lawcouncil.asn.au/docs/f13561ed-cb39-e711-93fb-005056be13b5/1103-Policy-Statement-Rule-of-Law-Principles.pdf [Accessed 23 August 2020]

Lynn, J., Harrell Jr, F. E., Cohn, F., & Hamel, M. B. (1996). Defining the 'Terminally Ill': Insights from Support. *Duquesne Law Review, 35*(1), 311–336.

Mackenzie, C., Rogers, W., & Dodds, S. (2014). *Vulnerability: New Essays in Ethics and Feminist Philosophy*. Oxford: Oxford University Press.

Mayo, D. J., & Gunderson, M. (2002). Vitalism Revitalized: Vulnerable Populations, Prejudice, and Physician-Assisted Death. *Hastings Center Report, 32*(4), 14–21.

Medical Board of Australia (MBA) (2014). *Good Medical Practice: A Code of Conduct for Doctors in Australia*. Available at: http://www.medicalboard.gov.au/Codes-Guidelines-Policies/Code-of-conduct.aspx [Accessed 5 March 2019]

Moore, M. (2018). Why does Lord Denning's Lead Balloon Intrigue Us Still? The Prospects of Finding a Unifying Principle for Duress, Undue Influence and Unconscionability. *Law Quarterly Review, 134*, 257–284.

Otlowski, M. (2000). *Voluntary Euthanasia and the Common Law*. Oxford: Oxford University Press.

Parliament of Victoria, Legal and Social Issues Committee (LSIC) (2016). *Inquiry into End of Life Choices: Final Report*. Melbourne: Victorian Government Printer.

Rietjens, J. A., Robijn, L., & van der Heide, A. (2014). Euthanasia for Minors in Belgium. *JAMA, 312*(12), 1258–1259.

Rurup, M. L., Smets, T., Cohen, J., Bilsen, J., Onwuteaka-Philipsen, B. D., & Deliens, L. (2012). The First Five Years of Euthanasia Legislation in Belgium and the Netherlands: Description and Comparison of Cases. *Palliative Medicine, 26*(1), 43–49.

Safyan, A. R. (2011). A Call for International Regulation of the Thriving "Industry" of Death Tourism. *Loyola of Los Angeles International and Comparative Law Review, 33*(2), 287–320.

Silvers, A. (1998). Protecting the Innocents from Physician-Assisted Suicide: Disability Discrimination and the Duty to Protect Otherwise Vulnerable Groups. In M. Battin, R. Rhodes, & A. Silvers (eds.), *Physician Assisted Suicide: Expanding the Debate*, 133–148. New York: Routledge.

Simpson, A. (2018). Equal Treatment and Non Discrimination through the Functionalist Lens. In R. Dixon (ed.), *Australian Constitutional Values*, 195–217. Oxford: Hart.

Skene, L. (2004). Disputes about the Withdrawal of Treatment: The Role of the Courts. *The Journal of Law, Medicine & Ethics, 32*(4), 701–707.

Smets, T., Bilsen, J., Cohen, J., Rurup, M. L., Mortier, F., & Deliens, L. (2010). Reporting of Euthanasia in Medical Practice in Flanders, Belgium: Cross Sectional Analysis of Reported and Unreported Cases. *British Medical Journal, 341*, c5174.

Stapleton, J. B. (2003). The Golden Thread at the Heart of Tort Law: Protection of the Vulnerable. *Australian Bar Review, 24*, 135–148.

Tamanaha, B. Z. (2004). *On the Rule of Law: History, Politics, Theory*. Cambridge: Cambridge University Press.

Toohey, J. L. (1992). A Government of Laws, and Not of Men? *Public Law Review, 4*, 158–174.

Victorian Government (2017). *Ministerial Advisory Panel on Voluntary Assisted Dying: Final Report*. Melbourne: Victorian Government.

White, B., & Willmott, L. (2018a). Future of Assisted Dying Reform in Australia. *Australian Health Review, 42*(6), 616–620.

White, B., & Willmott, L. (2018b). Double Effect and Palliative Care Excuses. In B. White, F. McDonald, & L. Willmott (eds.), *Health Law in Australia* (3rd ed.), 625–644. Sydney: Thomson Reuters.

White, B., Willmott, L., & Then, S. (2018). Adults Who Lack Capacity: Substitute Decision-Making. In B. White, F. McDonald, & L. Willmott (eds.), *Health Law in Australia* (3rd ed.), 207–270. Sydney: Thomson Reuters.

Willmott, L., & White, B. (2017). Assisted Dying in Australia: A Values-based Model for Reform. In I. Freckelton & K. Petersen (eds.), *Tensions and Traumas in Health Law*, 479–510. Sydney: Federation Press.

Willmott, L., White, B., Ko, D., Downar, J., & Deliens, L. (2020). Restricting Conversations About Voluntary Assisted Dying: Implications for Clinical Practice. *BMJ Supportive and Palliative Care, 10*(1), 105–110.

Willmott, L., White, B., Stackpoole, C., Purser, K., & McGee, A. (2016). Failed Voluntary Euthanasia Law Reform in Australia: Two Decades of Trends, Models and Politics. *University of New South Wales Law Journal, 39*(1), 1–46.

Willmott, L., White, B., & Then, S. (2018). Withholding and Withdrawing Life-Sustaining Medical Treatment. In B. White, F. McDonald, & L. Willmott (eds.), *Health Law in Australia* (3rd ed.), 571–623. Sydney: Thomson Reuters.

Part II

Ethics, morals and values

5 Assisted dying, ethics and the law

For, against, or somewhere in between?

Richard Huxtable

Introduction

> I think that the law should continue to criminalise assistance in suicide and I think that the law should … be broken from time to time. We need to have a law against it in order to prevent abuse but it has always been the case that this has been criminal and it has always been the case that courageous relatives and friends have helped people to die… I think that that is an untidy compromise of the sort that I suspect very few lawyers would adopt, but I don't believe that there is necessarily a moral obligation to obey the law and, ultimately, it is something that each person has to decide within his own conscience.
>
> Sumption (2019, 10)

Lord Sumption made these comments during his first 2019 Reith lecture, when replying to an audience member who had been investigated by the police for accompanying her terminally ill husband to Switzerland, where he sought assistance in suicide.

As a prominent public campaign suggests, "dying matters, let's talk about it" (Dying Matters 2019) and this particular "dying matter" – assistance in dying – is a "major moral issue" about which many competing words have been spoken and written (Sumption 2019, 9). Each side claims to be in the right, but, as his Lordship implies, a different response is also available, involving a compromise between those in favour of and those against assistance in dying. Compromise might be "untidy", but I will argue that it has its merits, in the hope that the ranks of those inclined to explore and endorse such a position might be swelled beyond those "very few lawyers" to whom his Lordship referred.

Echoing the "dying matters" refrain, I will first outline some preliminary matters, noting the treacherous terminological territory in which assistance in dying finds itself and summarising the basic legal position that obtains in England and Wales. Second, I will consider various ethical matters, including permissive arguments, which primarily concern the obligations to respect choice and remove suffering, as well as prohibitive arguments, which point

DOI: 10.4324/9780429329739-5

to the value of life, the integrity of medicine, and the risks of sliding down slippery slopes. Finally, I reflect on the case for compromise, the form(s) this might take and further questions to which future research might be directed.[1]

Preliminary matters

There are few, if any, aspects of the assisted dying debate that are not contested, including the language used to capture the practice(s) under discussion (Huxtable 2007, 3–9). Euthanasia – literally "a good death" – tends to refer to someone (often, but not necessarily, a doctor) intentionally ending the life of another person who is suffering. This may be consensual (voluntary) or non-consensual (involuntary), or it may involve someone who is not capable of making or expressing their choice (non-voluntary). A distinction is also sometimes drawn between active and passive euthanasia, although the line between the two, and even the existence of the latter concept, is disputed (Huxtable 2020). While the resultant six categories (active voluntary euthanasia, passive voluntary euthanasia, etc.) involve the second party taking the final fatal step, a seventh category – assisted suicide – involves the suffering individual doing so, albeit with the help of another.

Debates continue about not only the existence and meaning of these different categories but also the ethical rights and wrongs of such practices. Proponents prefer to avoid the term "suicide", with its potentially pejorative overtones, so much of the current focus is on "assisted dying", which either refers to both active voluntary euthanasia and assisted suicide, or else only to the latter concept.

Whichever label is used, English law makes clear that neither assisting someone in suicide nor active voluntary euthanasia is lawful. The law of homicide encompasses (inter alia) murder, which involves the intentional causation of death, and complicity in suicide, which (according to the revised Suicide Act 1961) involves assisting or encouraging a suicide. Numerous attempts to change the law – whether through the courts or Parliament – have failed, although the legal position has softened in recent decades. In the early 2000s, Diane Pretty's plea for assistance in suicide failed before the English courts; the European Court of Human Rights, however, accepted that her autonomy rights were engaged, although these could be limited by the State (*R (on the application of Pretty) v DPP* [2002] 1 FLR 268; *Pretty v UK* [2002] 2 FLR 45). By 2009, the English courts further acknowledged patients' rights to autonomy, specifically finding that citizens had a right to know when they might be prosecuted for assisting in suicide (*R (on the application of Purdy) v DPP* [2009] UKHL 45). The Director of Public Prosecutions (2010) accordingly issued guidance to prosecutors, which signalled that family members or other loved ones would be unlikely to be prosecuted, although healthcare professionals might well be. Although the prohibitive letter of the law had not changed, it appeared lenient in application – a trend that has long been evident in the law's dealings with "mercy killers", including medical professionals (Huxtable 2007). Although some judges are warming to reform, the courts have nevertheless confirmed that the stated prohibition will remain, unless Parliament decides otherwise (*R (on the application of Nicklinson and another) v Ministry of Justice; R (on the application of AM) v The Director of Public Prosecutions* [2014] UKSC 38; *R (on the application of Conway) v The Secretary of State for Justice* [2018] EWCA Civ 1431).

Ethical matters

Like a growing number of jurisdictions, England might yet come to permit assisted dying. There are numerous ethical arguments in favour of and against such a move, five of which appear particularly prominent.

The first, and probably the major, argument in favour of allowing assistance in dying essentially holds that *choice matters*. The main claim is that those who (autonomously) seek assistance in ending their lives should (lawfully) be entitled to receive such assistance. This argument depicts life as having a *self-determined value*: if the individual decides that her life no longer has value for her, then she should be at liberty to bring about its end, even with the assistance of some other. Dianne Pretty made the point powerfully: "The law needs changing so that I, and people like me, can choose how and when we die and not be forced to endure untold suffering for no reason" (Jukes 2016). The people in question should be autonomous, that is, they should have the requisite mental capacity and information to make the decision, and should make that decision freely. Even the Supreme Court has recognised that respecting such decisions may be consistent with "our belief in the dignity and autonomy of the individual" (*Nicklinson*, *supra*, [209]). The importance of (autonomous) choice also leads to the claim that we should heed the general will of citizens regarding assisted dying; opinion polls indicate there is considerable public support for permitting such practices, which is up to 93%, according to one recent poll (My Death, My Decision 2019).

The second argument in favour of assisted dying holds that *suffering matters*, such that it is permissible to end someone's suffering by ending her life, at least in suitably extreme cases. Here, life has (only) an *instrumental value*: life is a vehicle for reaching other goods, but the vehicle may be abandoned if it can no longer convey the individual to those goods. Singer (1994, 75) puts the point more directly when he refers to "an ethic that sensibly takes into account whether sustaining life will benefit or harm the human being whose life is to be sustained". The idea that a poor-quality life is "no longer worth living" underpins arguments in favour of non-voluntary euthanasia, that is, ending the life of an individual who is not autonomous (Doyal 2006, 66). The same idea can also join forces with the autonomy argument to support (voluntary) assistance in dying, thereby modifying the (bare) choice argument into one of *understandable* choice (Huxtable 2017).

Opponents of assisted dying typically invoke three contrary arguments. First, they argue that *life matters*: rather than self-determined or instrumental value, life has *intrinsic value*. The argument is sometimes put in the distinctively theological (Judaeo-Christian) terms of the sanctity of human life. This principle holds that it is impermissible intentionally to end life, whether by action or omission (Keown 2018). According to Keown, "the doctrine that human life possesses an intrinsic dignity grounds the principle that one must never intentionally kill an innocent human being" (Keown 1998, 257). However, the principle does not (vitalistically) require the protection or preservation of life at all costs: death may be foreseen, provided it is not intended, and fatal omissions may be permitted, provided that continued treatment is judged to be futile or more burdensome than beneficial (Keown 2018). Faith is also not required, as the central idea can be expressed in more secular terms of the inviolability of, or right to, life (ibid).

Second, opponents claim that *medicine matters*. The claim has empirical and conceptual dimensions. Empirically, opponents note how doctors are typically positioned as the appropriate providers of assistance in dying, but that many doctors are opposed to the practice, particularly (and tellingly?) those who work in palliative medicine. This opposition is certainly apparent in the UK, with Seale's (2006, 8) research finding a "lower relative rate of [end-of-life decisions] involving doctor-assisted dying in the UK", which "suggests a culture of medical decision making informed by a palliative care philosophy". Conceptually, opponents believe that assisting in dying is antithetical to the doctor's professional role and identity and, indeed, to the profession's integrity. The British Medical Association (BMA) has suggested that permissive reform "could fundamentally alter the ethos within which medical care is provided. The principal purpose of medicine is to improve patients' quality of life, not to foreshorten it" (British Medical Association 2019). Philosophers like Pellegrino (2001, 559) argue that the practice is incompatible with the "internal morality" of medicine, which he sees as requiring clinicians to promote and protect (in ascending order of importance) the medical good, the good as perceived by the patient, the good for the patient as a human being, and the spiritual good. Assisted dying, he argues, "may violate the good for humans or the spiritual good", and these concerns outweigh what the patient judges to be good for her (Pellegrino 2001, 572).

There are also empirical and conceptual versions of the third objection, which suggests that *consequences matter*. Opponents worry that permitting assisted dying in even an (apparently) appropriate case will – either in principle or in practice – open the floodgates to allowing this in inappropriate cases. It is better, they argue, not to take the first step onto a potentially slippery slope. Empirically, say opponents, permissive countries like the Netherlands show the slope in action. Beginning in the 1970s, the Dutch policy originally encompassed cases of incurable illness, where the affected individual was suffering unbearably and requested assistance in dying. By 1994, assistance was being provided in response to psychiatric suffering, for which a Dr Chabot was convicted, although he received no punishment (Griffiths 1995a). A similar result obtained in a 2001 case, in which the suffering individual was (merely?) "tired of life" (Huxtable and Möller 2007). A few years later, a Dutch hospital openly adopted a protocol allowing for euthanasia of critically ill children (Manninen 2006). Data from 2012 further indicates that the rate of euthanasia had tripled in ten years (from 1.1% of all deaths in 2002, to 3.3%) and that granted requests for assisted dying included (inter alia) "life fatigue" (6.8% of all cases) and psychological suffering (the sole basis for the request in 3.7% of cases) (Lerner and Caplan 2015). "For the inhabitants of such a flat country", says Keown (1997, 289), "the Dutch have proved remarkably fast skiers". Conceptually, the slide might not easily be halted, particularly given the emphasis on choice and the malleability of "suffering": "once voluntary euthanasia as performed by a doctor is allowed, then it may be difficult to draw a principled line restricting this to (seemingly) straightforward cases of 'medical' suffering" (Huxtable and Möller 2007, 126).

Complexity matters

Each of these ethical arguments commands support, and understandably so, as they each offer an important piece of the moral jigsaw puzzle. Respect for autonomy (and its neighbour liberty) is particularly dominant: the principle underpins much of contemporary English healthcare law and has been dubbed "first among equals" in one (prominent) account of biomedical ethics (Gillon 2003, 307). The obligation to remove, or avoid the infliction of, suffering arguably has a longer history, for example, featuring in the Hippocratic injunction "first, do no harm". As the BMA implied, this injunction continues to inform what doctors do and, at least if they are to be the intended providers of assisted dying, we should heed what doctors themselves – and the profession at large – think of the practice. Equally, the intrinsic value of life has long been venerated and perhaps sensibly so, since successful social co-existence seems, at a minimum, to require a prohibition on killing. So too we should be mindful of where our principles and policies might lead us and, more practically, of "the human tendency to test the limits of any regulation" (House of Lords Select Committee 1994, [238]).

Despite their appeal, the arguments on each side nevertheless also confront compelling challenges, which (again) we can organise into conceptual and empirical groupings. There are conceptual and definitional difficulties on each side of the debate. First, how are we to understand the principle which underlies the idea that choice matters? Proponents refer to "death with dignity" but so too do opponents, so dignity – one of the most elusive and "elastic" concepts in bioethics – might not get us far (Huxtable 2015a). Respect for autonomy is easier to grasp, but what this means and entails is also not entirely settled. Is an autonomous choice one based on the individual's current, "best" or "ideal" desires (Coggon 2007)? These different concepts can underpin different policies on assisted dying and send different messages. The first two accounts involve respecting the subjective choice(s) of the individual, although the first of these requires little-to-no interrogation of the individual's *reason* for making that choice. The third account, meanwhile, involves a more objective judgement about whether the individual is (in some sense) making the *right* choice – which might then encourage negative judgements of those who, despite existing in similar circumstances, do not make such a choice. The "best" desire model nevertheless seems to be dominant nowadays, but we might still ask where the limits of respect for autonomy, so understood, lie. Looking to Mill, the prospect of harm to others could serve to put the brakes on any permissive policy (Mill 1962). But some would go further and argue that the individualised understanding of autonomy trades on a myth, since it "necessarily ignores the relationships that characterize human life", so – put most boldly – we should "declare that autonomy is dead" (de Vries 2015, 205).

Second, what is the meaning and scope of the proposed obligation to address or remove suffering? What is to count as "suffering" in the relevant sense, whose account thereof matters, and (again) what messages might be sent by a permissive policy premised on the eradication of suffering? "As extreme as it might sound", arguments so founded "are essentially claiming that a patient enduring a poor quality existence might be better off dead" (Huxtable 2007, 15). According to some, such a judgement is not necessarily a problem, provided it is the individual herself who is making that judgement; indeed, it might even be "disablist" to deny people with disabilities access to assisted dying if this is what they autonomously seek (Shildrick 2015). But others detect troubling eugenicist undertones to this logic: "Despite protestations of 'merciful' motives, arguments in favor of euthanasia are really based on a deadly mix of emotion, economics (killing is cheaper than caring), and a negative view of the value of vulnerable people" (Davis 2004).

Third, the idea that life has an intrinsic value invites similar questions. If the injunction not to kill (or, strictly, not to murder) really originates in (particular) theistic beliefs, then it can have no hold over those of no – or another – faith. The precise formulation offered by the principle of the sanctity of human life also attracts criticism, since it draws some fine (potentially non-existent) lines between, for example, that which is intended and that which is not, and between actions and omissions. The ethic also offers very particular definitions of such key words as "burdensome" and "futile", which conceal some hidden value judgements. Indeed, the ethic might actually be making the very judgements it seeks to condemn: for example, to judge an intervention "futile" seems to rest on the idea that it is not worth providing this to this patient, presumably due to the poor quality of her life (Huxtable 2007, 21–24). If that interpretation stands up, then the central thrust of the ethic might only be rescued by going (too far?) in the opposite direction, that is, by vitalistically insisting that life must *always* be protected and preserved (ibid).

Fourth, the idea that medicine matters – and that its internal morality precludes assistance in dying – is also conceptually contested. Pellegrino's is not the only account of the core commitments of medical practice; Miller and Brody (1995), for example, believe that clinicians should heal, promote health and help patients to achieve dignified and peaceful deaths. The authors argue that the latter goal does not *necessarily* commit doctors to providing assisted dying, but they nevertheless conclude that the practice *is* consistent with the medical endeavour, at least "as a last resort" (Miller and Brody 1995, 12). However, the contributors on both sides seem to write their opposing conclusions on the defensibility of assisted dying into their accounts of the concept (and goals or values) of medicine, thus begging the question (Huxtable 2015a). Unfortunately, the concept of medicine is not easily pinned down in any case, such that "no single answer" as to the (il)legitimacy of assisted dying "appears (necessarily) to emerge from the concept of medicine" (ibid., 157).

The empirical claims made by both sides also have their shortcomings. First, how reliable are the supportive opinion polls and what influence should they have? The public are sometimes misinformed on this topic (Newman 2019), and researchers note how surveys revealing considerable support for assisted dying "are often designed with insufficient attention to framing effects; that is, effects on the respondents' stated attitudes caused by question wording and context" (Magelssen et al. 2016). Notably, some opponents of assisted dying have posed more nuanced questions in their polls, which have resulted in significantly lower support for assisted dying (Saunders 2014). Of course, these polls might also "frame" the questions, presumably to generate responses sympathetic to the opponents' cause. In any case, we might still ask what influence – if any – these or other findings should have. There may be a democratic mandate for heeding the will of the majority, but this requires people to be adequately informed and does not entirely settle *why* what people happen to believe *should* form the basis for policy.

Evidence revealing doctors' opposition should also be interrogated. Not *every* doctor is opposed to the practice, as the Royal College of Physicians (2019) (RCP) recently found. It is not even the case that every doctor practising in palliative medicine is opposed. European specialists may be united in their support for rolling-out palliative care, but their attitudes to assisted dying vary (Campbell and Huxtable 2003). Even UK specialists are not united in opposition (Lawrie et al. 2019), although some fear that the specialty's position of opposition is preventing doctors sympathetic to the practice from saying as much (Anonymous 2019).

The data that allegedly reveal the existence of a slippery slope are also contested. Opponents' version of the Dutch story is not told by everybody. Keown (2018, 102), for example, fixed on an early report which indicated that, in 1,000 cases, euthanasia had been performed in the absence of an explicit request from the patient. Others, however, have suggested that it was not necessarily the case that these patients did not consent (Griffiths 1995b). Recent studies cast further doubt on the opponents' fears. Lewis and Black (2013, 895), for example, reviewed the evidence from the Netherlands, Belgium and Oregon and found "that the legal criteria that apply to an individual's request for assisted dying are well respected". Slope fears nevertheless linger, given (for example) the aforementioned protocol allowing euthanasia of minors, which seems at odds with Dutch law's stated requirement that the patient (rather than some proxy, such as a parent) consent. Further evidence might yet help to settle the slope question, although Parker (2005, 523) warns that watchful waiting could amount to "a normative strategy, which is felicitous to the [prohibitive] status quo and further medicalises the end of life, but which masquerades as a value-neutral assertion about needing more knowledge".

Compromise matters

Despite their apparent weaknesses, all the ethical arguments surveyed continue to feature in the ongoing debates on this issue. Different arguments come to the fore at different times, with contemporary disputants tending to cast their arguments in terms of choice, consequences and medical integrity, rather than the competing obligations to prevent suffering and to protect life. Yet, none of these five arguments has gone away, and neither has either side decisively emerged victorious. Closure on the rights and wrongs of assisted dying appears as unlikely as agreement on the issue. Perhaps, then, it is time to explore an alternative to conquest or consensus, in the form of compromise.

Contemplating and crafting compromise on ethical matters may be contentious in principle, but it is not uncommon in practice. English law certainly appears to have struck a sort of a compromise between the two sides, its position(s) on end-of-life decisions drawing on each of the five arguments (Huxtable 2007). The importance of respecting autonomous choices finds expression in (for example) the right to refuse even life-sustaining treatment (*Re B (Adult: Refusal of Medical Treatment)* [2002] 2 All ER 449). The obligation to remove suffering permits doctors to withhold or withdraw life-sustaining treatment from incapacitated patients who are judged to have a poor quality of life. Yet, such decisions are also sometimes defended in terms of the sanctity of life, on the basis that continued treatment is futile or burdensome (Keown 2018, 35–49). That ethic then further informs the legal position on the relief of symptoms in terminal illness, and it combines with concerns about protecting the vulnerable and preserving the integrity of medicine to underpin the prohibition on assistance in dying. As such, the current legal position is informed by the competing arguments on each side: sometimes the importance of respecting choice or addressing suffering informs the law; elsewhere, the law recognises the intrinsic value of life, the integrity of medicine and the risks of slippery slopes. The broad legal picture of decisions about death and dying is therefore a mosaic, composed of a plurality of competing ethical perspectives. The specific position on assisted dying is also an "untidy" compromise. The law-on-the-books might condemn the practice, but the law-in-action suggests a gentler response: ways are usually found to ensure that the accused does not bear the full weight of the stated homicide laws (Huxtable 2007). As such, those who have been investigated, prosecuted and even convicted of crimes arising from the provision of assistance in dying are very unlikely to serve the prison time that often follows other forms of killing.

Law may have good reason for being strict in letter but soft in deed. Building on Benjamin's (1990) work, there appear to be six conditions under which compromise on an ethically contested matter may be indicated, all of which appear to be met in this context (Huxtable 2012, 2014). First, the disputing parties (and positions) have a prudential reason to contemplate compromise if – through failing to do so – they risk losing out completely. Second, it is not possible, simultaneously, to honour the competing claims fully. Third, a decision on the matter in question is nevertheless needed and, fourth, the disputants cannot simply walk away, as they are bound to co-exist with their antagonists. The final two conditions, which are probably the primary drivers of compromise, are that there is sufficient uncertainty and complexity pervading the facts and values in issue that a victor on one side or the other cannot be established.

Benjamin has argued that, when such conditions are present, a compromise is appropriate, which he illustrates by reference to the position adopted by the Warnock Commission on research on human embryos. The Commission, which informed English (and other) law in this area, confronted diametrically opposed positions: "an extreme conservative, or prolife, view of the moral standing of the embryo", which would not allow research that was destructive of the embryo, and "a considerably more liberal, or utilitarian, view", which would support at least some such research (Benjamin 1990, 39). Warnock struck a balance between the two, by permitting research up to 14 days from fertilisation but prohibiting it thereafter.

The tireless to-and-fro on assisted dying reinforces the impression that the conditions are ripe for striking a balance in this context too. The *process* for reaching compromise is an important consideration (Huxtable 2012), but the main question here is *what* might a compromise on assisted dying look like? What we currently have seems to qualify: according to Calabresi (1985, 88), the law faces a "tragic conflict" of beliefs and has made a "tragic choice", which strives to "cover the difficulty and permit us to assert that we are cleaving to both beliefs in conflict". McCall Smith (1999) has commended the current law for seeking to occupy the middle ground. However, this is a rather unpredictable and covert compromise: not only is the law "a sprung trap" (Williams 1958, 292), but there are also considerations of fair labelling to address (Ashworth 2003, 89–92).

Perhaps, then, a more explicit compromise position is needed. Various options exist, although some err too far in one direction. Mullock (2012), for example, has argued that assisted suicide should lawfully be provided, but (as in Oregon) only to those consenting patients who are terminally ill and intractably suffering. She considers this "a compromise that would address some of the concerns of those opposed" (Mullock 2012, 22). This proposal, however, offers much to proponents but little to opponents, so it is difficult to see how this occupies the middle ground. An alternative proposal, based on the (English) policy applicable to armed response policy officers who kill in the course of their duties, might offer more to opponents. By analogy, doctors who assist in dying would have their employment paused during an investigation but would be retrospectively excused (and return to work) if they are found to have met the relevant criteria for lawful assistance in dying (Huxtable and Ives 2015). This seems to send a more prohibitive message but, as with Mullock's proposal, it too might ultimately offer too much to proponents.

Other proposals err too far in the opposite direction. Keown (2018), for example, argues that the sanctity of life position is itself a compromise, between vitalism on one side, and an ethic premised on quality of life considerations on the other. He accordingly believes that end-of-life policies should be based on the idea that life has intrinsic value, but this obviously offers little to proponents of assisted dying. Other proposals, which essentially support the prohibitive status quo, might similarly fail to engage proponents, and they might also miss the point. The provision of continuous deep sedation offers something of a compromise, but it does not tackle the contested practice (assisted dying) head on (Huxtable and Horn 2013). Equally, Benjamin's (2003, 145) own proposal – that the refusal of nutrition and hydration might "be a reasonable compromise between those favouring physician-assisted suicide and those opposing it" – fails to split the difference on the specific contested practice.

It is, nevertheless, possible to adopt an explicit position on assisted dying that splits the difference between proponents and opponents. Permitting individuals to travel from a prohibitive jurisdiction to a permissive one (such as Switzerland) – the so-called assisted suicide tourism – strikes in the right direction, although it does not arrive at a compromise that is available to everyone, since the option would still be denied in the originating country and would therefore only be available to those with the health and resources to make the trip (Huxtable 2009).

A compromise can, however, be reached *within* a jurisdiction, which will be accessible to its citizens. To reach that point, we should first reframe the terms of the debate. It is noticeable that most disputants cast their contributions in terms of what is or is not *justified*, that is, in terms of right and wrong. The alternative concept of *excuse* might better capture the "moral conflict" to which Calebresi (and, indeed, Benjamin [2003, 147]) has referred. An excuse conveys that the agent was involved in wrong-doing but that their responsibility is mitigated, for example, because they were also involved in right-doing.

Such an ethically pluralistic concept underpins the proposal I have in mind, which involves the creation of a new offence of "compassionate killing" (cf. Keating and Bridgeman 2012, 697). The new offence, which would also operate as a partial defence to other homicide charges, could split the difference between opponents and proponents, since it would preserve,

> the criminal prohibition (thus retaining something of the condemnation sought by opponents), whilst also signalling that this is a lesser crime than

> homicide per se, which merits lighter sentences (thus affording something to the proponents of assisted dying).
>
> Huxtable (2014, 476)

Non-custodial sentences could then be handed down, such as probation, counselling or (for healthcare professionals) re-training. Neither justified nor unjustified, assistance in dying would instead be excused.

End matters

Compromise on assisted dying therefore appears defensible in principle and conceivable in practice. Questions nevertheless remain. First, when are the circumstances ripe for compromise – what does each of the conditions require and must they all be met? Second, what counts as a compromise? Third, by whom and through which processes should compromise be wrought? Fourth, whose and which positions should be accommodated within any compromise? And, finally, what are the costs of compromise?

Some of these questions have recently surfaced in public, policy and academic circles. Lord Sumption's (2019) recent public comments, noted at the outset of the chapter, invite reflection on the second question and, in particular, on the "tidiness" of different sorts of compromises. In terms of policy, the first three questions (particularly) arise in relation to the recent decision of the RCP, following a poll of its members, to move from a position of opposition to one of neutrality (Royal College of Physicians 2019). This new position might appear to split the difference between respondents. Differences certainly remain, with 43.4% of respondents believing the RCP should be opposed to permissive reform (down from 44.4% in a 2014 poll), while 31.6% believe the RCP should be in favour (up from 24.6%). The strength of support on each side suggests a compromise *might* be merited. Yet, the majority of these respondents clearly favours a prohibitive law. Curiously, however, the RCP indicated that it would adopt a neutral position unless one side garnered 60% support. This third option was also put to voters, but it attracted only 25% support (down from 31% in 2014). In short, respondents had to choose between three options, −1 (opposed), 0 (neutral) or +1 (in favour); option −1 received most support, option 0 the least, yet option 0 was the position adopted. Others can comment on the statistical (and, indeed, democratic) defensibility of this methodology and conclusion. Ethically, however, we might query whether the process, including the requirement for a "super majority", meant that the dice were loaded against opponents (cf. Hurley 2019). It is open to question whether the outcome is a compromise and whether it arose from a principled process.

In academic circles, meanwhile, Parker acknowledges that the offence I propose avoids the current subterfuge, but he doubts that it captures a compromise. He agrees that Mullock's proposal offers too much to proponents, but considers my proposal to offer *neither* side "sufficient net benefit for the arrangement to qualify" (Parker 2015, 530). The proposal is condemned as "hypocritical" and beset by "contradictions and incoherency", with Parker ultimately doubting that compromise between different values or worldviews is possible (ibid, 531, 532; cf. Holm 2010). Parker certainly poses pertinent questions, for example, about the goals and nature of retraining, probation and counselling, which merit further thought. However, he seems to emphasise only one side of compromise – anticipated gains – while underplaying the need for each side also to incur losses. Benjamin defends the possibility of compromise – noting, for example, that the compromise exists at the level of practice or policy, rather than between the conflicting values themselves – and concedes that some incoherence will inevitably follow. He nevertheless considers this "part of the price we must pay to avoid the dehumanization of simple consistency in an unavoidably complex situation" (Benjamin 1994, 277). Parker's complaints might therefore be addressed, although he rightly invites reconsideration of the concept of compromise and of what, practically, counts as a compromise and what this should entail.

Conclusion

The concept, principles and practices of compromise invite further work, as does its relation to assisted dying and other "apparently intractable bioethical questions in pluralistic societies" (Parker 2015, 526). I nevertheless hope to have offered one possible way forward, via the creation of a distinct offence of "compassionate killing", which captures the compassion that proponents seek, while reflecting the killing side that so concerns opponents. An explicit attempt to attend to concerns on both sides seems merited, not least because the rights and wrongs of assisted dying appear so contested, complex and uncertain. Proponents continue to claim that choice and suffering matters, while opponents repeatedly argue that life, medicine and consequences matter. Rather than trundle along on these well-worn tracks, "there are worse places to be" than the middle ground between them (McCall Smith 1999, 207).

Note

1 This chapter is partly based on my inaugural lecture (Huxtable 2016), which summarised much of my work on this topic to date (hence the potentially indecent amount of self-citation).

References

Anonymous (2019) We Risk Our Careers If We Discuss Assisted Dying, Say UK Palliative Care Consultants. *British Medical Journal*, 365, I1494.

Ashworth, A. (2003) *Principles of Criminal Law*, 4th edn. Oxford: Oxford University Press.

Benjamin, M. (1990) *Splitting the Difference: Compromise and Integrity in Ethics and Politics*. Lawrence: University Press of Kansas.

Benjamin, M. (1994) Conflict, Compromise, and Moral Integrity. In C.S. Campbell and B.A. Lustig (eds) *Duties to Others* (261–278). Dordrecht: Kluwer Academic Publishers.

Benjamin, M. (2003) *Philosophy and this Actual World*. Maryland: Rowman & Littlefield.

British Medical Association (2019) *Physician-Assisted Dying*. Available: <https://www.bma.org.uk/advice/employment/ethics/ethics-a-to-z/physician-assisted-dying> (accessed 14 June 2019).

Calabresi, G. (1985) *Ideals, Beliefs, Attitudes, and the Law: Private Law Perspectives on a Public Law Problem*. Syracuse: Syracuse University Press.

Campbell, A.V., and Huxtable, R. (2003) The Position Statement and Its Commentators: Consensus, Compromise or Confusion? *Palliative Medicine*, 17, 180–183.

Coggon, J. (2007) Varied and Principled Understandings of Autonomy in English Law: Justifiable Inconsistency or Blinkered Moralism? *Health Care Analysis*, 15, 235–255.

Davis, A. (2004) Commentary: A Disabled Person's Perspective on Euthanasia. *Disability Studies Quarterly*, 24(3), Available: <http://dsq-sds.org/article/view/512/689> (accessed 14 October 2019).

de Vries, R.G. (2015) Bioethics in Academic Rooms: Hearing Other Voices, Living in Other Rooms. In R. Huxtable and R. ter Meulen (eds) *The Voices and Rooms of European Bioethics* (192–206). Abingdon: Routledge.

Director of Public Prosecutions (2010) *Policy for Prosecutors in Respect of Cases of Encouraging or Assisting Suicide*. Available: <http://www.cps.gov.uk/publications/prosecution/assisted_suicide_policy.html> (accessed 14 June 2019).

Doyal, L. (2006) Dignity in Dying Should Include the Legalisation of Non-Voluntary Euthanasia. *Clinical Ethics*, 1, 65–67.

Dying Matters (2019) *Dying Matters*. Available: <https://www.dyingmatters.org/> (accessed 14 June 2019).

Gillon, R. (2003) Ethics Needs Principles – Four Can Encompass the Rest – and Respect for Autonomy Should Be "First among Equals". *Journal of Medical Ethics*, 29, 307–312.

Griffiths, J. (1995a) Assisted Suicide in the Netherlands: The Chabot Case. *Modern Law Review*, 58, 232–248.

Griffiths, J. (1995b) Recent Developments in the Netherlands Concerning Euthanasia and Other Medical Behavior that Shortens Life. *Medical Law International*, 2, 347–386.

Holm, S. (2010) Euthanasia: Agreeing to Disagree? *Medical Health Care Philosophy*, 13, 399–402.

House of Lords Select Committee (1994) *Report of the Select Committee on Medical Ethics*, HL Paper 21. London: Her Majesty's Stationery Office.

Hurley, R. (2019) RCP Threatened with Judicial Review over Assisted Dying Poll. *British Medical Journal*, 364, I559.

Huxtable, R. (2007) *Euthanasia, Ethics and the Law: From Conflict to Compromise*. Abingdon: Routledge-Cavendish.

Huxtable, R. (2009) The Suicide Tourist Trap: Compromise across Boundaries. *Journal of Bioethical Inquiry*, 6(3), 327–336.

Huxtable, R. (2012) *Law, Ethics and Compromise at the Limits of Life: To Treat Or Not to Treat?* Abingdon: Routledge.

Huxtable, R. (2014) Splitting the Difference? Principled Compromise and Assisted Dying. *Bioethics*, 28(9), 472–480.

Huxtable, R. (2015a) Death on Demand: Proper Medical Treatment? In S. Fovargue and A. Mullock (eds) *The Power of 'Proper Medical Treatment': What Role for the Medical Exception?* (142–159). Abingdon: Routledge.

Huxtable, R. (2015b) Dignity's Steer, Dignity's Subjects, Dignity's Synonyms? Three Questions for Dignity's Supporter(s). *Journal of Medical Ethics*, 41, 936–937.

Huxtable, R. (2016) Inaugural Lecture: Assisted Dying, Ethics and the Law: For, Against, or Somewhere in Between? Available: <https://www.bristol.ac.uk/pace/public-events/inaugural/2016/huxtable/> (accessed 14 June 2019).

Huxtable, R. (2017) Putting the Black Dog to Sleep? Depression and Assisted Dying. In J. Herring and C. Foster (eds) *Dementia: Ethical and Legal Issues* (280–293). Oxford: Oxford University Press.

Huxtable, R. (2020) On Killing and Letting Die, Acts and Omissions: For and Against the Distinctions. In N. Emmerich, B. Gordijn, and P. Mallia (eds) *Contemporary European Perspectives on the Ethics of End of Life* (229–241). New York: Springer.

Huxtable, R., and Horn, R. (2013) Continuous Sedation at the End of Life: Balancing Benefits and Harms in England, Germany and France. In S. Sterckx, K. Raus and F. Mortier (eds) *Continuous Sedation at the End of Life* (160–176). Cambridge: Cambridge University Press.

Huxtable, R., and Ives, J. (2015) License to Kill: A New Model for Excusing Medically Assisted Dying? In J. Varelius and M. Cholbi (eds) *New Directions in the Ethics of Assisted Suicide and Euthanasia* (149–168). Dordrecht: Springer.

Huxtable, R., and Möller, M. (2007) "Setting a Principled Boundary"? Euthanasia as a Response to 'Life Fatigue'. *Bioethics*, 21(3), 117–126.

Jukes, K. (2016) We Need to Talk about the Right to Die. Available: <https://rightsinfo.org/need-talk-right-die/> (accessed 14 June 2019).

Keating, H., and Bridgeman, J. (2012) Compassionate Killings: The Case for a Partial Defence, *Modern Law Review*, 75(5), 697–721.

Keown, J. (1997) Euthanasia in the Netherlands: Sliding Down the Slippery Slope? In J. Keown (ed) *Euthanasia Examined: Ethical, Clinical and Legal Perspectives* (261–296). Cambridge: Cambridge University Press.

Keown, J. (1998) The Legal Revolution: From "Sanctity of Life" to "Quality of Life" and "Autonomy". *Journal of Contemporary Health Law & Policy*, 14(2), 253–285.

Keown, J. (2018) *Euthanasia, Ethics and Public Policy: An Argument against Legalisation*, 2nd edn. Cambridge: Cambridge University Press.

Lawrie, I., Proffitt, A., Willis, D., and George, R. (2019) Assisted Dying: Association for Palliative Medicine responds. *British Medical Journal*, 365, I2008.

Lerner, B.H., and Caplan, A.L. (2015) Euthanasia in Belgium and the Netherlands on a Slippery Slope? *JAMA Internal Medical*, 175(10), 1640–1641.

Lewis, P., and Black, I. (2013) Adherence to the Request Criterion in Jurisdictions Where Assisted Dying Is Lawful? A Review of the Criteria and Evidence in the Netherlands, Belgium, Oregon and Switzerland. *Journal of Law, Medicine & Ethics*, 41(4), 885–898.

Magelssen, M., Supphellen, M., Nortvedt, P., and Materstvedt, J.J. (2016) Attitudes towards Assisted Dying are Influenced by Question Wording and Order: A Survey Experiment. *BMC Medical Ethics*, 17(1), 24.

Manninen, B.A. (2006) A Case for Justified Non-Voluntary Active Euthanasia: Exploring the Ethics of the Groningen Protocol. *Journal of Medical Ethics*, 32, 643–651.

McCall Smith, A. (1999) Euthanasia: The Strengths of the Middle Ground. *Medical Law Review*, 7, 194–207.

Mill, J.S. (1962) On Liberty. In M. Warnock (ed) *Utilitarianism, On Liberty, Essay on Bentham (by John Stuart Mill), together with Selected Writings of Jeremy Bentham and John Austin* (126–250). London: Collins, The Fontana Library.

Miller, F.G., and Brody, H. (1995) Professional Integrity and Physician-Assisted Death. *Hastings Center Report*, 25, 8–17.

Mullock, A. (2012) Compromising on Assisted Suicide: Is Turning a Blind Eye Ethical? *Clinical Ethics*, 7(1), 17–23.

My Death, My Decision (2019) Available: <https://www.mydeath-mydecision.org.uk/wp-content/uploads/2019/03/Briefing-on-NatCen-assisted-dying-poll.pdf> (accessed 14 June 2019).

Newman, M. (2019) Noa Pothoven Wasn't Euthanised – But It Was What She Wanted. *British Medical Journal*, 365, l4142.

Parker, M. (2005) End Games: Euthanasia under Interminable Scrutiny. *Bioethics*, 19(5–6), 523–536.

Parker, M. (2015) Clayton's Compromises and the Assisted Dying Debate. *Journal Law Medical*, 22, 526–533.

Pellegrino, E.D. (2001) The Internal Morality of Clinical Medicine: A Paradigm for the Ethics of the Helping and Healing Professions. *Journal of Medicine and Philosophy*, 26, 559–579.

Royal College of Physicians (2019) No Majority View on Assisted Dying Moves RCP Position to Neutral. Available: <https://www.rcplondon.ac.uk/news/no-majority-view-assisted-dying-moves-rcp-position-neutral> (accessed 14 June 2019).

Saunders, P. (2014) Support for UK Assisted Dying Bill Plummets to 43% after Hearing Opposing Arguments. Available: <http://www.lifesitenews.com/pulse/support-for-uk-assisted-dying-bill-plummets-to-43-after-hearing-opposing-ar> (accessed 14 June 2019).

Seale, C. (2006) National Survey of End-of-Life Decisions Made by UK Medical Practitioners. *Palliative Medicine*, 20(1), 3–10.

Shildrick, M. (2015) XI. Death, Debility and Disability. *Feminism & Psychology*, 25(1), 155–160.

Singer, P. (1994) *Rethinking Life and Death: The Collapse of Our Traditional Ethics*. New York: St Martin's Press.

Sumption, L.J. (2019) The Reith Lectures 2019: Law and the Decline of Politics; Lecture 1: Law's Expanding Empire. Available: <http://downloads.bbc.co.uk/radio4/reith2019/Reith_2019_Sumption_lecture_1.pdf> (accessed 14 June 2019).

Williams, G. (1958) *The Sanctity of Life and the Criminal Law*. London: Faber & Faber.

6 Euthanasia as life-extension

Anthony Wrigley

Introduction

Although genuinely new and novel arguments surrounding the permissibility of euthanasia have been thin on the ground in recent years, the issue itself is going through a period of intense public scrutiny, with multiple attempts to secure a legal basis for a 'right to die' in the UK, as well as increasing legislation across the world.[1] Amidst such debate, I want to return to some foundational moral arguments and consider a potentially new approach. This involves taking a perspective on the overall life of an individual and arguing that euthanasia has the potential to *extend* rather than shorten life in certain cases. This seemingly paradoxical claim does not offer a definitive or knock-down argument in the euthanasia debate but it does offer an additional type of argument in favour of euthanasia. Furthermore, such a consideration might be particularly suited to understanding euthanasia's place within, for example, the medical profession, where intentionally seeking to shorten life is often seen as problematic when considered alongside the goals of medicine. This is not an argument for the prolongation of life at any costs. Instead, it forms part of a 'whole of life' view that an individual may have about themselves (Dworkin, 1994, pp. 222–229).

The inspiration for considering a life-extension approach is the case of the Belgian Paralympic medal-winning athlete Marieke Vervoort. Vervoort, who won medals at the London and Rio Paralympics, suffered from a form of progressive tetraplegia, an incurable degenerative spinal condition which causes seizures, rising paralysis, failing eyesight, and reflex sympathetic dystrophy resulting in constant and excruciating pain. Born in 1979, Vervoort was diagnosed with the condition when she was 15 and lived with the inexorable progress of her disease ever since. She signed her euthanasia papers in 2008 but it was not her intention to undergo euthanasia at that point, as her numerous medal successes clearly illustrate. It was Vervoort's repeated claim, that she would have already taken her own life if she had not had the option of planned euthanasia available to her in Belgium,[2] that has given such a strong practical realisation to this perspective as a potential line of argument in the euthanasia debate. This is made all the

DOI: 10.4324/9780429329739-6

more apparent as, it seems, Vervoort's view is not an isolated case of this way of thinking about one's own life and euthanasia, with similar cases subsequently also coming to light.[3] This raises a timely question as to whether this consideration genuinely offers us a form of new and persuasive argument in favour of (certain types of) euthanasia or whether it is simply an expression of the intentions of the individual? I will argue that not only does it provide a supporting argument in favour of euthanasia, but it also provides an important counter-argument to certain types of sanctity of life arguments that are often utilised as overriding considerations against any individual wanting to claim a right to end their life in this way.[4]

Definitions and concepts

The sorts of arguments that can be utilised either for or against euthanasia can change quite markedly depending on what we actually mean by 'euthanasia' or on what the circumstances and intentions surrounding certain acts are. This is particularly important in the case of the life-extension argument, as it directly supports only certain kinds of euthanasia.

Although there is no one, universally agreed definition, there are enough common or shared features among various definitions to allow euthanasia be broadly defined as,

> the intentional bringing about of the death (or shortening of life) of the patient where this is done for the patient's own sake (their best interests).[5]

However, different aspects also have to be distinguished in terms of:

- i how it is being done;
- ii to whom it is being done;
- iii what is being done; and
- iv why it is being done.

With respect to (i), euthanasia can be distinguished in terms of the way in which the euthanasia is carried out. This usually takes the distinction between active and passive forms of euthanasia. Active euthanasia is the deliberate killing or hastening of death of a patient by taking some action that is intended to bring about their death, for the patient's own sake (such as by administering a lethal injection). Passive euthanasia differs by allowing a patient to die intentionally by omitting to take some action which would, if performed, have lengthened the life of the patient or prevented their death. Passive euthanasia primarily occurs through withdrawing or withholding life-prolonging treatment. Although there is debate as to whether there is, practically or morally, any difference between active and passive forms of euthanasia (Rachels, 1975), I shall take the well-supported view that such a distinction can be usefully maintained (Garrard and Wilkinson, 2005).

As I shall discuss later, the life-extension argument for euthanasia will have most bearing on active euthanasia.

With respect to (ii), we gain another distinction between voluntary, non-voluntary, and involuntary euthanasia. Voluntary euthanasia is euthanasia autonomously requested by the patient. It requires the patient both (a) to be sufficiently informed and competent to request or consent to it and (b) does in fact consent to it. The issue of whether both of these requirements can be achieved through the use of advance directives or other means of substituted judgements, such as using proxies, has been an important contemporary topic.[6] The Vervoort case is one where a pre-existing advance decision has been used to voluntarily request euthanasia. However, this was a prudential rather than necessary step for Vervoort, where it is physical ability rather than mental competence which is primarily at stake. Non-voluntary euthanasia is where the individual is not sufficiently mentally competent to request euthanasia or may be competent but is unable to communicate their request or consent to it (such as with Locked-in syndrome). Involuntary euthanasia occurs against either the patients stated wishes or where the patient, although competent, is not consulted.

With respect to (iii), it is important to distinguish between ending one's own life, physician-assisted dying, and euthanasia. The definition of 'suicide' can itself be problematic and can carry implicit negative connotations. Therefore, I will use the phrase 'ending one's own life' instead, which I define as,

> the act of taking one's own life intentionally and voluntarily (without assistance from another person).[7]

Although the moral permissibility of ending one's own life is not the issue under discussion here, there is an important step between this and euthanasia that it is worth distinguishing – physician-assisted dying (PAD). PAD can be defined as,

> ending one's own life in a way that is carried out by that individual with assistance from another person (which, in the case of physician assisted dying, is a doctor or equivalent health professional).

The relevant classificatory distinction here is the involvement of another person, even though the act itself is carried out by the subject. For example, a third party could provide the means for carrying out the act of ending one's own life by setting up apparatus and a doctor prescribe the lethal drugs to be utilized. This involvement of a third party has raised a considerable number of additional issues compared to those associated with taking one's own life without assistance (Dworkin, Frey, and Bok, 1998; Battin, 2005).

While life-extension arguments are potentially applicable to the case of PAD, the focus here is on active voluntary euthanasia (AVE). One important reason for this is that questions surrounding involuntary or non-voluntary euthanasia take us away from any notion of individual choice. Life-extension considerations strongly imply they must be accompanied by consensual future-planning on the part of the individual involved. Furthermore, arguments concerning the ethical permissibility of AVE would apply *a fortiori* to passive euthanasia and PAD. The thought is that if PAD is deemed to be morally identical or even less ethically problematic than AVE, then arguments supporting the more ethically demanding procedure would also support similar but less ethically demanding procedures.[8]

It is worth noting that throughout all the different distinctions considered so far, nothing refers to any reasons that a subject may have for requesting euthanasia and very little as to the motivations of the third party carrying out (or assisting with if PAD) the termination of life. As such, these definitions remain neutral on distinction (iv), which often concerns whether euthanasia is only for those with a terminal illness and/or unbearable suffering caused by an uncurable condition. Although many might consider euthanasia to only be applicable in cases where all of these elements are present, as it holds in Vervoort's home country of Belgium, euthanasia is reserved for those suffering with incurable conditions, the account I offer here allows scope for euthanasia to be applicable to other individual circumstances. This might include cases where the person requesting euthanasia would not be considered terminally ill, such as permanent paralysis or progressive dementia, and potentially other circumstances, such as 'life fatigue' (Huxtable and Moller, 2007).

These distinctions allow a precise picture of the life-extension argument in the case of Vervoort. In Belgium, euthanasia has been legal since 2002 and takes the form of AVE, as the Act specifies that euthanasia means 'the intentional termination of life by a person other than the person concerned, at the latter's request.'[9] Not only must the person be competent when making the request and do so voluntarily, but the medical condition of the patient is also relevant. Belgian law requires that the patient must be in a persistent and unbearable state of physical or psychological suffering that cannot be otherwise alleviated. Furthermore, this state must be the result of a serious and incurable disease or accident-induced condition. Vervoort's condition, a form of aggressive and incurable tetraplegia causing progressive physical deterioration, rising paralysis, and unbearable pain, therefore long ago met these requirements to the satisfaction of her own physician and the independent consultant physicians who were also required to authorize the euthanasia request. As Vervoort's condition progresses past the point where she would be able to take her own life or even make use of PAD due to her increasing paralysis, she holds that her established euthanasia request has allowed her the extra years of life that she would otherwise have had to forego. Her reasoning is that this request can be enacted on at a point of her choosing, rather than limiting her only option to end her life to a point where she could still do so without assistance.[10] This is something Vervoort confirmed in an interview shortly after the Rio Paralympic Games:

> When I didn't have those papers, I would have committed suicide. I hope other countries like Brazil can talk about it. It makes people live longer.

> It doesn't mean that when people sign the papers, they have to die two weeks later. I signed my papers in 2008. Look now, 2016 and I won the silver medal.[11]

Applying life-extension considerations to key arguments surrounding the ethics of euthanasia

The question as to whether this sort of life-extension argument really does contribute to the debate as to the ethical permissibility of euthanasia is an intriguing one. By itself, it would form, at best, only a weak, rebuttable consequentialist line of argument that more life years might result for an individual if it were allowed on these grounds. However, that would be to miss the point of both the context in which it is being employed and the unusual intentional basis of the argument itself. Therefore, rather than considering it in isolation, I want to consider whether it can be a consideration that genuinely strengthens arguments in favour of the moral permissibility of AVE and whether it meets any of the objections offered against AVE.

There is no doubt that the practice of euthanasia puts great tension on our duty of care towards individuals. On the one hand, its practice seems to contradict a central guiding moral principle often found in medical settings of non-maleficence – do no harm. This line meets its most radical utilisation with sanctity of life arguments, the view that a person's life is inviolable and of value regardless of disability, pain and suffering. Supporters such as Keown (2002) and Gormally (2000) believe that this means intentionally killing an innocent person – even if they request it through euthanasia – can never be justified. As Keown puts it, 'The "right to life" is essentially a right not to be intentionally killed' (Keown 2002, p. 40).

On the other hand, the moral permissibility of euthanasia is implied by two other principles. One is respect for individual autonomy – where, for example, if I am a rational and well-informed person and decide that I want to die because I believe it is in my interests not to live anymore (such as to prevent further intolerable suffering) then my decision should be respected. The second is the promotion of beneficence or best interests, by preventing needless suffering in cases where, for example, a patient is terminally ill or suffering from physical and/or psychological pain that cannot be relieved. These ethical concerns are not the only ones in play, many of which break down into much finer, more nuanced arguments, but as basic and often-cited guiding ethical principles, they are the first areas for consideration for the applicability of life-extension arguments.

Sanctity of life

If we start with the most radical (secular) line of objection to the permissibility of euthanasia – sanctity of life arguments based on what is generally known as 'vitalism' – we are unlikely to find much ground given in response to a counter-argument utilising life-extension considerations.[12] Defending the view that a person's life has absolute, intrinsic, worth (and so is of value regardless of disability, pain and suffering) is a position granting no exceptions. It is therefore not subject directly to considerations of 'more' and 'less' when it comes to life. Although a supporter of the vitalism view would doubtless consider that a greater length of life for an individual is better than a shorter one, they would not be willing to accede to euthanasia requests. Rejecting euthanasia based on the intrinsic value of life holds, according to Dworkin (1988), regardless of whether it is in a person's best interests to die or whether a person has autonomously chosen to waive their own right to life. This is because the sanctity of life is not identical with the value that any one individual may have for their own life. Instead, it simply holds of all lives. The addition of a life-extension argument would therefore not add any further justification. To do so would effectively be offering a justification for what they view as an intrinsic wrong (euthanasia) by appeal to another intrinsic wrong ('suicide').

Although less radical than vitalist positions, many secular 'inviolability of life' arguments still premise themselves on the innate or intrinsic good of life, as opposed to any quality of life consideration. However, the way in which the basis for this intrinsic good is established can leave open a route for counter-argument based on life-extension considerations. Most often, the foundation of secular sanctity of life positions are provided by appeal to some innate human characteristic, such as rational capacity, which is seen to give humans their innate worth and which grounds their 'right to life'. This innate value is also characterised as an impersonal value of a human life, that is 'different from its personal value – that is, the value it has for the individual whose life it is … and of what the person himself autonomously desires his life to be like' (McMahan, 2002, p. 331).

One of the most prominent explanations as to what grounds the sanctity of human life is Dworkin's (1994, p. 84) account of the 'complex creative investment' that has been made in the life.[13] This means that, due to the time, energy, resources, effort, and so on that have been invested in both the creation and development of a human life by others and the individual themselves, such life has its intrinsic value. However, this view has been subject to substantial criticism by McMahan (2002), who argues appeal to the sanctity of life cannot be a plausible objection to euthanasia or taking one's own life on this basis, claiming, 'For the fact that an investment has been made in a life does not make it important that the life should be preserved irrespective of what its character will be' (2002, p. 465). Dworkin's account holds that taking one's own life or euthanasia would be a *waste* of this investment; but McMahan's point is that there is no waste of investment if that life has already yielded all the good that can come from such investment and will not yield any further good. Not only will prolongation of life in such cases fail to advance that investment, but further investment in prolonging a life of misery would be seen to be a squandering of investment on something that will yield no further value.

This criticism gives an interesting role for life-extension considerations for sanctity of life claims of this type. If we link sanctity of life to a fullness of investment with a life, then it would not offer a compelling basis for rejecting euthanasia claims in cases like Vervoort's. This is based on the rationale for euthanasia as life-extension: that it allows an individual to glean more life – life still able to continue to yield the goods of the investment in it – than they would otherwise have been able to if AVE was not available to them. Indeed, this actually makes the case stronger for AVE and, potentially, even PAD than it does for choosing to take one's own life without assistance.[14] This is based on a desire to not waste life opportunities until one is not only past the point of being able to self-intervene to take one's own life but also past the point of life having *any* opportunity whatsoever for that person. This means that life is not being wasted but is, instead, fuller because of a life-extension that AVE offers that individual, making it appear compatible with this type of sanctity of life position (or, at least, a means of addressing the concerns such a view has raised against AVE). Although this will not meet absolutist views as to the sanctity of life, such as vitalism, it does offer a response to a grounded secular account of sanctity of life position.

It may be objected that this use of the life-extension argument makes the error of conflating an intrinsic, impersonal value of the good of life with a qualitative, personal, or subjective value of the good of life. Although the life-extension argument can be used to support certain positions for AVE that do rely on appeal to quality and personal value of life, this particular use in the case of sanctity of life is not one of them. The reason it can avoid this charge is because Dworkin's complex, creative investment explanation as to why we may consider life inviolable or sacred only gains meaning if one considers what value is generated by appeal to such investment. It is not that a life-extension argument is being used to assert a further claim to being in the best interests of the person seeking AVE, or that it is another form of autonomously waiving a right to life, both of which are asserting a personal value to the value of life. Instead, it is respecting the basis of the impersonal value where the investment in that person's life is recognised to the point at which death would not be, to use Dworkin's phrase, a 'waste' of that investment. By extending the life to the point at which all potential has been realised; where all investment has been fully 'redeemed', and where nothing more can be achieved, the sanctity of life is being honoured. This is not a claim about the badness of a life for a given individual; something that would be a personal value rather than an impersonal one. It is a claim that AVE can allow an individual to travel to the point of their personal negative evaluation of their life but also that of the more objective position as to what counts as determining that sanctity. This is the point where, due to both physical and cognitive decline, that life has maximally accomplished all that the creative investment involved in it could ever have yielded.[15]

Appeals to autonomy

Life-extension considerations can also be utilised as part of a positive argument in support of euthanasia when working in tandem with other important pro-euthanasia arguments. Given the prominence of arguments for AVE based on promoting individual autonomy, it is apt to consider how appeal to a life-extension argument can be used in such cases.

Appeals to respecting individual autonomy are relatively straightforward.[16] They build from the premise that an autonomous individual has a right to determine and shape their own life through their own choices. Accordingly, such an individual's decisions carry an overriding moral weight when it comes to determining what treatments and actions should or should not be carried out towards them. It is their own values that determine what worth they give their continued existence and, should they decide to do so, they can request that their life ends. Furthermore, should there be such a thing as a right to life, it is part of being an autonomous agent that allows us to waive such a right concerning our own lives.[17]

Certain caveats apply to the application of autonomy arguments for euthanasia, even where it is held that our autonomous views as to our continued existence should be respected. One is that autonomy-based arguments only support voluntary (active or passive) euthanasia. As discussed, it is the defining feature of involuntary and non-voluntary euthanasia that they do not seek to respect the autonomous views of the individual. The other notable caveat is that while autonomy arguments support the right of an individual to end their own life, they do not settle the question of the manner of death. They may support taking one's own life but not PAD or any form of euthanasia. The major reason for this is that PAD and all forms of euthanasia involve a third party. As respect for autonomy does not extend to simply fulfilling any request an autonomous individual may make, additional arguments need to be in place to support the role of a third party in such cases. This would require that much of the groundwork for the moral permissibility of PAD or AVE already be in place, as it would not be possible to generate a third-party obligation on the basis of respecting the autonomy of the patient if that request is to participate in an immoral action.[18]

However, leaving aside the debate concerning third parties, the question at hand is whether life-extension arguments themselves are able to support autonomy-based arguments for AVE. The first, and simplest, way this might be achieved is simply by providing the basis for a rational, considered, autonomous decision. This is exactly the sort of rationale offered in the Vervoort case, where an individual knows they have a degenerative condition and also has a firm conviction that they would not wish to continue living after a certain point of physical or cognitive decline but, nevertheless, values the experience of living past the point where they might be able to take their own life. By allowing such future-orientated preparation for a decision to request AVE at a certain point in their condition, individuals like Vervoort can exercise their autonomy through maximising the values they have regarding their own lives.

There would also be additional advantages for autonomy-related concerns that might arise through this future-orientated process of requesting AVE. Notably, it allows substantial scope to determine the soundness of the expressed autonomous wish to die. This occurs in two ways. One way is that the individual can experience more of life with a declining state and thereby allow themselves a greater understanding as to what it is to live with such a condition. As such, they will be able to form an accurate as possible picture of their conviction that life would not be worth living after a certain point with a degenerative condition. Another is that they also have the greatest possible amount of time to reflect on and to rescind (should they wish) the request for AVE. Hence, the quality of their autonomous decision is given every opportunity to form or be rejected because they are able to live past a point where they would otherwise have taken their own life. This does not, of course, mean that all problems surrounding appeals to autonomy as a basis for euthanasia are met. Substantial safeguards still need to be in place to ensure genuine autonomous decisions to request AVE are being made. Some of the potential problems may even be exacerbated by protracted life span after a request for AVE has been appropriately created but not yet initiated. For example, certain groups may be subject to certain kinds of emotional or psychological pressures to make a choice to end their life, genuine or perceived, even where this does not amount to coercion.[19] Therefore, additional questions of, for example, 'authenticity' for autonomous decisions may be additional vital considerations.[20]

Appeals to beneficence

The other major line of supporting argument for the permissibility of euthanasia is an appeal to beneficence. The moral principle of beneficence is one that requires us to prevent avoidable suffering in others by contributing to or promoting their welfare.[21] When used in support of euthanasia, this line of argument is advanced on the basis that sometimes the suffering (be it physical, psychological, etc.) that a person is experiencing can only be relieved through death. In such cases, it may therefore be that what will most benefit the patient is to bring about their death. In keeping with the principle, such a person's death should be brought about as swiftly and painlessly as possible to avoid any additional suffering. It is therefore often the case that appeals to beneficence promote active rather than passive forms of euthanasia.[22]

Appeal to beneficence is rarely utilised by itself but rather usually in conjunction with respect for autonomy considerations.[23] Even where the focus is solely on beneficence, the types of argument raised by including life-extension considerations are markedly similar to those that support autonomy-based ones. This is largely due to the nature of the predicted suffering made by the individual also being a part of their value-based considerations that inform their autonomous judgement. In beneficence terms, the advantages are more about providing additional scale of support rather than a new type of beneficence consideration. The specific support life-extension considerations offer beneficence arguments is primarily twofold. First, by enabling a person to live longer than they otherwise would have, they are able to experience more of a life that they still consider worth living, thereby increasing the sum-total of positive experiences. It is not something that has to be cut short by the requirements of physical or cognitive limitations that might impede taking one's own life. Second, not only is the individual able to secure a release from what they hold to be a state of unbearable suffering, but they also gain the psychological benefits that such pre-planning brings with it. Hence, beneficence-based arguments in support of euthanasia that make use of life-extension considerations offer individuals more experience of positive welfare and a guaranteed end to suffering once a certain state has been reached. In this sense, life-extension considerations help maximise the benefits that beneficence arguments attempt to bring.

Challenges to considering euthanasia in terms of life-extension

Although life-extension considerations offer both support to existing arguments in favour of euthanasia and counter-arguments to certain sanctity of life objections, their application still presents challenges. One notable problem is a moral debate about the nature of life-extension. Such debates usually focus on the ethics of *substantially* extending the term of one's natural life, often through utilising advances in technology to enhance the human body so that the natural life span is extended by a significant number of years (Ackerman, 2009). However, in the euthanasia context it is life-extension in the sense of a prevention of artificial *curtailment* of life (e.g. taking one's own life) rather than an artificial *prolongation* of natural life span (via, for example, genetic enhancements).[24] This leaves open debate on what, if any, the moral difference might be between the prevention of the curtailment of someone's life (their taking their own life) and the active prolongation of life (through treatment, enhancement, etc.). The answer to this question may impact on the use of life-extension arguments in the euthanasia debate if, for example, it turns out that actions preventing threats of taking one's own life do not form a basis for constituting actions that genuinely extend life.

There is a related issue that concerns intentions to take one's own life. For AVE to be seen as life-extending in the sense discussed here, the threat of taking one's own life at an earlier stage if denied access to AVE has to be genuine. However, the only way of accessing the veracity of such a claim is by assessing the intentional state of the individual making the claims of their intention to take their own life. There are two significant reasons why this might pose difficulties for allowing AVE on these grounds. First, because it is difficult to verify a purely intentional claim. However, although difficult, it is far from an insurmountable problem, as all sorts of claims about values, attitudes, intentions, etc. are regularly assessed in many areas of life without undue problem. The second reason, perhaps only a particular aspect of the first problem, is a concern that because the life-extension consideration is based on an intentional claim to taking one's own life, it might be subject to abuse. The thought here is that if what is justifying the request for AVE is an individual claiming they would otherwise take their own life, to what extent can that claim be considered a voluntary one arising from an individual's own desires? Again, I do not think this an insurmountable problem, but it is certainly one that would require attention when considering any safeguards surrounding the use of a policy that accepted life-extension arguments as a legitimate consideration when requesting AVE.

Conclusion

Vervoort's case is remarkable because it illustrates how someone can be living an extremely full and successful life and yet still rationally want to choose euthanasia as a way of making sure they maintain control over their life in the knowledge that they do not want to continue to live under certain circumstances. While only a few key arguments have been discussed here, there remain numerous aspects of the euthanasia debate on which life-extension considerations might have some bearing. These include arguments that centre on the use of advance directives, slippery slope arguments, concerns about the impact on palliative care and end-of-life services, and the nature of the relationship between patient and health care professionals. However, it would seem that the possibility of seeing AVE as life-extension rather than life-shortening has the potential to advance the euthanasia debate in terms of both supporting exiting pro-euthanasia arguments and meeting certain types of sanctity of life objections.[25]

Notes

1 There are numerous examples. Concerning euthanasia in the UK: *R v Cox* [1992] 12 BMLR 38; *R v Inglis* [2010] EWCA Crim 2637; *R (Nicklinson) v Ministry of Justice* [2012] EWHC 2381 (Admin). Concerning assisted suicide in the UK: *R (on the application of Pretty) v Director of Public Prosecutions* [2001] UKHL 61; *Pretty v United Kingdom* (2002) 35 EHRR1; *R (on the application of Purdy) v Director of Public Prosecutions* [2009] UKHL 45; *R (Martin) v Director of Public Prosecutions* [2012] EWHC 2381 (Admin); *Airedale NHS Trust v Bland* [1993] AC 789; *R (Conway) v Secretary of State for Justice* [2017] EWHC 2447 (Admin) and *R (Conway) v Secretary of State for Justice* [2018] EWCA Civ 1431. There have also been a number of attempts to change the law in the UK in recent years, including the Assisted Suicide (Scotland) Bill (2013), Lord Falconer's Assisted Dying Bill (2014), Rob Marris's Assisted Dying Bill (2015), and Lord Haywards's Assisted Dying Bill [HL] (2016).

Outside of the UK, euthanasia is legal in Belgium (since 2002), Canada (known as 'medical assistance in dying' since 2016), Colombia (since 1997 but not implemented until clarified by their Ministry of Health in 2015), Luxembourg (since 2008) and the Netherlands (since 2002); while assisted suicide (but not euthanasia) has been permitted in Switzerland since 1942. A number of states in the United States have made assisted dying legal (but not euthanasia) including Oregon (since 1994), Washington (since 2008), Vermont (since 2013), California (since 2015), and more recently Hawaii (since 2018) and New Jersey (since 1 August 2019).

2 https://www.rt.com/sport/359065-belgian-paralympian-euthanasia-paralympics/ (accessed 20/05/21).

3 Such as that reported by Alexandra Johnston concerning her brother's suicide following his decline from Parkinson's disease, at: https://www.stuff.co.nz/national/health/101604023/if-euthanasia-were-legal-my-brother-might-have-lived-longer (accessed 20/05/21).

4 Notably, Dworkin's (1994) 'creative investment' account of the inviolability of life.

5 These essential elements of the concept are widely accepted across all accounts of euthanasia, both in the ethical and the legal domains. See, for example, McMahan (2002, p. 456), Jackson (2009, pp. 874–975) or Keown (2002, pp. 9–17).

6 One of the most substantial discussions of this is Buchanan and Brock (1990). There is a wealth of other discussion, including Buchanan (1988), Degrazia (1999), Dworkin (1988), Dworkin (1994), and Wrigley (2007a, 2007b, 2015, 2018).

7 This definition, with minor variations of expression, is an *intentional* account and is found in numerous important philosophical discussions on the issue, for example: Brandt (1975), McMahan (2002), Paterson (2003) and Cholbi (2011).

8 For arguments that AVE is no more morally demanding than PAD, see Dixon (1998).

9 The definition of euthanasia is given in Chapter 1, Article 2 of the Belgian Act, available at: http://www.ejustice.just.fgov.be/cgi/article_body.pl?language=-nl&pub_date=2002-06-22&numac=2002009590&caller=summary (accessed 20/05/21). For a detailed discussion of the legislation, see Cohen-Almagor (2009).

10 Interview from *The Telegraph*, 21/12/17, 'Exclusive Marieke Vervoort interview – Paralympics star preparing for euthanasia: "I'm in so much pain. I'm done"', available at: https://www.telegraph.co.uk/paralympic-sport/2017/12/21/marieke-vervoort-paralympics-star-preparing-euthanasia-much/ (accessed 20/05/21).

11 Interview from *The Guardian*, 11/09/16, 'Marieke Vervoort denies planning to kill herself straight after Rio Paralympics', available at: https://www.theguardian.com/sport/2016/sep/11/marieke-vervoort-now-my-fear-of-death-is-gone (accessed 20/05/21).

12 I am here restricting discussion to secular accounts. Religious accounts are the province of theological rather than ethical debate.

13 The difference between something being *instrumentally* important and something being *intrinsically* important is discussed by Dworkin (1994, Ch. 3) as a means of capturing what a secular account of the sanctity of life might be. This position is critically assessed by McMahan (2002) alongside various other approaches to secular accounts of the sanctity of life, such as high cognitive and rational capacities, experiences, and biological complexity.

14 Taking one's own life would require that the person choose to do so when still able to both physically and mentally, PAD allows a longer time span but still requires some ability (arguably, both physical and cognitive) to carry out the final act of taking one's own life, even with assistance. AVE does not require either of these elements as long as a suitable advance decision has been created establishing a point of decline that might take an individual past their ability to physically participate in the manner of their death or past their cognitive ability to reason

or communicate their wishes. This would presumably encompass every last scrap of potential that may be yielded from such a life. Even with no advance directive, AVE still allows life to continue past the point of complete loss of physical ability to participate.

15 It may be thought that those with severe cognitive or physical disability who are not declining but in a steady state might, under this account, be seen to have already accomplished all that they could. To avoid the 'objective' devaluation of their existence, it may therefore be argued that 'being' is itself an accomplishment and continued being the route to maximal accomplishment. Doubtless, supporters of the sanctity of life view would readily make such a case. However, I am here emphasising the use of this argument within the Active *Voluntary* Euthanasia (AVE) debate, where euthanasia is requested by a mentally competent person. This interpretation could therefore be applied as desired by any autonomous agent concerning their own life but for those people unable to request AVE it would simply be inapplicable. I am grateful to Sue Westwood for drawing this important concern to my attention.

16 The nature and role of autonomy is, however, a substantial topic which would take us way beyond the issue at hand. The classic foundational readings on the modern view of personal autonomy are Dworkin (1988) and Frankfurt (1971) There remain other accounts of the concept and the moral duty to respect autonomy which can lead to different views surrounding the intentional ending of one's life. For example, Kantian conceptions of autonomy often reject the moral permissibility of taking one's own life.

17 Right to life as an aspect of the euthanasia debate is discussed by, e.g., Feinberg (1978), Gray (1999) and Biggs (2001).

18 The role of third parties is discussed in Brock (1993).

19 Feminist authors have raised concerns about women who, as a group, are more likely to not wish to be a burden on carers or family. Minority ethnic groups may also have communal, rather than individual autonomous, decision-making processes. I am grateful to Sue Westwood for highlighting these cases.

20 There is a great deal of important feminist literature on the nature of autonomy, including accounts of its social-relational nature and how oppression of agents can affect autonomy. A good selection of material on this topic can be found in Mackenzie and Stoljar (2000). See also Westwood (2017) for a discussion of how vulnerable groups can be disadvantaged or lack appropriate voice when considering 'right to die' issues.

21 This is a principle that received a great deal of attention from Utilitarian thinkers. However, its prominence in modern health care ethics can be seen in Pellegrino and Thomasma (1988) and in Scanlon (1993). There remains a good overview of the principle in Beauchamp and Childress (2001, Ch. 5).

22 It is worth noting, however, that while beneficence might support active euthanasia as morally preferable to passive, it may also support on certain readings involuntary and non-voluntary euthanasia if beneficence is the sole – or primary – moral principle being considered.

23 Brock (1993) discusses not only patient well-being but also how autonomy-based arguments directly link to issues of suffering as a basis for arguments in favour of assisted dying. Whether patient well-being or best interests may be treated as objective and independent of self-determining choices remains an interesting question (Bullock, 2015).

24 There may be another, third, interpretation of 'life-extension' in this context if it is seen as akin to 'saving lives'. Standing debates about the saving lives aspect of euthanasia focus on organ donation after assisted dying (Shaw, 2015). AVE might be an unusual variant of the saving lives debate here, where the person who dies and the person who has their life saved are one and the same.

25 This chapter was originally conceived and written just prior to the news that Marieke Vervoort died by euthanasia on 22 October 2019, in accordance with her express wishes. I dedicate this chapter to her memory.

References

Ackerman, F.N. (2009). Death is a Punch in the Jaw. In B. Steinbock (ed). *The Oxford Handbook of Bioethics* (324–348). Oxford: Oxford University Press.

Battin, M.P. (2005). Euthanasia and Physician-Assisted Suicide. In H. LaFollette (ed). *Oxford Handbook of Practical Ethics* (673–704). Oxford: Oxford University Press.

Beauchamp, T. and Childress, J. (2001). *Principles of Biomedical Ethics*. 5th ed. New York: Oxford University Press.

Biggs, H. (2001). *Euthanasia, Death with Dignity, and the Law*. Oxford: Hart Publishing.

Brandt, R. (1975). The Morality and Rationality of Suicide. In S. Perlin (ed). *A Handbook for the Study of Suicide* (61–76). Oxford: Oxford University Press.

Brock, D.W. (1993). *Life and Death: Philosophical Essays in Biomedical Ethics*. Cambridge: Cambridge University Press.

Buchanan, A. (1988). Advance Directives and the Personal Identity Problem. *Philosophy and Public Affairs* 17(4), 277–302.

Buchanan, A.E. and Brock, D.W. (1990). *Deciding for Others: The Ethics of Surrogate Decision Making*. Cambridge: Cambridge University Press.

Bullock, E.C. (2015). Assisted Dying and the Proper Role of Patient Autonomy. In M. Cholbi and J. Varelius (eds). *New Directions in the Ethics of Assisted Suicide and Euthanasia* (11–25). Basel: Springer International Publishing.

Cholbi, M. (2011). *Suicide: The Philosophical Dimensions*. Peterborough, ON: Broadview.

Cohen-Almagor, R. (2009). Belgian Euthanasia Law: A Critical Analysis. *Journal of Medical Ethics* 35(7), 436–439.

Degrazia, D. (1999). Advance Directives, Dementia and the 'Someone Else Problem'. *Bioethics* 13(5), 373–391.

Dixon, N. (1998). On the Difference between Physician-Assisted Suicide and Active Euthanasia. *Hastings Center Report* 28(5), 25–29.

Dworkin, G. (1988). *The Theory and Practice of Autonomy*. Cambridge: Cambridge University Press.

Dworkin, G., Frey, R.G., and Bok, S. (1998). *Euthanasia and Physician-Assisted Suicide: For and Against*. Cambridge: Cambridge University Press.

Dworkin, R. (1994). *Life's Dominion: An Argument about Abortion, Euthanasia, and Individual Freedom*. New York: Vintage Books.

Feinberg, J. (1978). Voluntary Euthanasia and the Inalienable Right to Life. *Philosophy and Public Affairs* 7(2), 93–123.

Frankfurt, H.G. (1971). Freedom of the Will and the Concept of a Person. *Journal of Philosophy* 68(1), 5–20.

Garrard, E., and Wilkinson, S. (2005). Passive Euthanasia. *Journal of Medical Ethics* 31(2), 64–68.

Gormally, L. (2000). Euthanasia and Assisted Suicide: 7 Reasons Why They Should Not be Legalized. In D. Dickinson, M. Johnson, and J. Samson Katz (eds). *Death, Dying and Bereavement*, 2nd ed. (286–289). Sage: London.

Gray, W. (1999). Right to Die or Duty to Live? The Problem of Euthanasia. *Journal of Applied Philosophy* 16(1), 19–32.

Huxtable, R., and Moller, M. (2007). 'Setting a Principled Boundary?' Euthanasia as a Response to 'Life Fatigue'. *Bioethics* 21(3), 117–126.

Jackson, E. (2009). *Medical Law: Text, Cases, and Materials*. Oxford: Oxford University Press.

Keown, J. (2002). *Euthanasia, Ethics and Public Policy: An Argument against Legalisation*. Cambridge: Cambridge University Press.

Mackenzie, C., and Stoljar, N. (eds) (2000). *Relational Autonomy: Feminist Perspectives on Autonomy, Agency, and the Social Self*. New York: Oxford University Press.

McMahan, J. (2002). *The Ethics of Killing: Problems at the Margins of Life*. New York: Oxford University Press.

Paterson, C. (2003). On Clarifying Terms in Applied Ethics Discourse: Suicide, Assisted Suicide and Euthanasia. *International Philosophical Quarterly* 43(3), 351–358.

Pellegrino, E., and Thomasma, D. (1988). *For the Patient's Good: The Restoration of Beneficence in Health Care*. New York: Oxford University Press.

Rachels, J. (1975). Active and Passive Euthanasia. *New England Journal of Medicine* 292(2), 78–80.

Scanlon, T. (1993). Value, Desire and Quality of Life. In M.C. Nussbaum and A. Sen (eds). *The Quality of Life* (185–200). Oxford: Clarendon Press.

Shaw, D.M. (2015). Saving Lives with Assisted Suicide and Euthanasia. In M. Cholbi and J. Varelius (eds). *New Directions in the Ethics of Assisted Dying and Euthanasia* (185–192). Springer International Publishing.

Westwood, S. (2017). Older Lesbians, Gay Men and the 'Right to Die' Debate: 'I Always Kee a Lethal Dose of Something Because I Don't Want to Become an Elderly Isolated Person'. *Social & Legal Studies* 26(5), 606–628.

Wrigley, A. (2007a). Personal Identity, Autonomy and Advance Statements. *The Journal of Applied Philosophy* 24(4), 381–396.

Wrigley, A. (2007b). Proxy Consent: Moral Authority Misconceived. *The Journal of Medical Ethics* 33(9), 527–531.

Wrigley, A. (2015). Moral Authority and Proxy Decision-Making. *Ethical Theory and Moral Practice* 18(3), 631–647.

Wrigley, A. (2018). Consent for Others. In A. Muller and P. Schaber (eds). *The Routledge Handbook of the Ethics of Consent* (322–333). Abingdon: Routledge.

7 A pro tanto moral case for assisted death

Isra Black

Introduction

This chapter makes a pro tanto case for the moral permissibility of assisted death. It is pro tanto in the sense that my principal interest is the *other things equal* moral evaluation of the dimension of assisted death that comprises one individual, who wishes to die with assistance, and another, who either grants or refuses to grant the former's wish and who provides assistance or does not provide assistance, respectively. Put another way, this is not a case for assisted death *all things considered*. Specifically, I shall not consider the detail of other-regarding matters relevant to the all things considered moral permissibility of assisted death. In making a pro tanto moral case for assisted death only, I have a substantive aim: to set out a universal foundation for the moral permissibility of assisted death, which, in turn, contributes to discussion of the *all things considered* moral permissibility of assisted death, and which structures (in part) the institutionalisation of assisted death in law or policy.

I argue that, other things equal, it is morally permissible for an agent to assist an individual to die just when their wish to die is autonomous and assisting their death is what an agent has most reason to do, where the latter is determined by the intrinsic values of the courses of action available to the agent in the individual's regard.[1] More formally, it is, other things equal, morally permissible for *Q* to assist *P* to die if *P*'s decision to die is autonomous and *Q* has most reason to assist *P*'s death.

I reach my conclusion that assisted death is pro tanto morally permissible through discussion of Ralph Wedgwood's (2009) account of how intrinsic values—specifically those instantiated by states of affairs—generate reasons for action, that is, how such values explain what an agent *ought* to do (for a state of affairs, at a time). This metaethical view offers a promising starting point for discussion of the morality of assisted death. It is compatible with the best explanation of the value of death for an individual who dies: the deprivation account (Feldman 1991, 1992). Wedgwood's theory attends to non-consequentialist concerns going to the—causal or intentional—role an agent plays in bringing about a state of affairs. Specifically, it is sensitive to the different ways in which an agent may causally contribute to another's death

DOI: 10.4324/9780429329739-7

and the intention-foresight distinction, both of which are often thought relevant to the moral permissibility of assisted death. Finally, on a methodological note, I suggest that it is advantageous to foreground discussion of the nature and source of the moral reasons relevant to the permissibility of assisted death.

By way of plan, I shall first treat some preliminary matters. I then outline Wedgwood's view of intrinsic values and reasons for action. I then make the case for the pro tanto morality of assisted death. In the conclusion, I set out in brief some factors relevant to the *all things considered* moral permissibility of assisted death.

Preliminaries

It is important to settle some preliminary matters, which should help to clarify the target of my argument and what I hope to achieve.

For brevity, I shall refer to an individual who dies as *P*, and an individual (or individuals) who is (or are) causally involved in *P*'s death as Q(s). For simplicity, I shall assume only one Q in what follows. I shall often refer to courses of action as *A* and consequences of or the state(s) of affairs resulting from *A* as *S*. *S* includes all relevant facts about the world for time *t*.

By assisted death, I mean voluntary euthanasia or assisted suicide (Black 2020, 2021).[2] The concepts of suicide and of assistance are, respectively, complex, perhaps surprisingly so. I shall have to rely on an intuitive grasp of what it means for Q to assist *P*'s suicide. To amount to euthanasia, Q must deliberately *cause* *P*'s death and death must be *good for P*. If we wish to exclude relevant instances of assisted suicide from the concept of euthanasia, some further specification as to causation is necessary. Something along the lines that Q must be the *most proximate* cause of *P*'s death should suffice. Other things equal, euthanasia is voluntary when *P* makes an autonomous positive decision—that is, consent or request—in respect of Q's causing *P*'s death; it is involuntary when *P* makes an autonomous negative decision—refusal—in respect of Q's causing *P*'s death. I take it that an individual's decision is autonomous just when they have adequate information in respect of *S*, have capacity to decide what to do in *S*, and are not subject to autonomy-undermining third party influence. Other things equal, euthanasia is non-voluntary when *P* is presently unable to take an autonomous decision in respect of Q's causing *P*'s death and has no prior autonomous decision that would make euthanasia voluntary or involuntary. I shall argue that involuntary euthanasia may be pro tanto morally permissible, but that it is usually pro tanto morally impermissible to pursue a course of action that involves involuntary killing. My discussion leaves open the morality of non-voluntary euthanasia.

I shall assume a non-absolutist position in respect of the morality of conduct that intentionally causes or contributes to death. There are many defences of the view that assisted death is absolutely morally wrong (Finnis 1995; Keown 2002), specific replies (Harris 1995), and a literature that engages critically with the underlying normative machinery of absolutist views

(McIntyre 2001; Scanlon 2008). There is little to gain from rehearsing these arguments. In my view, non-absolutism is more interesting—it seeks to map the contours of assisted death, some instances of which will be morally permissible and others morally impermissible. Non-absolutism is also more appropriate in the context of a volume that is largely friendly to the moral, legal, and social permissibility of assisted death.

Finally, I shall not directly defend Wedgwood against other accounts of reason for action. I shall attempt to set out Wedgwood's view in sufficient detail so that readers may gauge its plausibility. I also aim to provide indirect support for the argument that intrinsic values generate reasons for action, insofar as I aim to show that it fares well in reflective equilibrium (Daniels 1979). Wedgwood's theory is compatible with the deprivation account of the value of death; it is sensitive to non-consequentialist intuitions; and, importantly for our purposes, it yields a plausible account of the morality of assisted death.

Wedgwood's intrinsic values and reasons for action

What is a reason for action? As Wedgwood explains, '[a] "reason for agent x to do act A at time t" is some fact about A (in relation to x's situation at t) that plays a certain sort of role in *explaining* what x *ought* to do at t' (2009, 321).[3] As the 'ought' signifies, reasons for action, at least in the sense relevant here, are normative: they explain—or justify—what counts in favour of or against a course of action over any other (Raz 1999).[4]

According to Wedgwood, 'all reasons for action are grounded in facts about how courses of action available to the relevant agent at the relevant time are related to *intrinsic values*' (2009, 323). Of course, more needs to be said to explain this theory. In this section, I attempt to provide an outline of its moving parts in three stages. I start by detailing what Wedgwood means by intrinsic value and the states of affairs that bear intrinsic value. I then explain how Wedgwood establishes the intrinsic values of courses of action using examples relevant to assisted death. Finally, I explain how the intrinsic value of courses of action generates reasons for action.

Intrinsic value and states of affairs

On Wedgwood's view, we can express intrinsic value in terms of *absolute* goodness or value (2009, 324). One way to explain that something has absolute value is by appeal to its being the fitting object of an *agent neutral* pro-attitude:

> an item x has [absolute value] if and only if it is appropriate for *anyone* who adequately considers x to have the corresponding … pro-attitude of some fairly straightforward kind [eg *admiration*]. If it is really is appropriate for absolutely *anyone* who adequately considers x to have this sort

> of pro-attitude towards *x*, this pro-attitude must be an essentially *disinterested* pro-attitude, that is, a pro-attitude that does not depend for its appropriateness on the particular relation that the thinker has towards *x*.
> 325

The bearers of intrinsic values within this theory are *states of affairs* (327), that is, the sets of circumstances that serve as a description of something. For example, we might describe the state of affairs that concerned Tony Nicklinson—who challenged the legal prohibitions on assisted death in England and Wales—immediately prior to his death as: aged 51 years, suffering from 'locked-in' syndrome (*R (oao Nicklinson v Ministry of Justice* [2014] UKSC 38). Three important clarifications are necessary.

First, the description of a state of affairs must be sufficiently detailed so as to permit a determination of its intrinsic value:

> the state of affairs of *x*'s having *P* [where *P* is the property that makes it the case that *x* has value *V*] must … be sufficient for that state of affairs having the corresponding value *V*': that is, it is impossible for this state of affairs to exist without having that value *V*'. In that sense, this value *V*' is an intrinsic feature of this state of affairs.
> Wedgwood (2009, 328)

The above description of Tony Nicklinson's circumstances seems insufficient to determine its intrinsic value. An evaluatively adequate description might be: man, aged 51 years, paralysed save for the ability to move his head and his eyes, able to communicate via eye blink computer, regarding his life as 'dull, miserable, demeaning, undignified and intolerable', wishing to die (*Nicklinson* [3] (Lord Neuberger)).

Second, the intrinsic values instantiated by states of affairs come in degrees, that is, one state of affairs may instantiate intrinsic values to a greater or lesser extent than another (Wedgwood 2009, 329). The upshot of this idea is that 'each of these values generates a *ranking* of states of affairs' (329), that may permit their comparison.

Third, on Wedgwood's theory the states of affairs that bear intrinsic value are *abstract* entities (327, 329). That is, a state of affairs may '*exist* even if it does not *obtain*' (327). This is important for our purposes, since when considering the moral permissibility of assisted death, it is necessary to rank the degrees of intrinsic value of mutually exclusive states of affairs—*P* receives assistance to die or receives no such assistance, respectively. For example, had Tony Nicklinson succeeded at first instance, he might have received assistance to die; it transpired that he died of pneumonia having refused 'all nutrition, fluids, and medical treatment' (*Nicklinson* [6] (Lord Neuberger)). More generally, as Wedgwood observes, it seems 'of great importance to ethical theory to be able to *compare* states of affairs that do not actually obtain' (2009, 329).

The intrinsic value of courses of action involving assisted death

The states of affairs relevant to reasons for action (and our discussion of the moral permissibility of assisted death) are *courses of action*, broadly construed to include omissions as well as acts, and sufficiently detailed such that the relevant values are an intrinsic feature of the agent's conduct. A general way of describing such a detailed course of action is, 'acting in such a way that a state of affairs that instantiates value *V* to degree d_1 results' (Wedgwood 2009, 333). Because courses of action are complex states of affairs, that is, made up of other states of affairs, the degree of intrinsic value instantiated in a course of action is complex—is a function of the intrinsic value of the other intrinsically valuable states of affairs the course of action comprises (332).

Two elements determine the intrinsic values of courses of action on Wedgwood's theory. First, there is the intrinsic value of the individuated states of affairs that count as a consequence of a course of action (333–334). Second, there is the degree of agential involvement in bringing about each of the consequences of a course of action (334–336).

The intrinsic value of the each of the consequences of a course of action is determined *comparatively* (333). The explanation of how such a comparison might take place is somewhat complex, but the idea is intuitive. For the set of alternative courses of action available to an agent at a time, there exists a *benchmark of comparison* for each of the consequences that exemplifies an intrinsic value:

> For every agent and every time when the agent is capable of acting, and for every intrinsic value *V* that is exemplified by some of the consequences of courses of action that are available to that agent at that time, there is a relevant "benchmark of comparison" for *V* with respect to the situation of the agent at that time.
>
> 333

One way to determine this benchmark of comparison, for example, is to average the degree to which each of the consequences of the alternative courses of action exemplifies an intrinsic value (333). I shall proceed on this basis. Once we have established the benchmark of comparison, the positive or negative degree of intrinsic value of a consequence of a course of action is a function of its situation above or below the benchmark, respectively:

> When a consequence of a course of action is *superior* to the benchmark (with respect to the relevant value), the consequence exemplifies this value to a *positive* degree: in other words, having this consequence counts as a *good* feature of the course of action. When a consequence of a course of action is *inferior* to the benchmark (with respect to that value), the consequence exemplifies this value to a *negative* degree; and that counts as a *bad* feature of the course of action.
>
> 333

The upshot of measuring the intrinsic value of the consequences of courses of action comparatively is that 'there is a *separate* benchmark for every practical situation of an agent at a time [and] no unique zero-point that divides *all* states of affairs that instantiate the relevant value' (341).

To make the discussion a little more concrete, imagine that there are two courses of action available to Q: A_1 and A_2. A_1 involves Q assisting *P* to die, with the consequences that $S_{1.1}$: *P*'s wish to die is fulfilled; and $S_{1.2}$: *P* suffers for t_1 but avoids suffering for t_2.[5] A_2 involves Q not assisting *P* to die, with the consequences that $S_{2.1}$: *P*'s wish to die is fulfilled by refusing life-prolonging treatment; and $S_{2.2}$: *P* suffers for t_1 and t_2. I stipulate that the exercise of autonomy instantiates the intrinsic value of well-being to some degree—I shall discuss the intrinsic values relevant to assisted death shortly. So $S_{1.1}$ and $S_{2.1}$ instantiate the value of well-being to some degree. In both states of affairs *P*'s wish to die is fulfilled, but in $S_{1.1}$, *P*'s exercise of autonomy extends, through the receipt of assisted death, to deciding how and when to die, whereas in $S_{1.2}$, *P*'s exercise of autonomous refusal of life-prolonging treatment cannot control the manner of their death or its exact timing. If the benchmark of comparison is the average of the degree to which $S_{1.1}$ and $S_{2.1}$ exemplify the value of well-being, $S_{1.1}$ is superior to the benchmark and is an intrinsically good feature of A_1, and $S_{2.1}$ is inferior to the benchmark and is an intrinsically bad feature of A_2. I also stipulate that there is some inverse association between suffering and well-being such that $S_{1.2}$ and $S_{2.2}$ fail to instantiate the value of well-being to some degree. If the benchmark for comparison is the average of the degree to which $S_{1.2}$ and $S_{2.2}$ fail to instantiate the value of well-being, given that *P* suffers more in $S_{2.2}$, $S_{1.2}$ is an intrinsically good feature of A_1, whereas $S_{2.2}$ is an intrinsically bad feature of A_2. On this analysis, A_1 ranks higher than A_2 on both dimensions of intrinsic value considered.

The second element that determines the intrinsic values of courses of action is what Wedgwood terms 'the agent's *degree of agential involvement* in bringing about each of the consequences' (334), to which there is a *causal* and an *intentional* dimension.

In respect of the causal dimension, the—perhaps familiar—idea is that there are degrees to which an agent may contribute to a state of affairs coming to pass (334–335).[6] For example, it seems plausible that in A_1, Q is more causally agentially involved in *P*'s death through their provision of assistance to die than in A_2, in which they refuse to provide assistance to die (and presumably decline to intervene to prevent *P*'s death by refusal of treatment). In A_1, Q ends *P*'s life, whereas in A_2, *P* refuses life-prolonging treatment (and dies) following Q's refusal to assist *P*'s death. And suppose that Q could assist *P*'s death in one of two ways, either $A_{1.1}$: euthanasia; or $A_{1.2}$: suicide assistance.[7] It seems plausible that Q's degree of causal agential involvement is greater in $A_{1.1}$ than it is in $A_{1.2}$. For in $A_{1.1}$, Q ends *P*'s life whereas in $A_{1.2}$, *P* ends their own life with Q's assistance.

In respect of the intentional dimension, Wedgwood argues that

> Other things equal, your degree of agential involvement in bringing about a state of affairs is greater if you directly *intend* that state of affairs than if you merely *foresee* that that state of affairs will result from your action.
> 335[8]

For example, in A_1, if we grant that Q intends the course of action that involves *P*'s death,[9] Q's degree of agential involvement is greater than it is in A_2, assuming Q merely foresees that *P* might refuse life-prolonging treatment (and die).

The two elements of the intrinsic values of courses of action combine in the following way: we adjust the intrinsic value of each of the consequences of a course of action relative to the benchmark for the degree of agential involvement. If *S* is an intrinsically bad feature of a course of action, it is made more or less bad according to the agent's high or low degree of agential involvement, respectively (336), mutatis mutandis—with the necessary changes—if *S* is an intrinsically good feature of a course of action. For example, between the options $A_{1.1}$ and A_2, if Q intends to assist *P*'s death by euthanasia in $A_{1.1}$, this increases the goodness of the—intended and proximate—consequences $S_{1.1}$ and $S_{1.2}$, whereas if Q intentionally refuses to assist *P*'s death in A_2 with the foreseen and less proximate consequence that *P* dies by refusal of life-prolonging treatment, this decreases the badness of the consequences $S_{2.1}$ and $S_{2.2}$.

Reasons for action

It is now possible succinctly to state the relation between intrinsic values and reasons for action. On Wedgwood's theory, 'a reason in favour of a course of action is simply an intrinsically good feature of that course of action' (2009, 336), mutatis mutandis for reasons against a course of action. As explained above, whether consequence *S* counts as an intrinsically good or bad feature of course of action *A* is determined by the degree to which the relevant consequence instantiates the relevant intrinsic value, weighted for the agent's degree of agential involvement. This gives the *agentially weighted value* of *S* (337). Whether an agent has a reason for or against *A* is a function of the respective positive or negative agentially weighted value of *S* (337). In addition, Wedgwood's account of reasons for action provides a basis for establishing the relative strength of reasons:

> Other things equal, the higher the positive agentially-weighted value, the stronger this reason for *A* is; the lower the negative agentially-weighted value, the stronger the reason against *A*. (The qualification 'other things equal' is important here, because there will be many cases of *interactions* between reasons …).
> 337

Having outlined how intrinsic values generate reasons for action on Wedgwood's view, I am now in a position to provide an account of the pro tanto moral permissibility of assisted death.

The pro tanto case for assisted death

In this section, I make the case for the pro tanto moral permissibility of assisted death at a general level. I argue that, other things equal, it is morally permissible for an agent to assist an individual to die just when their wish to die is autonomous and assisting their death is what the agent has most reason to do, where the latter is determined by the intrinsic values of the courses of action available to the agent in the individual's regard. More formally, it is, other things equal, morally permissible for Q to assist P to die if P's decision to die is autonomous and Q has most reason to assist P's death.[10]

For the purposes of what follows, I take as the criterion of moral rightness that a course of action is morally permissible iff—if and only if—it accords with what an agent has *most* reason to do.[11]

I shall argue that the key to understanding the morality of assisted death lies in the intrinsic value of well-being. I then consider how this value explains the value of death and death-related reasons for action. I then explain why involuntary killing is usually morally wrong. Finally, I account for the pro tanto moral permissibility of assisted death.

Well-being and assisted death

The way I see it, one intrinsic value is key to the pro tanto moral permissibility of assisted death: the value of well-being—or prudential value or welfare. I regard the exercise of autonomy as 'one of the elements of well-being' (Mill 2002, 131–136). I shall not take a stance here on whether autonomy has instrumental—as a means—value *and* intrinsic value. If autonomy has intrinsic value (see, e.g., Hurka 1987), it provides reasons for action relevant to the pro tanto moral permissibility of assisted death in its own right. But since autonomy is one of the elements of well-being, treating it independently would likely involve some degree of double counting, even if autonomy instantiates well-being in a complex way. I suggest that it is unnecessary to introduce this complication. Either way, autonomy remains a formal and substantive element of my view, respectively: assisted death, by definition, requires an autonomous wish to die; and the exercise of autonomy is one way to instantiate the intrinsic value of well-being.

I shall not defend a particular conception of well-being or welfare (see, e.g., Parfit 1984, appendix I; Tiberius 2015). The simple idea is this: well-being is that which is *good for* an individual. Their faring well to some degree is a matter of standing in a positive relation to the prudential goods that comprise well-being, and that relation is net positive against the prudential ills that comprise ill-being (Kagan 2014).

To draw the intrinsic value of states of affairs and well-being together: faring well consists in the positive instantiation of the value of well-being—however conceived—for the state of affairs that is an individual's life at a time—synchronically—or over time—diachronically, mutatis mutandis in respect of what it means to fare poorly. States of affairs that involve faring poorly *may* include chronic or terminal illness, mental disorders including anxiety and depression, trauma, the absence of pleasurable experience, the absence of love or friendship characterised by close personal relationships etc. To be clear, my claim is not that these states of affairs *necessarily* involve ill-being. Rather, I suggest that a certain kind of negative affective attitude that possibly accompanies such states of affairs is what makes for ill-being. That is, certain states of affairs may involve *suffering*, and suffering may be one of the consequences of a state of affairs that instantiates the value of well-being to some negative degree.[12] Since I only need *P* to fare poorly or to fare well to make my argument, I shall leave open what facts precisely make for states of well- or ill-being.

The value of death and reasons for action

Many of us will fare poorly—perhaps even very poorly—during some stage of our lives. Yet it does not follow that pursuing a course of action whose consequence is death is what we have most moral reason to do in such circumstances. This is because death, relative to the alternative outcomes achievable in our regard, is often thought to be *bad for us*; it deprives us of goods such as well-being that we would otherwise (expect to) enjoy.[13] Understood in this way, the value of death is *extrinsic*; it derives from,

> The difference between the intrinsic value for [*P*] of the life [*P*] would lead if [they die at t_1] and the intrinsic value for [*P*] of the life [*P*] would lead if [they die at t_2].
>
> Feldman (1992, 150)

Helpfully, this explanation of the value of death is compatible with Wedgwood's account of reasons for action. The deprivation account relies on the determination of the relative intrinsic value of lives. We can characterise lives as complex states of affairs that instantiate intrinsic values. To determine the value of death for *P*, we compare the relative intrinsic values of the states of affairs comprising *P*'s life should they die at either an earlier or a later time. To determine whether Q has a reason to *cause* *P*'s death, we compare the agentially weighted value of the courses of action involving *P* dying at either an earlier or a later time with the relevant degree of Q's involvement.

On this basis, we can show that Q has a reason not to pursue a course of action that produces *P*'s death, if, other things equal, death would be extrinsically bad for *P*. Suppose that the courses of action available to Q are A_3 and A_4. A_3 involves Q pursuing a course of action that causes *P*'s death.

The relevant consequence of A_3 is S_3: *P* is deprived of a life in which they fare well to some degree. A_4 involves Q letting *P* alone, with consequence S_4: *P* has a life in which they fare well to some degree. It seems clear that, other things equal, A_3 has negative agentially weighted value, whereas A_4 has positive agentially weighted value. In light of the value of well-being, S_3 is an intrinsically bad feature of A_3 and S_4 is an intrinsically good feature of A_4, relative to the benchmark of comparison, respectively, and adjusted for Q's degree of agential involvement. Given the relation between intrinsic values and reasons for action, Q has, other things equal, a reason against A_3 and in favour of A_4.

Mutatis mutandis, we can show that Q has a reason to pursue a course of action that produces *P*'s death, if, other things equal, death would be extrinsically good for *P*.

Why involuntary killing is usually morally wrong

Understanding how the value of well-being, the value of death, and Wedgwood's account of reasons for action relate to each other provides the basis for explaining why courses of action that involve involuntary killing are usually pro tanto morally wrong. I shall argue that *actual* cases of involuntary euthanasia are pro tanto morally permissible, however. This discussion illustrates the general plausibility of my view and will help us to understand the morality of assisted death.

I argue elsewhere that if autonomy is one of the elements of well-being, 'every violation of autonomy results in a pro tanto diminishment of welfare' (Black 2018, 311). One might interpret this as a claim that *P*'s autonomous wish to remain alive is *wholly* constitutive of their well-being. But if this were true, there could not be such a thing as involuntary euthanasia, since killing *P* against their wishes could not be *good for* them. All instances of involuntary euthanasia would just be instances of involuntary killing. For there to be conceptual space for involuntary euthanasia, we should instead hold that *P*'s wish to remain alive is *partly* constitutive of their well-being or may provide *evidence* that they fare well to some degree.

I can show that involuntary euthanasia is pro tanto morally permissible but that other involuntary killing is pro tanto morally impermissible. Consider two variants of A_3 that involve involuntary killing: $A_{3.1}$ and $A_{3.2}$. On $A_{3.1}$, Q kills *P* with the intention that death is good for *P*, against *P*'s wish to remain alive. The relevant consequence of $A_{3.1}$ is $S_{3.1}$: *P* is deprived of a life in which they fare *well* to some degree—because the wish to remain alive is *sufficient* to make it that they fare well or *sufficient evidence* that they fare well. On $A_{3.2}$, Q again kills *P* with the intention that death is good for *P*, against *P*'s wish to remain alive. But $A_{3.2}$ causes $S_{3.2}$: *P* is deprived of a life in which they fare *poorly* to some degree—because the wish to remain alive is *insufficient* to make it that they fare well or *insufficient evidence* that they fare well. $A_{3.1}$ is just an involuntary killing. Only $A_{3.2}$ involves involuntary euthanasia.

The alternative course of action to $A_{3.1}$ is A_4: Q lets *P* alone with the consequence S_4 that *P* fares *well* to some degree. The alternative course of action to $A_{3.1}$ is A_5: Q lets *P* alone with the consequence S_5 that *P* fares *poorly* to some degree. Against their respective benchmarks of comparison, $S_{3.1}$ instantiates the value of well-being to some negative degree and $S_{3.2}$ instantiates the value of well-being to some positive degree. For both $S_{3.1}$ and $S_{3.2}$, Q's pursuit of $A_{3.1}$ and $A_{3.2}$ involves high, albeit different, degrees of agential involvement: in $S_{3.1}$, Q is the *most proximate* cause of *P*'s death and Q intends to kill *P*, but does not intend to deprive *P* of a life in which *P* fares well to some degree; in $S_{3.2}$, Q is the *most proximate* cause of *P*'s death, Q intends to kill *P* and intends to deprive *P* of a life in which *P* fares poorly to some degree. Relative to A_4, pursuing $A_{3.1}$ has negative agentially weighted value, whereas relative to A_5, pursuing $A_{3.2}$ has positive agentially weighted value. Put in terms of—moral—reasons for action, there are, other things equal, pro tanto reasons in favour of involuntary euthanasia and against other involuntary killing. It would therefore seem that involuntary euthanasia is pro tanto morally permissible.

Even if involuntary euthanasia is pro tanto morally permissible, it does not follow that it is morally permissible to attempt it. The reason for this is that if *P*'s exercise of autonomy—the wish to remain alive—is partly constitutive of *P*'s well-being or is evidence that they fare well, this will affect the degree to which the value of well-being is instantiated relative to the benchmark of comparison. If the positive intrinsic value of $S_{3.2}$ is close to the benchmark, Q ought to have less confidence that they are in fact pursuing $A_{3.2}$ (involuntary euthanasia), as opposed to $A_{3.1}$ (other involuntary killing), whose consequence is $S_{3.1}$. It may be the case that Q brings about an intrinsically *good* state of affairs ($S_{3.2}$), but the converse may obtain ($S_{3.1}$). And given the high degree of Q's agential involvement in $S_{3.2}$ and $S_{3.1}$, respectively, their killing of *P* may be *very good* or *very bad*, respectively. Given this uncertainty and the irreversibility of death, I argue that an agent must be *very confident* in which course of action involving involuntary killing they would, in fact, pursue. Since agents should rarely have such confidence, any involuntary killing is usually pro tanto morally impermissible, for *epistemic reasons*. But epistemic confidence that Q pursues involuntary euthanasia may sometimes be justified. As Jonathan Glover writes,

> It does not seem plausible to say that there is no conceivable amount of future misery that would justify killing someone against his will. If I had been a Jew in Nazi Germany, I would have considered very seriously killing myself and my family, if there was no other escape from the death camps. And, if someone in that position felt that his family did not understand what the future would feel like and so killed them against their wishes, I at least am not sure that this decision would be wrong.
>
> 1990, 82[14]

The pro tanto moral permissibility of assisted death

I am now able to account for the pro tanto moral permissibility of assisted death. I stated above that it is morally permissible for an agent to assist an individual to die just when their wish to die is autonomous and assisting their death is what an agent has most reason to do. This can be explained in short order.

Death is extrinsically good for *P* if the comparison of the intrinsic value for *P* of the life they would lead if they die and the intrinsic value for *P* of the life they would lead if they do not die is favourable to death. The intrinsic value for *P* of the state of affairs that is their life is determined by the intrinsic value of well-being. Autonomy is one element of the value of well-being. The intrinsic values exemplified by courses of action generate reasons for action. The direction and strength of these reasons is a function of the agentially weighted value of the consequences of a course of action: the degree to which each consequence instantiates a relevant intrinsic value, adjusted for the agent's degree of agential involvement. An act is morally permissible if and only if it accords with what an agent has most reason to do.

Putting all this together, if among the courses of action available to *Q*, assisted death for *P* has the highest (positive) agentially weighted value, it is what *Q* has most reason to do: assisted death is pro tanto morally permissible. For example, in the explanation of A_1 and A_2 above, in which the available courses of action were *Q* assisting *P* to die and *Q* refusing to assist *P* to die, respectively, assisted death is pro tanto morally permissible, because of the way in which pursuing A_1 with the said consequences and to said degree of agential involvement most instantiates the value of well-being.

In what remains, I shall briefly treat three further relevant issues: the weight of *P*'s wish to die, and whether there are moral differences between voluntary euthanasia and assisted suicide, and assisted death and refusal of treatment, respectively.

How much credence should we give the wish to die in determining whether assisted death would, among the available courses of action, be what *Q* has most reason to do? Consistent with what I argue above, I take it that *P*'s autonomous wish to die is *partly* constitutive of their well-being or may provide *evidence* that they fare poorly to some degree. It may be that *P*'s wish to die and the other elements of their well-being align to a great degree such that no other available course of action exemplifies the value of well-being more than assisted death. In such cases—the plight of Tony Nicklinson is perhaps an apt example—assisted death may be uncontroversially morally permissible. Significantly more difficult are the cases in which *P* wishes to die but other elements of her well-being provide reasons against assisted death. In such circumstances, *Q* risks a course of action in which they assist *P* to die without that course of action instantiating the value of well-being more than any other available course of action.

In the event of tension between the wish to die and the other elements of well-being, I submit that the argument I made in respect of involuntary euthanasia applies, mutatis mutandis. If the elements of well-being—including the wish to die—conflict, any reason that Q has to assist *P*'s death will be weaker, because the degree to which the consequences of assisting *P* to die exemplify the value of well-being will be closer to the benchmark. If this is true, Q ought to have less epistemic confidence that they are in fact pursuing a morally permissible instance of assisted death. Because death is irreversible, in cases in which the elements of well-being are in tension, I argue that assisting *P* to die is pro tanto morally impermissible, and this is for *epistemic reasons*.[15]

Voluntary euthanasia involves a greater degree of causal agential involvement than assisted suicide. It seems that, other things equal, an agent has a stronger reason to provide voluntary euthanasia than to participate in assisted suicide. The other things equal qualification is important here. Assuming both voluntary euthanasia and assisted suicide are available, Q only has a stronger reason to provide voluntary euthanasia if it is the course of action *P* prefers. Otherwise, it is plausible that providing voluntary euthanasia would exemplify the value of well-being to a lesser degree than providing assisted suicide because in so doing *P*'s autonomous wishes are fulfilled to a lesser degree.

In a similar vein, in A_1 and A_2 above, Q has more reason to assist *P*'s death than she has reason to refuse *P*'s death with the foreseen consequence that *P* refuses treatment (and dies). This example shows that assisted death may be pro tanto morally *preferable* to other courses of action whose consequence is *P*'s death. It is important to note that this is not a general conclusion, but arises from the fact that in A_2, *P*'s wish for assistance to goes unfulfilled.

Conclusion

In this chapter, I advanced a pro tanto case for the moral permissibility of assisted death. My principal concern was the *other things equal* moral evaluation of the dimension of assisted death that comprises one individual, who wishes to die with assistance, and another, who either grants or refuses to grant the wish and who provides assistance or does not provide assistance, respectively.

I argued that, other things equal, it is morally permissible for an agent to assist an individual to die just when their wish to die is autonomous and assisting their death is what an agent has most reason to do, where the latter is determined by the intrinsic values of the courses of action available to the agent in the individual's regard. I relied on Ralph Wedgwood's (2009) account of how intrinsic values—specifically those instantiated by states of affairs—generate reasons for action, that is, how such values explain what an agent *ought* to do (for a state of affairs, at a time).

If we are to have *death rights* in the style of this volume, we require a pro tanto account of the moral permissibility of assisted death that provides a normative foundation for discussion of whether we have (assisted) death rights, and that partly structures the institutionalisation of assisted death (rights) in law or policy. My aim in this chapter was to advance a plausible moral theory of the permissibility of assisted death grounded in reasons for action. It is clear, however, that an account such as mine is not *sufficient* for us having a subset of death rights pertaining to assisted death. In order to do this, we must attend to those factors that are relevant to the *all things considered* (political) morality of assisted death.

The relevant all things considered factors may include normative concerns, such as the alleged logical slippery slope from assisted death to non-voluntary euthanasia or assisted death on demand (Keown 2002; cf. Lillehammer 2002), as well as mixed empirical and normative concerns, such as the 'expressivist' objection (see, e.g., Hansard, HL Deb, 'Assisted Dying Bill [HL]' 2014 vol 754 col 809 (Baroness Campbell)), the protection of 'the vulnerable' from coercion or undue influence or ill-considered decisions (Battin et al. 2007), and the empirical slippery slope (Lewis 2007a, 188; 2007b). We need to determine whether any of these concerns would materialise as consequences of individual instances of assisted death or of permitting assisted death in law or policy, and to determine the intrinsic value of any consequences that would obtain. Institutional design will also be highly relevant to whether assisted death is all things considered morally permissible.

I shall conclude the chapter with two general observations on the role of empirical factors and on institutionalisation as they both relate to death rights. The relevant empirical facts that influence whether assisted death is all things considered morally permissible may vary in time and space. Assisted death may not be all things considered *universally* morally permissible. However, it may be all things considered morally permissible in various places, at various times. It seems plausible, therefore, that possession and nature of death rights may be a local, rather than a universal, matter. In respect of institutionalisation, I take it that an institutional regime for assisted death that fails to approximate to a plausible moral view (and address its political justification) or attend to relevant other-regarding matters would be deficient in these senses. But the detail of institutionalising assisted death—*how* it is permitted—seems a jurisdiction-specific question—even if there may exist a global supply of possible legal ingredients (Frankenberg 2010). Death rights of the same nature may take different legal or policy forms.

Acknowledgements

Lisa Forsberg, Dimitrios Tsarapatsanis, Sue Westwood, and students who took *Health care law* in 2020–21 at York Law School all helped me to improve this chapter—thank you! The responsibility for errors is mine only.

Notes

1 I am using they/them/their and so on in a singular, gender-neutral sense.
2 Many authors (e.g. Coggon 2010; Lewis 2007a) use 'assisted dying' to refer to voluntary euthanasia and assisted suicide. I note elsewhere that 'within the public

debate on the legalisation of end-of-life decision-making and assistance [in England and Wales], certain organisations and politicians have attempted to redefine assisted dying as (physician) assisted suicide only. Whatever its political merits, this move has not served the ends of conceptual clarity' (Black 2021). As such, I prefer the term 'assisted death'.

3 All emphases in quotations are original, unless stated otherwise.

4 There is a specific sense 'ought' takes within Wedgwood's theory of reasons for action (2009, 322)—what ought is about and what ought comprises. First, ought is *practical*, in that it relates, in a general all things considered way, to the end or starting points of deliberation about what to do (322). Second, ought is *objective* in that 'what an agent … ought to do is determined by *all* practically significant facts about the agent's situation—regardless of whether the agent in question actually knows those facts, and even of whether the agent is in a position to know these facts' (322).

5 Three clarifications on notation: (1) course of action A_1 … has consequence S_1, courses of action A_2 … A_n have consequences S_2…S_n respectively; (2) if A_1 has multiple consequences, I individuate these using decimal points, $S_{1.1}$, $S_{1.2}$ …, mutatis mutandis—with the necessary changes—for A_2 … A_n with multiple consequences; and (3) t_1, t_2 … t_n refer to non-identical time periods.

6 Wedgwood characterises these degrees of causal agential involvement along the lines of *failing to prevent* and *actively causing* (2009, 334), which he suggests 'many philosophers think of as the distinction between *doing* and *allowing*). For a helpful summary and critique of these distinctions, see (Woollard 2012a, 2012b). To avoid additional complication, I shall speak in terms of *relative* degrees of causal agential involvement without further classification, since, in my view, that is all we require to make Wedgwood's view work.

7 A further clarification on notation: if course of action A_1 is pursuable by alternative means, I individuate these using decimal points, $A_{1.1}$, $A_{1.2}$ …, mutatis mutandis for A_2 … A_n pursuable by alternative means.

8 For discussion of intentional agential involvement and reasons for action, see Wedgwood (2011).

9 The formulation of Q's intention here is deliberately broad to capture cases of suicide assistance in which Q does not intend that *P* die (Gavaghan and King 2016, 362–364).

10 For simplicity, I shall assume that there are no facts about Q—for example, taking pleasure in killing or susceptibility to moral distress—that would give Q more or less reason to assist or not to assist *P*'s death, respectively. Thanks to my students for inviting me to clarify this point.

11 This criterion prescribes a narrow range of morally permissible possible courses of action: those with the *most* agentially weighted value. If this is a bullet, I am happy to bite it, at least in this context. Were we to hold that the criterion of moral rightness is that a course of action is morally permissible if it accords with what an agent has *some* reason to do, this might entail the moral permissibility of assisted death in cases in which there is less—but still some—reason to provide assisted suicide or euthanasia relative to other courses of action available to the agent. This does not seem plausible. Thanks to Dimitrios Tsarapatsanis for suggesting that I clarify this point.

12 Of course, consistent with folk accounts of the experience of suffering, suffering itself may have consequences that in turn instantiate the value of well-being to some positive or negative degree.

13 This is commonly known as the deprivation account of the badness of death: Feldman (1991, 1992).

14 Glover is speaking of the trade-off between autonomy and well-being, each of which has intrinsic value on his view. In my view, his point holds for the

threshold at which we can be confident that a course of action involves involuntary euthanasia, as opposed to other involuntary killing.

15 To reinforce this conclusion, I would note that when an agent refuses to assist an individual in their projects, the agent may have a low degree of agential involvement in the consequences that ensue. We can see this in A_2 above.

References

Battin, M. P., Van der Heide, A., Ganzini, L., Van der Wal, G., & Onwuteaka-Philipsen, B. D. (2007). Legal physician-assisted dying in Oregon and the Netherlands: evidence concerning the impact on patients in "vulnerable" groups. *Journal of Medical Ethics, 33*(10), 591–597.

Black, I. (2018). Refusing life-prolonging medical treatment and the ECHR. *Oxford Journal of Legal Studies, 38*(2), 299–327.

Black, I. (2020). Patients, physicians and law at the end of life in England and Wales. In R. E. Board et al. (eds), *End of Life Choices for Cancer Patients* (28–40). Oxford: EBN Health.

Black, I. (2021). Novel beings and assisted nonexistence. *Cambridge Quarterly of Healthcare Ethics, 30*(3), 543–555.

Coggon, J. (2010). Assisted dying and the context of debate: "medical law" versus "end-of-life" law. *Medical Law Review, 18*(4), 541–563.

Daniels, N. (1979). Wide reflective equilibrium and theory acceptance in ethics. *The Journal of Philosophy, 76*(5), 256–282.

Feldman, F. (1991). Some puzzles about the evil of death. *The Philosophical Review, 100*(2), 205–227.

Feldman, F. (1992). *Confrontations with the Reaper: A Philosophical Study of Nature and Value of Death*. New York: Oxford University Press.

Finnis, J. (1995). A philosophical case against euthanasia. In J. Keown (ed) *Euthanasia Examined: Ethical, Clinical and Legal Perspectives* (23–35). Cambridge: Cambridge University Press.

Frankenberg, G. (2010). Constitutional transfer: the IKEA theory revisited. *International Journal of Constitutional Law, 8*(3), 563.

Gavaghan, C., & King, M. (2016). Can facilitated aid in dying be permitted by 'double effect'? Some reflections from a recent New Zealand case. *Journal of Medical Ethics, 42*(6), 361–366.

Glover, J. (1990). *Causing Death and Saving Lives: The Moral Problems of Abortion, Infanticide, Suicide, Euthanasia, Capital Punishment, War and Other Life-or-Death Choices*. London: Penguin.

Harris, J. (1995). The philosophical case against the philosophical case against euthanasia. In J. Keown (ed) *Euthanasia Examined: Ethical, Clinical and Legal Perspectives* (36–45). Cambridge: Cambridge University Press.

Hurka, T. (1987). Why value autonomy? *Social Theory and Practice, 13*(3), 361–382.

Kagan, S. (2014). An introduction to ill-being. In M. Timmons (ed) *Oxford Studies in Normative Ethics Volume 4* (261–288). Oxford: Oxford University Press.

Keown, J. (2002). *Euthanasia, Ethics, and Public Policy: An Argument against Legislation*. Cambridge: Cambridge University Press.

Lewis, P. (2007a). *Assisted Dying and Legal Change*. Oxford: Oxford University Press.

Lewis, P. (2007b). The empirical slippery slope from voluntary to non-voluntary euthanasia. *Journal of Law, Medicine & Ethics, 35*(1), 197.

Lillehammer, H. (2002). Voluntary euthanasia and the logical slippery slope argument. *Cambridge Law Journal, 61*(3), 545.

McIntyre, A. (2001). Doing away with double effect. *Ethics, 111*(2), 219–255.

Mill, J. S. (2002). *Utilitarianism and On Liberty: Including Mill's Essay on Bentham' and Selections from the Writings of Jeremy Bentham and John Austin.* 2nd edn. Oxford: Blackwell.

Parfit, D. (1984). *Reasons and Persons.* Oxford: Clarendon Press.

Raz, J. (1999). *Engaging Reason: On the Theory of Value and Action.* Oxford: Oxford University Press.

Scanlon, T. (2008). *Moral Dimensions: Permissibility, Meaning, Blame.* London: Belknap Press.

Tiberius, V. (2015). Prudential value. In I. Hirose and J. Olson (eds) *The Oxford Handbook of Value Theory* (158–174). Oxford: Oxford University Press.

Wedgwood, R. (2009). Intrinsic values and reasons for action. *Philosophical Issues, 19*, 321–342.

Wedgwood, R. (2011). Defending double effect. *Ratio, 24*(4), 384–401.

Woollard, F. (2012a). The doctrine of doing and allowing I: analysis of the doing/allowing distinction. *Philosophy Compass*, 7(7), 448–458.

Woollard, F. (2012b). The doctrine of doing and allowing II: the moral relevance of the doing/allowing distinction. *Philosophy Compass*, 7(7), 459–469.

Part III

Rights claims

8 Understanding rights in the context of a "right to die"

Sharon Young

Introduction

Freedom to determine the manner and timing of one's own death, and to request assistance to die, is more frequently being discussed in terms of having a "right to die". But what is meant when a "right" to something is expressed? The interpretation and application of human rights seems to vary according to who is articulating the rights and, as Dembour (2010, 2) argues, "[d]ifferent people hold different concepts of human rights". The ways in which the end of life is spoken about has the potential to influence public opinion and to challenge the law, policy and practices. However, there is little analysis of *how* rights are understood or have come to be appropriated in an end-of-life context and scarce explanation of why rights appear to be holding traction in the current UK debate.

The purpose of this chapter is to explore the ways in which human rights could be understood in an end-of-life context and, as a result of this, explain how a right to die may be envisioned. It contributes to the collection as a whole by illuminating perspectives on rights and clarifying positions from which various arguments can be made when rights are used to debate end-of-life issues. A broad social constructivist approach using a qualitative strategy was adopted to explore these different perceived understandings of rights in written and spoken texts. The research design included; three focus group discussions with Death Café Hampstead[1] participants, examination of UK law and policy documents, and a case study on the UK-based organisation *Dignity in Dying* who campaign to legalise assisted dying (Young, 2017).

The chapter is divided into three parts starting with a foundational position on rights. Within this perspective, a right to die can be grounded in conceptions of innate personal liberty and human dignity that could explain or support end-of-life decision-making. Selected contributions from Death Café Hampstead participants are used to illustrate this position. The second and third parts of this chapter explore an anti-foundational perspective which rejects the foundational assumptions of human rights, arguing instead that rights are time and context specific. An anti-foundational position includes both a legal approach to rights and a social constructivist approach. A legal

DOI: 10.4324/9780429329739-8

approach regards the role of the nation state important to define and legislate human rights. The landmark case of Diane Pretty is used as an example to evaluate the boundaries and scope of rights arguments in a legal understanding of the right to die. Social constructivism is explored in the final part of this chapter in relation to how different actors, in particular, *Dignity in Dying*, use recognised discursive strategies to influence how assisted dying is thought about.

Foundational approach to rights

A foundational or essentialist approach to rights embraces the most common interpretation of human rights: individuals are the bearers of human rights solely by virtue of their humanity. A foundational perspective that encompasses natural law and liberal tradition, typically considers innate personal liberty and human dignity as foundations for the existence of rights.

Individual liberty

Key philosophers John Locke and Immanuel Kant have formulated principles of liberty within different frameworks. Locke, as the founder of liberalism, traditionally argued from his belief in a divine perspective on natural law that "all men" (and women) are born free and equal. Human beings possess natural rights that are those values and moral norms deemed worthy of protection in a hypothetical "state of nature" independent of outside influence (Locke [1689] 1970). Locke's contribution grounded liberty in Western liberal theory and natural law tradition, but he also situated his idea of natural rights within a political context whereby the legitimacy of a government depended on the respect that it accorded these rights (Locke [1689] 1970). Locke elaborated on the concept of liberty arguing that all human beings are entitled to certain rights derived from their own moral nature and considered one's individual property. He argued this property to include one's own person:

> Though the earth and all inferior creatures be common to all men, yet every man has a "property" in his own "person". This, nobody has any right to but himself.
>
> Locke, 1689 Bk II Ch V (1970, 27)

This highlights an important point relevant to the end-of-life debate. Through the notion of the body as personal property, Locke emphasises that *individuals*, and only these individuals, have a right to decide over their own bodies. If the body belongs to the self, it follows that at the heart of liberty is the right to determine one's own existence or indeed non-existence.

Kant's perspective regards individual liberty as living by one's own values and beliefs, informed by a voluntary, rational choice. In contrast to Locke, Kant argues that the right of autonomy is not necessarily intrinsic to human beings, but is dependent on their "rational nature" (Kant [1797] 1996, 436). In this regard, autonomy is an exercise of evaluative choice, requiring individuals to consider their options and possible consequences. From a contemporary perspective, Carel (2008, 73) links understandings of individual liberty to human agency as a means to assert oneself and for Lawton (2000, 81), this sense of self involves the "ability to act as the agents of their embodied actions". These arguments support the idea that human beings as freely choosing individuals are able to make decisions about their lives, over their own bodies, and also about the manner and timing of their death.

Human dignity

Dignity as a concept is generally associated with a natural law perspective on rights and dignity is often perceived as the basis for human rights (Kateb 2011; Rosen 2012). As one particular example, the contribution of political scientist, Jack Donnelly (2003, 2007), grounded rights in respect for the inherent dignity of human beings. He argued that rights ought to be enjoyed "simply because one is a human being" (Donnelly 2003, 10). This was suggested earlier by Kant who associated the concept of dignity with an innate human worth. In his *Metaphysics of Morals* Kant notes the inherent nature of "dignity in the person", claiming "all worth, must for that very reason have a dignity, that is, an unconditional, incomparable worth" and this, he states, is deserving of respect from others (Kant [1797] 1996, 440, 436). For Kant, dignity has an unconditional value.[2] In contrast to the divine perspective adopted by Locke, he associates dignity as the basis for morality from a secular position that may closely resonate with contemporary and humanist perceptions of dignity and rights.

A foundational understanding of human dignity and rights is highlighted as the very first paragraph in the Preamble to the Universal Declaration of Human Rights 1948, which states,

> Whereas recognition of the inherent dignity and of the equal and inalienable rights of all members of the human family is the foundation of freedom, justice and peace in the world.
>
> UDHR (1948, 1)

Human dignity could offer a credible basis for the existence of human rights and through the generally desirable notion of a dignified death, an understanding of dignity grounded in rights suggests a plausible basis for a right to die. However, the definition and phenomenology of dignity are ambiguous. Given that the values of dignity and freedom of choice have become important and relevant to contemporary dying in the UK, there is a surprising lack of philosophical interest in dignity as a concept and a lack of scholarly discussion on what human dignity is or why it matters for rights.

The notion of dignity is frequently coupled with choice in the context of dying using rights as the common basis for this association, as in this example:

> … the right to choose is a basic expression of one's dignity and there is no more fundamental expression of one's dignity than the right to make life-saving or life-terminating choices.
>
> Beyleveld and Brownsword (2001, 242)

Respect for dignity that encompasses dignity in dying is prioritised by some people as illustrated in the research examples below. The protection of dignity is also argued by others, including campaigning organisations, who suggest a right to die can enhance human dignity through the avoidance of an undignified death. A right to die could be conceived through a foundational approach to rights by emphasising values of personal liberty and human dignity, not only in life but also in death. From this perspective, individuals have the right to make end-of-life choices over their own bodies.

Focus group discussions

To explore understandings of rights, dignity, choice and suffering in relation to the end of life, individuals on the Death Café Hampstead mailing list were invited by the author to participate in focus group discussions during the period from September 2014 to February 2015. The groups represent a London-based sample of 19 people of a varied age range and background, who identified themselves as having a specific interest in speaking about death and dying. A funnel approach including key themes, standardised questions and prompts was used and the findings contribute towards a wider narrative informing the UK debate.

All group discussions began with a quote and the open question, "What does dignity mean to you?" There was a swift and enthusiastic level of engagement with the concept of dignity. Comments included the following.

> Dignity is being able to take care of yourself and feel comfortable with it.
>
> Denise, aged 67

> I believe it's the ability to live according to the principles of one's mind ….
>
> Beth, aged 30

> … control over your own bodily functions.
>
> Petula, aged 50

> respect and self-respect for me is what dignity is about and it includes also respectful care, caring.
>
> Josefine, aged 63

Speaking about the experience of her 91-year-old father who had recently died in a care home, one participant explained her understanding of innate and bestowed dignity:

> … there was something about how carefully they treated him. The nurses there were just so nice and they also thought what a lovely man he was. He had dignity because he had a dignity within him.
>
> Beverley, aged 61

Participants readily identified concepts of both inherent human dignity and bestowed dignity through relationships with others. This also informed their own perceptions of dying well. Examples of dignified death were considered as "being allowed to go in your own time" (Martin A. aged 65), and,

> … to have that sense that you've done what you can, that you've enjoyed what you can and that you are going with a sense of completion.
>
> Brenda, aged 67

Their responses demonstrated that dignity in an end-of-life context was highly valued.

With the exception of three participants across the groups, all indicated the importance of individual choice in end-of-life decision-making as a fundamental value. The few comments that rejected this understanding were defended from a religious or cultural background. The following contributions were typical of those who defended their right to die through freedom of choice underpinned by respect for human agency:

> I think we should be able to choose. It's us that's choosing. If you've got to the point where your quality of life is not as you've had it then you want to go.
>
> Martin B, aged 75

> …you are the only person who should be allowed to decide. Everyone should be able to decide for themselves.
>
> Luke, aged 60

> Control is very much a part of it, in the sense of control of what happens.
>
> Carol, aged 75

The underlying assumption for many of the participants discussing choice, was that human beings are rational, free-thinking and selective individuals. This conception of liberty reflects a foundational position on rights and suggests that in the same way that individuals decide how to live their lives, control of their own death should also be free from interference by others.

Perhaps surprisingly, given the topical discussions and political debates at this time on the "right to die", members of the public appeared to have difficulty defining *rights* and referring to rights explicitly in an end-of-life context. In asking the key question "So what do you understand by a 'right to die', what is a right to something?" there was only one direct response across all groups: "It comes back to the issue of having control" (Beth, aged 30). Despite a general reluctance to engage with human rights per se, focus group participants did reference concepts of liberty and dignity as grounded in a foundational position on rights and this suggested an understanding of the essence of rights. Focus groups consistently highlighted that at the end of life the opportunity to die well and experience a "good death" was desirable. Participants thought this to be enhanced through respect for individual liberty, beholding a sense of identity based on human dignity and maintaining the feeling of being in control to achieve the death that would be reflective of their personal values in life.

Anti-foundational approaches

Anti-foundational approaches view human rights as constructed and relative to a specific time and social/ political/cultural context. Rights are understood without metaphysical grounding either on the basis of natural law relating to God, as in the tradition of Locke, or on the basis of reason and logic, as proposed by Kant. Anti-foundationalism or constructivism can be helpful to explain historic variations in the nature of human rights claims and the institutions or mechanisms designed to protect them. This section is divided into two parts. The first examines legal positivism as one basis for understanding legal rights. The second explores a social constructivist approach that grounds and analyses claims to rights through an emphasis on the social rather than legal context.

Legal positivism

A legal positivist position on rights assumes human rights and subsequent claims to rights as solely defined and protected through the action of a nation state enshrining them in law. Legal positivism looks to the recommendations of the political and legal systems for guidance on permissible conduct in relation to complex dilemmas. On this basis, law and policy has an important role; statutory and policy provisions will determine the options available at the end of life and help shape how the public thinks about these options.

From a legal positivist perspective, realisation of a right to die would potentially involve the amendment of statutory UK law, legislation of a new right or, perhaps more likely, extending the boundaries of and appropriating existing rights into a new area. Should this happen, the status of the dying person meeting the eligibility criteria[3] and requesting an assisted death would be classified as a "rights-holder". Feinberg (1980, 151) suggests that to think of oneself as a rights-holder is empowering, it involves elements of pride and self-esteem, and deserves respect from others. Classifying the dying person as a rights-holder also positions the state and others who could include members of the community, as duty-bearers who may be responsible for discharging legal obligations or duties associated with these rights. For most human rights theorists, duties are not considered a precondition to human rights, but rights do often involve duties both to fulfil moral, practical or social obligations and to facilitate the rights of others (Etzioni and Brodbeck 2012; Freeman 2011). If there was granted a legal right to die, the state would become responsible for discharging obligations that would include nominating a duty-bearer to assist the death to enable the right of the rights-holder to be fulfilled. In the UK, in light of continuing opposition from the medical professional bodies, and lack of suitable, alternative proposals, there is currently no consensus on who has an obligation to act as a duty-bearer and it is undetermined where, or with whom, the claim would be lodged.

The normative principles of human rights may motivate some rights adherents towards legal entrenchment. However, human rights are sometimes contradictory in nature where fulfilment of one right adversely affects or conflicts with another already established right or new rights may infringe on the rights of other members of society (Freeman 2011, 6). Legal recognition of a right to die, for example, might directly conflict with an already established right to life, an absolute right protected under national and international human rights mechanisms that the UK has ratified, including the Human Rights Act 1998 and the European Convention on Human Rights 1950. Nevertheless, the boundaries of rights may be open to interpretation by actors and circumstances that may either develop and extend existing rights or impede their legal implementation, as highlighted in the example below.

Case of Diane Pretty 2001

In November 1998, the Human Rights Act (HRA) received Royal Assent and enshrined the principles of the 1950 European Convention on Human Rights (ECHR) within UK law. Section 6(1) of the HRA provides a method for which individuals in complex cases, including requests for an assisted death, have the option to challenge a decision already made in court through the process of judicial review. Diane Pretty, diagnosed with motor neurone disease, wanted to end her life with the help of her husband before reaching the stage which she considered would involve unbearable suffering. She sought prior immunity from prosecution for her husband if he assisted in her death (*Pretty v DPP* [2001] UKHL 61). Diane Pretty grounded her motion on the basis of their marital status, her physical inability to end her own life due to disability, and the right to privacy in regard to her own decision-making ability on this personal matter. Pretty was the first individual to challenge legislation by suggesting that Section 2 of the 1961 Suicide Act, if it prohibits this help from her husband and prevents the Director of Public Prosecutions undertaking not to prosecute if he does, is incompatible with the recently enshrined ECHR 1950 (*Pretty v DPP* [2001] UKHL 61). Citing violation of the Convention rights soon after the HRA 1998 entered into force and petitioning an application for assistance to die positions the case of *Pretty* as an important legal landmark.

The case of *Pretty* principally invoked respect for the right to self-determination at the end of life as a reflection of individual liberty and an attempt to maintain human dignity. In essence: a foundational understanding of rights was used to launch a legal challenge. Her appeal cited violation of the ECHR 1950 Article 2 the right to life; Article 3 prohibition of torture and inhuman or degrading treatment; Article 8 right to respect for private and family life; Article 9 freedom of thought, conscience and religion, and Article 14 prohibition of discrimination. The right to life is central to the debate on assisted dying and its inviolable nature has been challenged in a number of ways. Pretty's case began by questioning the inalienable status of the right to life and suggested that individuals who are suffering or dying may rationally choose not to avail themselves of this rightful entitlement. Counsel for *Pretty* argued that Article 2 protects the *right to* life rather than life itself, and, on this basis, it is for the individual to choose whether or not to claim this right. It was thus proposed that interpreting the scope of a right to life should include being able to waive the right to life.

Counsel for Pretty challenged the juridical framework for end-of-life decision-making by suggesting a new concept, namely, the *right not to live* as a conjunction of the right to life and the right to self-determination. A right not to live, in effect a right to die, would be applied in practice in the same manner that individuals may refuse life-saving or life-prolonging medical treatment, or may lawfully choose to commit suicide if they are physically able. Pretty argued further that the right to die is not the antithesis of the right to life but the corollary of it, and that the state has a positive obligation to protect both (*Pretty v DPP* [2001] UKHL 61). The secretary of state replied with a number of objections to this interpretation of the right to life, which were upheld by the Court. Lord Bingham, reflecting on arguments made by the secretary of state, confers,

> The article protects the right to life and prevents the deliberate taking of life save in very narrowly defined circumstances. An article with that effect cannot be interpreted as conferring a right to die or to enlist the aid of another in bringing about one's own death.
>
> *Pretty v DPP* [2001] UKHL 61 (paragraph 5)

Diane Pretty also cited ECHR, Article 8(1) the right to respect for private and family life as a means to sanction an assisted death. This is a key argument in the debate but one that only appears to surface in relation to individual appeals. Counsel for *Pretty* suggested extending the boundaries and context of this right to a private life to include a right to determine one's own death. Lord Bingham explains further:

> This right embraces a right to choose when and how to die so that suffering and indignity can be avoided. Section 2(1) of the 1961 Act interferes with this right of self-determination ....
>
> *Pretty v DPP* [2001] UKHL 61 (paragraph 17)

A right to privacy highlights and protects individual liberty through permitting individuals to self-determine their own actions within their private, family and home environment. However, the boundaries of privacy rights remain subject to interpretation and especially in relation to the end of life, the right to privacy has been under-theorised both historically and philosophically. It is not always clear where and when legally valid expectations of privacy exist, how they are defined, nor how they fare in relation to other legally recognised interests including public morality and national security.

Counsel for *Pretty* argued that her right to die was also grounded in the indignity of human suffering associated with physically not being able to end her life herself and being refused assistance to do this. The debilitating nature of the dying process that characterised Ms Pretty's condition, prolonging the actual or anticipated undignified conditions under which she must remain alive might constitute inhuman or degrading treatment. Through the prohibition of "inhuman or degrading treatment," Article 3 of the ECHR 1950 confers respect for personal integrity and human dignity and links this with the avoidance of suffering. Although the importance of dignity is implied through Article 3, the concept of dignity did not inform the language of law and jurisprudence pre twentieth century (McCrudden, 2008). There is no legal right to dignity per se, but it has increasingly featured in a range of international legal documents since the 1948 Universal Declaration of Human Rights (see, e.g., McCrudden's (2008) analysis that also notes in regard to judicial review, the nature of dignity as "an interpretive principle to assist the further explication of the catalogue of rights generated by the principle" [681]).

Losing her appeal in the UK House of Lords, Diane Pretty applied to the European Court of Human Rights in 2002 where she was partially successful, in that it was held that her desire to end her life did engage Article 8.1, suggesting that the UK legislation on assisting suicide was not compliant with European human rights law (Case of *Pretty v. United Kingdom* Application no. 2346/02). The European Court noted that member states enjoy a wide margin of appreciation on the issue of assisted dying and the concept of "private life" is a broad term not susceptible to exhaustive definition (Case of *Pretty v. United Kingdom* Application no. 2346/02, paragraph 61). In disagreement with the earlier opinion of the secretary of state, cited by Lord Bingham that private life refers to "the manner in which a person conducts his life, not the manner in which he departs from it" (*Pretty v DPP* [2001] UKHL 61 at para 18) the assessment by the European Court[4] decided,

> ... that the ability to conduct one's life in a manner of one's own choosing may also include the opportunity to pursue activities perceived to be of a physically or morally harmful or dangerous nature for the individual concerned.
>
> Case of *Pretty v. United Kingdom* Application no. 2346/02 (paragraph 62)

The case of *Pretty* suggests that attempts to expand human rights principles in relation to assisted death, are most persuasive through the right to privacy that promotes a sense of self and respect for autonomous decision-making *in private* over individual bodily integrity.[5]

Analysis of the *Pretty* judgement reveals the law as a blunt instrument in defining human rights principles, especially in hard cases that necessitate close scrutiny and a degree of interpretation. It also raises further questions about rights including who "owns" our bodies in regard to end-of-life decision-making; the state or the individual. Diane Pretty's condition deteriorated shortly after the above judgement and she went into a coma following breathing difficulties and died in May, 2002. Her case exemplifies an anti-foundational approach to rights in that it argued concepts of human rights are fluid, open to interpretation and deliberation, and could be appropriated in a new context, namely, in relation to the right to die.

Social constructivism

A social constructivist theory of rights emphasises that rights are a product of their environment, and that they are generated and shaped through social/political/cultural interaction and reflect a specific time and context. In contrast to legal or foundational perspectives that base an understanding of rights on positive law or human nature, a social constructivist approach suggests that certain rights or claims expressed as rights emerge in particular social settings and are instead based on the culture and context of the community in which they operate (O'Byrne 2003, 39). From this perspective, understandings of human rights are subject to interpretation; meanings are both evident and constructed by different actors who adapt these to suit their own purposes and practice.

One powerful way in which attitudes towards death and dying are shaped is through discourse. A discursive approach to rights is part of a social constructivist position that regards rights as a linguistic expression. Theorising the language structure of human rights, O' Byrne (2012, 835) argues that the,

> ... language of human rights provides us with a set of ethical validity claims which we as individuals and on behalf of ourselves and others make against society as a whole.

Human rights discourses have, in regard to specific issues, been instrumental in shaping how society thinks about a complex dilemma.[6] Merry (2006, cited in Freeman 2011, 110) highlights this ability of rights discourses to "subvert and displace prior discourses." Framing human rights as claims to something, for example, a "*right to* die" does appear to increase their validity and make them less politically negotiable so that framing processes are a central dynamic in understanding how people develop a particular conceptualisation of an issue or reorient their thinking about an issue (Benford and Snow 2000; Chong and Druckman 2007). In contemporary society, rights discourses are becoming increasingly salient to the extent that they could inflate and sustain a challenge to medical practice and political institutions that determine permissible frameworks for end of life.

A significant contribution towards understanding rights was made by Miller (2010) who used a social constructivist perspective to analyse what had commonly been referred to as "rights-*based* approaches" in the context of campaigning non-governmental organisations (NGOs) and instead proposed "rights-*framed* approaches". Rights-framed approaches offer an alternative strategy where rights discourses are adopted as a campaign tool to interpret and transform an issue for their own purpose, being underpinned by ideology rather than reference to international human rights mechanisms (Miller 2010, 923). "Rights talk" is incorporated strategically through a human rights frame, and more usually at an operational level to promote and advance the campaign objectives so that rights are used as a "*tool* to *serve* the NGO's official approach" (author's emphasis) as demonstrated, in part, by the case study below (Miller 2010, 925).

Dignity in dying

Dignity in Dying (hereafter DiD) is a UK-based organisation with over 25,000 active members who support their campaign to change the law "to legalise assisted dying within upfront safeguards for terminally ill, mentally competent adults" (DiD, 2016a). DiD were selected for a case study on the basis of their historic foundation, significant reach, and their ability to stimulate debate on the right to die in both the public and political arena. Dr Charles Killick Millard founded DiD in 1935 under the name The Voluntary Euthanasia Society. He played a key role in placing the issue of assisted death on the political agenda when he proposed the first Bill for the legalisation of voluntary euthanasia in his Presidential Address to the Society of Medical Officers of Health in October 1931 (Millard, 1931). His speech emphasised that this act "should be regarded not merely as an act of mercy, *but as a matter of elementary human right*" (author's emphasis) (Millard 1931, 12). This appears to have been the first time that euthanasia was thought of as a personal "right" and a right to die had been articulated as such.

Campaign messages placed on the London Underground and mainline railway stations in the late 1950s highlighted the "right to choose a Merciful Death" that demonstrates some understanding of rights throughout the history of DiD (see Kemp 2006 for more details of the British euthanasia movement). In 2006 when the organisation changed its name to *Dignity in Dying*, the value of human dignity was centralised and the act of assisting death clearly positioned in terms of rights. The emphasis on dignity by DiD serves to transform an understanding of the debate through linking the right to die with the right to a dignified death that is shown in the above analyses to be generally desirable.

Textual analysis of DiD's mediated communication over the period of study 2012–2016 demonstrated that rights discourses have remained central to the organization but the application of rights, has at times been extended or different conceptions of rights brought forward in order to advance their objectives. For example, in May 2016, DiD stated, "We believe everybody has the right to a good death. Including the option of assisted dying for terminally ill, mentally competent adults" (DiD, 2016a). A shift in nuance here suggests permitting a right to die can help promote a good death. This inference is strengthened through the 2016 campaign aims that articulate the notion of a right, not only to a dignified death and to a good death, but "[t]he right, when dying, to die well" (DiD, 2016b).

Concepts of suffering not usually associated with rights, have more recently been engaged as part of the discourse on dying through emphasising the values of dignity and choice. In June, 2016, the DiD "About us" website page was revised to demand "greater choice and control to alleviate suffering at the end of life." This indicated a potential shift at DiD away from explicit references to rights as the direction of the organisation began to focus more on the alleviation of suffering as an argument to change the law. Reasons for this are not apparent but may be related to defeat of the 2014 House of Lords Assisted Dying Bill and 2015 House of Commons Assisted Dying (No. 2) Bill. The findings demonstrate a carefully considered use of rights discourses and the foregrounding of rights to a greater or lesser extent at different times that is indicative of a social constructivist position and rights-framed approaches (RFAs) proposed by Miller (2010) above. Rights discourses are applied, or in the case of DiD, prioritised in specific contexts where they are considered for a variety of reasons to be strategically advantageous.

DiD chronicles personal narratives of individuals who are living with a serious condition, are dying or have been bereaved under the "Personal stories" section of their website. Each of the 36 personal stories selected from London and the South East region vividly describes their own experience that is assumed to resonate widely with the public interest because dying is a universal phenomenon and all are susceptible to serious illness. The purpose of these individual stories is to engage readers on a personal level, arouse sympathy, enhance proximity to the debate and potentially transform readers' perceptions on the right to die. Coded NVivo10 analysis of the language in these personal stories revealed frames of "choice", "dignity", "suffering" and "rights" that provided an insight of *how* the issue of assisted death was positioned, thought about and given meaning. The strategic use of a rights frame linking notions of choice and dignity understood as rights was evident. Narratives are crucial in constructing a shared meaning and identity and these particular frames resonate across a broad spectrum of target audiences. To an extent, the case study findings suggest that rights discourses, now more widely used by the organisation have become central to defining the terms and clarifying the arguments in the end-of-life debate. Assisted dying has been redefined as an individual "right to die" based on the values of choice and dignity, providing an opportunity for everyone to experience what they consider to be a good death and avoid suffering.

Conclusion

Both foundational and anti-foundational approaches to rights could arguably support a "right to die". Different understandings of rights at the end of life are being applied to support the idea that individuals are sovereign over their own bodies and are able to self-determine, *not only how they live but how they die*. From a foundational perspective, rights are understood through inherent concepts of individual liberty and human dignity grounded in human nature. Freedom to determine the manner and timing of one's own death could be defended through this approach on the basis of human beings as rational, freely choosing individuals. A right to die could, similarly, be conceived through the desire to maintain a sense of dignity of the person, especially in the face of suffering, or to avoid potential indignity at the end of life.

Anti-foundational approaches to human rights include legal positivism and social constructivism that argues rights are not a static phenomenon but become defined through legal, social, political and cultural factors. From a legal positivist perspective, rights arise as a product of political and legal institutions that serves to increase the legitimacy of a right, customise normative standards of behaviour and guide social conduct. In the UK, established legal instruments, including the HRA 1998 and ECHR 1950, currently protect individual liberty rights relevant to the end of life. Analysis of the prominent case of Diane Pretty revealed how new configurations of rights that include a right to die and a right to waive the existing right to life challenged the scope of existing rights. Driven by this and similar appeals together with wider debates involving the interpretation of rights at the end of life, in particular the right to privacy and application of human dignity, a right to die has become so tangible that there is a possibility of the UK law courts making a Declaration of Incompatibility, or using the principles of statutory interpretation to override existing provision. In this way, a right to die could be established through setting a legal precedent.

A social constructivist approach that analyses human rights in a social context can also help explain how new rights claims arise and become normalised practice. Human rights discourses can be used selectively and interchangeably to embed rights at the end-of-life. A range of social actors and organisations have incorporated rights discourses to appropriate and proliferate new sets of rights claims and to successfully facilitate institutional, organisational and legal change. Through framing the notion of requested death as a *right* to die to reflect ideals of choice, human dignity and relief of suffering, *Dignity in Dying*, as one example, has constructed a new and empowering narrative of assisted dying. This case study demonstrates how a national campaigning organisation has used rights discourses strategically to construct and articulate the right to an assisted death through a common desire to experience a dignified and good death. The above analysis offers answers to the questions posed at the beginning of this chapter; what is understood when a "right" to something is expressed and how a "right to die" may be conceived. It is clear that a notion of rights at the end of life has impacted our perception of dying and substantiated a "right to die", but in ways that are complex and arise as a reflection of dying at a specific period in time.

Case law

Pretty v United Kingdom Application no. 2346/02 [2002] ECHR 427.
Pretty v DPP [2001] UKHL 61.

Statute

Human Rights Act 1998.

Notes

1 Death Cafe was originally conceptualised by a Swiss sociologist Bernard Crettaz, under the name Café Mortel and then developed in London by Jon Underwood in 2011. It operates as a not for profit social franchise with the objective "to increase awareness of death with a view to helping people make the most of their (finite) lives" (Death Café, 2014). Groups of people meet to enjoy refreshments and discuss death with no agenda, objectives or themes but agree to rules of respect and confidentiality (see, e.g., https://deathcafe.com/profile/20932).

2 Conceptions of rights, dignity, respect and duty are central to Kant's morality, and these underpin his condemnation of suicide that is well known and presented in his lectures on ethics (Kant [1775–1780], 1963, 147–154).

3 Proposals debated most recently in the 2014 House of Lords Assisted Dying Bill specify eligibility criteria as age, terminal illness and rational capacity as requirements, meaning that the right to die would not be equally or universally available to all.

4 Joint statement by the Court.

5 In three subsequent decisions, the European Court has stated in clear terms that Article 8.1 encompasses the right to decide how and when to die, and in particular the right to avoid a distressing and undignified end to life provided that the decision is made freely (see *Haas v Switzerland* (2011) 53 EHRR 33, para 51, *Koch v Germany* (2013) 56 EHRR 6, paras 46 and 51, and *Gross v Switzerland* (2014) 58 EHRR 7, para 60).

6 Anti-discrimination rights that now afford protection for equality on the basis of disability and sexuality, and the extension of women's rights that encompasses a right to choose in the case of permitted abortion are suggested examples of how rights discourses have proliferated a range of claims that have facilitated an increased scope and provision of rights in national and international mechanisms.

References

Benford, R. D. and Snow, D. A. (2000). Framing processes and social movements: An overview and assessment. *Annual Review of Sociology, 26*(1), 611–639.

Beyleveld, D. and Brownsword, R. (2001). *Human Dignity in Bioethics and Biolaw.* Oxford: Oxford University Press.

Carel, H. (2008). *Illness: The Cry of the Flesh.* Durham: Acumen.

Chong, D. and Druckman, J. N. (2007). A theory of framing and opinion formation in competitive elite environments. *Journal of Communication, 57*(1), 99–118.

Death Café (2014). *What is Death Café?* Available at: https://deathcafe.com/what/ Accessed 28.05.19.

Dembour, M-B. (2010). What are human rights? Four schools of thought. *Human Rights Quarterly, 32*(1), 1–20.

Dignity in Dying (DiD) (2016a). *Welcome.* Available at: http://www.dignityindying.org.uk/ Accessed 28.04.16.

Dignity in Dying (DiD) (2016b). *Support Us.* Available at: https://www.dignityindying.org.uk/support-us/what-is-campaign-dignity-in-dying/ Accessed 28.04.16.

Donnelly, J. (2003). *Universal Human Rights in Theory and Practice,* 3rd Edition. London: Cornell University Press.

Donnelly, J. (2007). The relative universality of human rights. *Human Rights Quarterly, 29*(2), 281–306.

Etzioni, A. and Brodbeck, L. (2012). Rights and responsibilities: The intergenerational covenant. *Journal of Comparative Social Welfare, 28*(2), 113–117.

Feinberg, J. (1980). *Rights, Justice and the Bounds of Liberty.* Princeton: Princeton University Press.

Freeman, M. (2011). *Human Rights,* 2nd edition. Cambridge: Polity Press.

Kant, I. [1724–1802] (1996). *The Metaphysics of Morals,* edited/translated by Mary Gregor. Cambridge: Cambridge University Press.

Kateb, G. (2011). *Human Dignity.* London: The Belknap Press.

Kemp. N. D. A. (2002). *"Merciful Release" The History of the British Euthanasia Movement.* Manchester: Manchester University Press.

Lawton, J. (2000). *The Dying Process: Patients' Experiences of Palliative Care.* London: Routledge.

Locke, J. [1689–1690] (1970). *Two Treaties of Government.* Cambridge: Cambridge University Press.

McCrudden, C. (2008). Human dignity and judicial interpretation of human rights. *The European Journal of International Law, 19*(4), 655–724.

Millard, C. K. (1931). *Euthanasia: A Plea for the Legalisation of Voluntary Euthanasia under Certain Conditions.* London: The CW Daniel Company.

Miller, H. (2010). From "rights-based" to "rights-framed" approaches: A social constructionist view of human rights practice. *International Journal of Human Rights, 14*(6), 915–931.

O' Byrne, D. (2003). *Human Rights: An Introduction.* London: Pearson Education Ltd.

O' Byrne, D. (2012). On the sociology of human rights: Theorising the language-structure of rights. *Sociology, 46*(5), 829–843.

Rosen, M. (2012). *Dignity: Its History and Meaning.* Cambridge: Harvard University Press.

Young, S. (2017). *A Right to Die? Examining the Centrality of Human Rights Discourses to End of Life Debate and Policy in the UK.* PhD dissertation, Kingston University, UK.

9 Dying with conscience

The potential application of Article 9 ECHR to assisted dying

Elizabeth Wicks

Introduction

The manner in which we die is an issue of fundamental importance to us and our opinions and choices about it are likely to be coloured by our personal values and belief systems. In light of this, it is surprising that the human right of freedom of conscience and religion has been absent from the assisted dying debate for so long, particularly when quasi-religious concepts such as sanctity of life[1] are so overtly present. This chapter will investigate the potential role of Article 9 of the European Convention of Human Rights (ECHR) which protects the freedom of thought, conscience and religion, including a right to manifest a religion or belief. The ECHR is a regional human rights treaty to which all members of the Council of Europe, including the UK, are parties. There has, to date, been little attention paid to the issue of Article 9 ECHR's application to assisted dying but two significant developments in the European Court of Human Rights' interpretation of the Convention suggest that the time might be ripe for such consideration. First, the application of human rights in general, and Article 8's right to respect for private life in particular, to end-of-life decision-making has come to the forefront of the assisted dying debate. That there is a (prima facie) right to a dignified death under Article 8 of the Convention is no longer in doubt following cases such as *Pretty v United Kingdom* in which this was recognised,[2] although its protection in the face of the need for the state to take positive steps to protect the lives of vulnerable members of society remains the subject of debate. Second, the meaning of a manifestation of belief under Article 9 has evolved to encompass actions closely connected to, but not required, by the belief (such as the wearing of a crucifix).

These two developments necessitate some consideration of whether dying with assistance in order to ensure a dignified death could amount to the manifestation of a belief and thus be protected under Article 9. Such a manifestation is not, of course, protected in absolute terms under this provision. Interference by the state with any manifestation of a belief can be justified under Article 9(2) if prescribed by law and necessary in a democratic society for one of four specified legitimate aims, including significantly the

DOI: 10.4324/9780429329739-9

protection of health and morals and the protection of the rights and freedoms of others. The balancing exercise required under the second paragraph is not the focus of the discussion in this chapter, however. It may indeed be justified under Article 9(2) for the state to restrict a freedom to manifest beliefs by dying with assistance, because such restrictions might be regarded as necessary in a democratic society, to use the wording of that provision. However, this assessment of necessity is likely to raise similar issues to those already being considered in the context of Article 8.[3] The present discussion will focus, instead, on the preliminary issue of whether Article 9 is engaged at all by the assisted dying debate. In doing so, it is hoped to illuminate some of the weaknesses in the current treatment of non-religious beliefs under Article 9.

The discussion begins with the problematic question of whether a non-religious and individualistic belief is entitled to any protection under Article 9. Following this, there will be consideration of the link between a belief and its manifestation, taking into account judicial developments on this topic. Focus will then turn to an evaluation of whether a desire for assistance in dying is capable of being regarded as a manifestation of belief, or indeed as an aspect of a broader freedom of conscience, under Article 9.

Defining 'belief'

It is clear that Article 9's protection of freedom of thought, conscience and religion extends beyond religion to provide vital protection for other non-religious beliefs. Indeed, the most famous statement of the European Court of Human Rights on Article 9 emphasised this very fact:

> Freedom of thought, conscience and religion is one of the foundations of a 'democratic society' within the meaning of the Convention. It is, in its religious dimension, one of the most vital elements that go to make up the identity of believers and their conception of life, but it is also a precious asset for atheists, agnostics, sceptics and the unconcerned. The pluralism indissociable from a democratic society, which has been dearly won over the centuries, depends on it.
>
> *Kokkinakis v Greece* (1993)[4]

Furthermore, it is not only a right not to hold religious beliefs that falls within the ambit of Article 9, although that certainly does so (*Buscarini v San Marino* (1999)),[5] but also other specific secular beliefs such as pacifism (*Arrowsmith v UK* (1978)).[6] The ambit of Article 9 does have limits, however, as was apparent in *Pretty v United Kingdom* (2002). In that case, the Court summarily rejected the applicant's claim that her desire to die with dignity by means of assisted suicide was a 'belief' included within Article 9, stating merely that 'not all opinions or convictions constitute beliefs in the sense protected by Article 9(1)' (*Pretty*, 82).[7] What becomes clear therefore is that the significant distinction under the terms of Article 9 is not, as we might instinctively have expected, one between religious beliefs and non-religious beliefs, but rather one between 'beliefs' and opinions or convictions falling short of 'beliefs'.

How, then, might a mere opinion or conviction be elevated to a 'belief'? In the landmark case of *Eweida*, the Court confirmed its approach of protecting only those views that 'attain a certain level of cogency, seriousness, cohesion and importance' (*Eweida v UK*, 2013).[8] These requirements have been poached from another Convention right entirely. Article 2 of the First Protocol to the European Convention of Human Rights (which contains further rights beyond those in the Convention) protects, inter alia, the right of parents to ensure their children's education and teaching in conformity with their own religions and philosophical convictions. It is in this context, as a means of defining what amounts to a religious or philosophical conviction, that the requirements of cogency, seriousness, cohesion and importance were first articulated (*Campbell and Cosans v UK*, 1982).[9] Under Article 9, they have been set to a different purpose: to distinguish a belief from a conviction. Although the four requirements of cogency, seriousness, cohesion and importance will apply to all beliefs under Article 9, the test is much easier to satisfy for certain types of beliefs than for others. Most notably, a belief that stems from a mainstream religion is likely to bypass these requirements easily. Indeed, in the domestic case of *R v Secretary of State for Education and Employment, ex parte Williamson* (2005),[10] Lord Nicholls acknowledged that the requirement of seriousness was 'readily satisfied' by a religious belief (23). It may also present little difficulty for well-established schools of thought beyond religion, and therefore atheism and pacifism will similarly pass the test easily. It will be much harder for a single-issue belief to qualify for protection. In *McFeeley v United Kingdom* (1980), a political prisoner's objection to wearing prison uniform did not fall within the ambit of Article 9.[11] A more surprising exclusion was apparent in *X v Federal Republic of Germany* (1981).[12] The applicant wished to have his ashes scattered in a garden rather than in a graveyard. That wish did not fall within the ambit of Article 9, with the Commission noting that, while the applicant's desired action had 'a strong personal motivation', it did not express a 'coherent view on fundamental problems' (138). This requirement is somewhat problematic for it seems to set an extremely high standard for something to qualify as a 'belief' and arguably presupposes a quasi-religious approach to belief systems. As Carolyn Evans notes (2001, 59), the applicant in this case objected to lying in a graveyard that was full of Christian symbols. Such an objection would, undoubtedly, have been looked on more sympathetically if he had professed to an established non-Christian religion, and yet the belief remained unchanged and undiminished by its isolation from the mainstream. One means of elevating a personal belief to one more likely to fall within the ambit of Article 9 appears to be the formation of an association which will imply a level of formality that may assist in satisfying the *Campbell and Cosans* requirements (M. Evans, 1997, 292). In *Plattform Ärzte* (1988), an association of doctors with anti-abortionist views seemed to be viewed as falling within the scope of Article 9 even though it was a single-issue pressure group.[13] It is certainly a factor that may be of relevance to a belief in assisted dying, as will be discussed further below.

In terms of defining beliefs that fall within the ambit of Article 9, it appears that non-religious beliefs, and particularly those which are not in a formalised structure, are at a disadvantage. A reluctance to investigate, in a reasoned manner, what qualifies as a belief under Article 9 means that all too often the line reverts to a 'religion-plus-other-isms' (such as atheism and pacifism) position, excluding without reason the entire gamut of personalised non-religious beliefs. Regrettably this fails to make full use of the potential of Article 9s protection for a broader concept of freedom of conscience. It must be remembered that categorising something as a belief under Article 9 is only the first hurdle. The remaining hurdles of its manifestation, and a balancing with other societal interests to determine what is necessary in a democratic society, could serve to prevent the ambit of Article 9 becoming too wide without the need to define non-religious beliefs so restrictively.

'Manifesting' a belief

The boundaries between the different issues under consideration here are often fluid in court judgments. Thus, the question of whether there is a manifestation of belief will sometimes be answered with reference to whether the belief warrants protection under Article 9 rather than whether it is being manifested by the applicant. Indeed, this appears to be what occurred in the *Pretty* judgment, where the Court proclaimed that not all opinions or convictions constitute beliefs but then immediately followed this by concluding that the applicant's claims did not involve a form of manifestation of a religion or belief as required by Article 9 (*Pretty v UK*, 2002, 82). The impression is given therefore that the applicant's opinion did not qualify as a belief merely because it was not manifested by her desired action. Whether this is the approach intended by the Court or merely the result of the thoughtless drafting of its judgment is unclear.

Article 9(1) specifies four forms of manifestation of a religion or belief: through worship, teaching, practice or observance. It has been noted that these 'protected manifestations are connected to relatively traditional religious practices (particularly worship and observance)' (Evans, 2001, 66). While the use of the word 'practice' is broader than mere 'worship and observance', it too can present difficulties for non-religious beliefs. This is because different types of belief will require very different steps to be taken by their adherents to give effect to the belief system, and those steps taken by non-religious believers may look more like social or political action. The definition of a manifestation of belief was, until recently, focussed on an early European Commission of Human Rights' decision. *Arrowsmith v United Kingdom* involved the conviction of a pacifist for distributing, outside an army base, leaflets that promoted desertion and criticised the British army's involvement in Northern Ireland. While the Commission was willing to accord pacifism the status of a 'belief' under Article 9, it did not regard the distribution of the leaflets as a manifestation of that belief. The Commission held that the term 'practice' in Article 9 'does not cover each act which is motivated or influenced by a religion or belief' (1978, 71).[14] Its conclusion that the applicant's actions were not so covered seems to be based on the fact that the leaflets 'do not actually express the belief concerned' (71). Instead of generally proclaiming the idea of pacifism, the leaflets were specifically tailored to a campaign to end the violent conflict in Northern Ireland. For the Commission this meant that they could not be regarded as a manifestation of a pacifist belief. For the applicant, on the other hand, her belief in pacifism 'was not an abstract hope or wish … but was integrally and inseparably bound up with political action' (31). The Commission was swayed by the fact that other people, not sharing the applicant's pacifist belief but opposed to UK government policy in Northern Ireland, could have distributed the leaflets in question.

This, however, must be a red herring because it should not matter why other people might have undertaken the act in question when it is abundantly clear why the particular applicant has done so. She did it because of her pacifist belief, as the Commission recognises when stating that her actions were motivated by her belief. Why, then, is that not a manifestation of her belief, merely because others might have been motivated by other considerations to perform the same action? Mr Opsahl, in a separate opinion to the decision, was entirely correct to argue for a more contextual approach in which the actions are looked at in the individual circumstances of the case, such that the distribution of these leaflets could be a manifestation of belief for the applicant, but not for others (Separate Opinion, *Arrowsmith*, 3).

Such a contextual approach was adopted by the Court in *Jakobski v Poland* (2010).[15] The applicant had been denied a meat-free diet in prison, which he claimed was contrary to the requirements of his Buddhist faith. Although there are many reasons why a person might request a vegetarian diet, and not all would necessarily be a manifestation of belief, the Court looked specifically at why the applicant had made such a request and recognised that 'the applicant's decision to adhere to a vegetarian diet can be regarded as motivated or inspired by a religion and was not unreasonable' (45). This was undoubtedly a step forward in terms of defining what can amount to a manifestation of belief, although the Court did moderate this statement with recognition that 'Buddhism is one of the world's major religions officially recognised in numerous countries' (45), thus implying that a manifestation of this belief might be easier to establish than a manifestation of a non-religious belief or a minority religious-belief.

The contextual approach requires that the applicant's individual motives be investigated. As Article 9 does not only protect the manifestation of a religious belief but also, at the very least, manifestation of secular principles akin to religion, vegetarianism for principled moral reasons (such as a view that it is morally wrong to kill animals for food) should also be protected. It is hard to avoid the conclusion that this would be a higher hurdle to overcome, however. By analogy, one might compare the proselytising in *Arrowsmith* with that in *Kokkinakis*, involving a Jehovah's Witness: a very similar action, namely, a focussed attempt to convert others to one's cause, is treated as a manifestation when motivated by a religious belief, and not when motivated by a secular belief. It would be possible, however, to select a vegetarian diet not only for a religious or philosophical reason (such as a moral objection to killing animals for food) but also for a non-principled reason – because one does not like meat, for example, or because it is cheaper – and it is here where the line would more appropriately be drawn between actions falling within the ambit of Article 9 and those outside of it.

In the landmark case of *Eweida and others v United Kingdom*, the European Court of Human Rights had the opportunity to re-think its approach to the question of defining a manifestation of belief. The case involved four applicants sharing a Christian faith and complaining of interference with their desire to either wear a crucifix at work or to decline to offer their professional services (as a registrar or relationship counsellor) on an equal basis irrespective of sexuality. Although the four applications are varied on their facts, all shared a common problem that their desired actions were not explicitly required by their faith. A narrow approach to manifestation of Christian belief might well have excluded these activities from the ambit of Article 9, but the Court adopted a much broader approach, holding that manifestation requires only that the act in question 'be intimately linked to the religion or belief' (82). The Court further explained that 'the existence of a sufficiently close and direct nexus between the act and the underlying belief must be determined on the facts of each case' (82). This removes all doubt that the proper approach to the question of the manifestation of a belief is a contextual one that considers why the applicant seeks to perform the act in question and assesses only the closeness of the link between the act and the belief, rather than enquiring more generally into the appropriate way of manifesting a specific faith or belief. With this broader approach to manifestation, the wearing of a cross in public was accepted as a manifestation of belief, even though not all Christians will feel compelled to do so. This must be the correct approach, and again leaves scope for a line to be drawn between the applicants and others who may choose to wear a cross for reasons of fashion or provocation.

As Carolyn Evans has noted (2001, 122), for individualistic beliefs, 'there may be no higher authority or set of rules that can be consulted to determine what behaviour is required by the belief.' For this very reason, a focus on the applicant's motives for acting and an enquiry as to the connection between the underlying belief and the subsequent action is a vital step forward for individualistic believers. *Eweida* opens the door to a more relaxed approach to defining a manifestation of belief, that focusses on the extent of the connection between a belief and an act that the applicant seeks to perform due to that belief. In theory, therefore, and despite the lack of solid support from the case law, a secular belief, without an 'ism' attached, could be sufficiently closely connected to a desired action to afford it some protection under

Article 9. The way in which such an approach could be applied to end-of-life decision-making will now be considered.

Manifesting a belief by requesting assistance to die with dignity

The increasing influence of human rights on health care decisions has added an important new dimension to end-of-life decision-making. It has become clear that choices about how to die, including seeking a dignified death by means of suicide, fall within the protection of Article 8's right to respect for private life (*Pretty v UK*, 2002).[16] States have a wide margin of appreciation on this issue, and conflicting obligations under Article 2's right to life (*Haas v Switzerland*, 2011, 54), but when assisted suicide is permitted by a state, there will be procedural obligations surrounding its imposition to ensure, for example, that there has been a voluntary decision made by a person with capacity.

Given the potential applicability of these two Articles, there has been little focus on Article 9's relevance to end-of-life decisions. And yet, the cases that are brought to the national courts often highlight the significance of issues of faith, belief and conscience to the dying process. For example, a refusal of life-saving treatment may be based on a religious belief as, for example, in respect of a refusal of a blood transfusion by a Jehovah's Witness. In addition, a determination of the best interests of a patient who lacks capacity is required under the Mental Capacity Act 2005 to take into account his or her beliefs and values – a broad phrase which is not defined – alongside his or her wishes and feelings.[17] Thus a previous belief system may be relevant to a decision to withdraw life-sustaining treatment from a patient who is no longer capable of manifesting those beliefs. In its religious context, therefore, Article 9 has significant potential application to end-of-life decisions. However, the focus of this chapter is on the manifestation of non-religious beliefs in the context of assisted dying and in this context the application of Article 9 faces greater obstacles.

The desire to be assisted to die is increasingly being asserted in cases brought before domestic courts and informed by the ECHR, but generally to little avail. In *Pretty v UK* (2002), the European Court of Human Rights held that the interference with the applicant's Article 8 rights was justified in order to protect other vulnerable members of society. Although this position was explicitly doubted by some members of the Supreme Court in *R (Nicklinson) v Ministry of Justice; R (AM) v Director of Public Prosecutions* (2014), a majority were not prepared to declare the existing law to be incompatible with the Convention. The cause is not helped by the inherent ambiguity in the concept of dignity generally,[18] and specifically in its application to the dying process. As noted above, in the *Pretty* case, the European Court of Human Rights summarily rejected the argument that the applicant's views on assisted suicide amounted to 'beliefs' protected under Article 9, and that her claims involved a form of manifestation of beliefs. As discovered above, while Article 9's protection explicitly extends beyond religion, the ECHR institutions have been reluctant to investigate, in any reasoned way, what qualifies as a belief under this Article, leading to a tendency to protect only 'religion-plus-other-isms' and exclude other personalised non-religious beliefs. This presents a problem for an applicant in a position such as Dianne Pretty or Tony Nicklinson, from the cases mentioned above. Their desire to die a dignified death is fundamental to their lives, but does not immediately appear to fall within the narrow, and inflexible, scope of 'beliefs' as interpreted in Strasbourg. Is it possible that a wish to die with dignity could qualify as a 'belief'?

The elemental nature of such a desire is well-expressed by Ronald Dworkin, who famously stated (1993, 217) that '[m]aking someone die in a way that others approve, but he believes a horrifying contradiction of his life, is a devastating, odious form of tyranny.' He takes this view because of a recognition that while 'we live our whole lives in the shadow of death; it is also true that we die in the shadow of our whole lives' (199). Thus it is important that we die 'appropriately' – 'that death keeps faith with the way we want to have lived' (199). Decisions about life and death are therefore of vital importance to us because 'we think it crucial to make them in character, and for ourselves' (239). The *Nicklinson* case highlighted the tragic impotence felt by some individuals who were denied the possibility of dying in the manner they chose by English law's criminal prohibition of assisted suicide and voluntary active euthanasia, when one claimant took drastic action after his case failed before the High Court. As explained in the Court of Appeal,

> Sadly, following the judgment below in which he was unsuccessful, Tony Nicklinson took the view that he was condemned to a life of increasing misery. He refused nutrition, fluids and medical treatment and died of pneumonia less than a week later, on 22 August 2012.
>
> *Nicklinson* (2013, 12)[19]

Such an immediate and tragic response further highlights the significant role that the timing and manner of death represents in the lives of such claimants.

As noted above, 'belief' under Article 9 must 'attain a certain level of cogency, seriousness, cohesion and importance' (*Eweida*, 81). The requirements of both seriousness and importance seem to be satisfied in the context of a right to be assisted in dying. A wish to die with dignity is sufficiently serious to qualify as it is far from a trivial matter, and the personal consequences will be profound. Choices about life and death, as well as the dying process are similarly important, if not fundamental. It is hard to imagine a more important issue for a human being. It is also an opinion, or desire, that tackles the harder issues in life, and thus might be compared in that sense to more traditional religious belief systems.

However, the other two requirements of cogency and cohesion are much harder to satisfy. Whether a wish to be assisted to die presents a coherent and cogent view on the fundamental problem of dying is highly debatable. There are conflicting opinions on whether a quicker death by means of intervention by others is more or less dignified than a palliative approach to care. The concept of human dignity is becoming more and more visible as an underlying foundation for all human rights but its application will remain ambiguous while it is utilised both to empower individual choice and to constrain it (Beyleveld and Brownsword, 2001). In the context of end-of-life decision-making by adults retaining capacity, it is the empowerment interpretation of dignity that is called into battle to bolster the case for legalised assisted dying. However, its role of constraining individual choices to act in undignified manners means that the inherent ambiguity about dignity in the dying process remains, and might preclude the classification of a wish to die with dignity as a coherent and cogent approach to dying. The case would be stronger with a more formalised belief system to support it. As with the anti-abortionist doctors in *Plattform Ärzte* (discussed above), an organisation provides formality, and thus arguably cogency, to a single-issue belief that is inherently individualised and ambiguous. In the context of assisted dying, such organisations undoubtedly exist, with the most prominent one being 'Dignity in Dying' which is campaigning for the legalisation of assisted dying for those with less than six months to live.[20] The British Humanist Association also explicitly supports the right of each individual to make his or her own judgment about whether life should be prolonged in the face of pointless suffering.[21]

As discussed above, the question of whether a belief in the right to die in the manner and at the time of one's own choosing would be 'manifested' by the action of dying with assistance would now be answered solely by looking at why a specific individual wishes to seek assistance in dying. Not everyone that does so will be able to establish that intimate link with an underlying belief. It may well require proof of an underlying belief in the right to die to exist independently of the request for assistance but to be closely connected to it. Although Article 9 protects the freedom to change religion or belief, it seems likely that some enduring belief in the importance of a death with dignity, achieved by intervention if necessary, would be beneficial. It appears, however, that, post-*Eweida*, the major obstacle will not be the connection between the belief and its manifestation, but rather the preliminary problem of gaining 'belief' status for something as intangible and ambiguous as choosing how to die.

Respecting conscience rather than belief

If a wish to die with dignity falls short of qualification as a belief, is there any other protection that could be offered to it under Article 9? Could it be conceived as a conscientious objection? Nehushtan (2008, 245) defines this concept by explaining that

> the conscientious objector seeks an exemption from the law not because of his status ... but because he holds an alternative set of basic values or an

> alternative way of balancing basic values – which are all part of his conscience, or the result of it – that conflicts with the ends, the means or the values of a specific law and ultimately contradict the demands of that law.

The most obvious example of a conscientious objection is to military service, and the European Court of Human Rights has acknowledged that such an objection may find protection under Article 9. In *Bayatyan v Armenia*, a case brought by a Jehovah's Witness who was imprisoned for his refusal to perform military service on conscientious grounds, the Grand Chamber noted that Article 9 does not explicitly include a right to conscientious objection, but held that opposition to military service could constitute a belief under Article 9 in circumstances 'where it is motivated by a serious and insurmountable conflict between the obligation to serve in the army and a person's conscience or his deeply and genuinely held religious or other beliefs' (110). In *Bayatyan*, the Court acknowledged that the applicant's objection to military service was motivated by his religious beliefs as a Jehovah's Witness, and the Court recognised that those beliefs were 'genuinely held and were in serious and insurmountable conflict with his obligation to perform military service' (111). The lack of any alternative to military service in Armenia at the relevant time meant that the restriction on the applicant's right to manifest his religious beliefs was not a proportionate limitation of his Article 9 rights.[22] The Court may, as usual, have been swayed by the existence of a recognised religion providing the foundation for the applicant's conscientious objection. The reasoning should hold, however, without this foundation. It is possible to imagine a 'serious and insurmountable conflict' between the state's prohibition of dying with assistance, and a person's conscience or 'deeply and genuinely held' beliefs. Exemptions from legal obligations are not restricted to military service and may also apply to equal treatment provisions, drug use, and animal slaughter (Nehushtan, 2008, 246). In the health care context, there is already a precedent relating to participation in terminations of pregnancy,[23] while proposals to legalise a form of assisted dying invariably include a conscientious objection clause to enable members of the medical profession to avoid acting contrary to their conscience in assisting a death.[24]

In *Bayatyan*, the Court distinguished the applicant's situation from one that concerns a legal obligation 'which has no specific conscientious implications in itself, such as a general tax obligation' (111). Assisted dying seems to carry analogous conscientious implications as military service, and is easily distinguishable from the obligation to pay tax. The very nature of conscientious exemptions from general legal rules presupposes, in the words of Nehushtan (2008, 253),

> that the ruler does not share the conscientious objector's values or his way of balancing between values, and considers that it would be unbearable and indeed intolerable if everyone shared the objector's kind of conscience and reasoning.

Viewing assisted dying as such an exemption from the general rules about death and dying would be an effective way of securing the state's commitment to (an already limited) sanctity of life principle, and to the positive obligations of an international right to life. It could send a message that seeking an early, or 'unnatural' death is not the preferred option by society, and that all life is valued, but that there is tolerance of the views of a minority whose conscience dictates otherwise. In western societies where the generally applicable law is frequently founded on Judaeo-Christian values, a limited exemption for those whose belief systems have different priorities (e.g. human dignity over sanctity of life) could serve a vital role in ensuring that we can all live freely, guided by our own consciences in relation to the dying process. It could even be viewed, perversely perhaps, as a better option for the permissibility of assisted dying than by virtue of Article 8 because the latter provision's focus on individual autonomy would potentially open the door to anyone who chose this type of death, while Article 9 would only protect those whose conscience genuinely requires a limited exemption from the usual legal rules. A workable right to assistance in dying built on Article 8's protection for autonomy would necessitate the imposition of boundaries to restrict the right along the lines of terminal illness or unbearable suffering, which would sit uneasily within an autonomy context, whereas a right built on Article 9 comes complete with integrated restrictions along the lines of the strength of the connection with an individual's conscience.

The categorisation of a wish to die as an element of 'conscience' rather than 'belief' might even have stronger implications. In a controversial 'Joint Partly Dissenting Opinion' in the *Eweida* case, Judges Vučinić and De Gaetano argued that there is a fundamental difference between freedom of religion and freedom of conscience. They suggested that the omission of the word 'conscience' from Article 9(2) in the context of manifestation is significant. In their view, while the prescriptions of religion may be subject to limitations, those of conscience cannot be so limited. These judges explain conscience as 'moral conscience': 'what enjoins a person at the appropriate moment to do good, and to avoid evil' (2). Actions based on such a conscience are not, in their view, subject to limitation by the state (3). Applying this approach, the dissenting judges regarded the issue raised by the applicant Ms Ladele who, as a registrar, refused to officiate over civil partnerships, to be one of conscientious objection, as well as manifestation of a religious belief. The desire to exempt herself from the equality laws which protected same-sex couples might indeed be viewed more fittingly as a conscientious objection rather than a manifestation of a Christian belief. The sheer objectionability of it fits well with this being an exception to the mainstream; an opinion not shared by society as a whole nor by the laws of the state. Nonetheless, these judges go too far in arguing that the right of conscientious objection is not subject to the usual proportionality restrictions in Article 9(2), and there are other weaknesses in their opinions that raise significant concerns.[25] Freedom of conscience is indeed an important value, but not an absolute one.

Conclusion

Ultimately it seems unlikely that an individualistic belief in assisted dying will be afforded protection as a 'belief' under Article 9 under the Court's current interpretation of it. This is regrettable not only in the context of assisted dying (which will, after all, gain some recognition, albeit divorced from a personal belief system, under Article 8) but also more broadly for what it tells us about the place of non-religious and non-formalised beliefs under Article 9. This provision, as it has been interpreted thus far, does not do a good job of protecting freedom of conscience alongside freedom of religion. The developments in the interpretation of the word 'manifestation' have signalled a relaxation in limits on actions in the public sphere motivated by religious beliefs. The focus now is almost exclusively on the balancing of individual faith with public interests under Article 9(2) as, for example, with the cases concerning religious dress and symbols (*S.A.S. v France*, 2014).[26] These are vital issues and this discussion should not be seen to underplay them. However, Article 9 as drafted explicitly extends beyond freedom of religion and into the wider, and yet more personalised, sphere of individual conscience. Although there may be some scope for formalised non-religious 'isms' to gain protection under Article 9, most notably atheism, other fundamental aspects of a person's conscience seem to remain excluded from the provision. While it is true that often these other aspects may fall within the ambit of other Convention rights, such as a right to respect for private life (with its protection for autonomous choices) or freedom of expression (with its protection for expression of ideas and opinions), there is no legitimate reason why they should not also be respected as aspects of a person's conscience under Article 9's freedom of thought, conscience and religion.

Religion is often fundamental to a person's life and death, but so too are other secular ideas such as dignity, autonomy, pacifism, atheism, compassion and equality. A person who chooses to live their life guided by a non-religious principle should have the importance of that principle recognised as they face death. A conscientious objection to laws about dying, especially when those laws are built on Christian foundations and reasoning, would be a restrained but welcome response to the present assisted dying debate. The dissenting judges in *Eweida* go too far in regarding it as an absolute right because one's conscience, the same as one's religion, must, in a democratic society, be able to co-exist with other people in society with different beliefs and potentially conflicting needs. But a limited right to conscientious objection to the criminal prohibition on assisted dying is worth further consideration. It would be not only more demanding of the individual wishing to assert it than an autonomy-based right to die under Article 8 but also more respectful of the fundamental role of beliefs when one faces death. If there is merit in a general prohibition on assisted dying, then a narrow exception for those whose conscience genuinely requires it might be a better first step than a more general prioritisation of autonomous choices about how to die. The manner and timing of our deaths are not issues to be taken lightly, and no one facing such a decision would do so. Guided by religious faith or secular principles, our reasoned and fundamental choices will reflect our conscience. It is time that this was duly recognised in the interpretation of Article 9, which is, after all, a right to freedom of conscience as well as to freedom of religion.

Notes

1 The sanctity of life, an ethical principle which originally stemmed from religious doctrine, refers to a recognition of the special value inherent in human life. However, the principle is now also widely respected on a secular basis.
2 *Pretty v United Kingdom* (App. 2346/02), 29 April 2002, (2002) 35 EHRR 1, ECHR 2002-III.
3 Protection of the rights of other vulnerable members of society is accepted as a legitimate aim for state interference with autonomous choices to die with assistance, and the existence of a wide margin of appreciation on this topic means that states are given significant discretion to regulate assisted dying. See *Pretty v United Kingdom*, (App. 2346/02), 29 April; 2002, (2002) 35 EHRR 1, ECHR 2002-III, paras. 68–78 and *Haas v Switzerland* (App. no. 31322/07) Judgment of 20 January 2011, ECHR 2011, para. 55.
4 *Kokkinakis v Greece*, (App. 14307/88), 25 May 1993, Series A No 260-A, (1994) 17 EHRR 397 at [31].
5 *Buscarini and others v San Marino*, (App. 2464 5/94), 18 February 1999, (2000) 30 EHRR 208, ECHR 1999-I; *Grzelak v Poland* (App. 7710/02), 15 June 2010.
6 *Arrowsmith v United Kingdom* (App. 7050/75), Decision of 12 October 1978 (1980) 19 DR 5.
7 *Pretty v United Kingdom* (App. 2346/02), 29 April 2002, (2002) 35 EHRR 1, ECHR 2002-III at [82].
8 *Eweida and others v United Kingdom (App. 48420/10, 59842/10, 51671/10 and 36516/10) 15 January 2013, ECHR 2012 (extracts).*, para. 81. See also *Lautsi v Italy* (App. 30814/06), 18 March 2011 [GC], ECHR 2011 (extracts), 50 E.H.R.R. 42 at [58]; *Jakobski v Poland* (App 18429/06) 7 December 2010 at [44]; and *Bayatyan v Armenia* (App. 23459/03), 7 July 2011 [GC], ECHR 2011 at [110].
9 *Campbell and Cosans v United Kingdom* (1982) Series A, No. 48 (25 February 1982).
10 *R v Secretary of State for Education and Employment, ex parte Williamson* [2005] UKHL 15.
11 *McFeeley v United Kingdom* Applic. 8317/78, Decision of 15 May 1980, (1980) 20 D.R.44.
12 *X v Federal Republic of Germany* Applic. 8741/79, Decision of 10 March 1981, (1981) 24 D.R.137.
13 *Plattform "Ärzte für das Leben" v. Austria* (App. 10126/82), 21 June 1988, Series A no. 139.
14 *Arrowsmith v United Kingdom* App. 7050/75, Decision of 12 October 1978 (1980) 19 DR 5 at [71].
15 *Jakobski v Poland* (App. 18429/06) 7 December 2010.
16 In addition to *Pretty*, see *Haas v Switzerland*; *Koch v Germany*, and, at a domestic level, *R (Purdy) v Director of Public Prosecutions* [2009] UKHL 45; *R (Nicklinson) v Ministry of Justice; R (AM) v Director of Public Prosecutions* [2014] UKSC 38.
17 Mental Capacity Act 2005, Section 4(6)(b).
18 See McCrudden (2008), Dupre (2009) and Beyleveld and Brownsword (2001).
19 *R (on the application of Nicklinson and another) v A Primary Care Trust* [2013] EWCA Civ 961 at [12].

20 The organisation's website (https://www.dignityindying.org.uk/) (last visited 27 June 2019) claims an active membership of over 20,000.
21 See https://humanism.org.uk/campaigns/public-ethical-issues/assisted-dying/ (last visited 27 June 2019).
22 The Court has found similar violations in relation to conscientious objection in two cases against Turkey: *Erçep v Turkey* (App.43965/04), 22 November 2011 and *Savda v Turkey* (App.42730/05), 12 June 2012. More recently, see also *Adyan and Others v. Armenia* (App.75604/11), 12 October 2017.
23 Abortion Act 1967 (as amended), Section 4.
24 Smith (2015) has also investigated doctor's claims of conscience in relation to the withdrawal of life-sustaining treatment.
25 The intemperate language used by these partially dissenting judges in *Eweida* does somewhat detract from the general weight to be attached to their opinions. The joint opinion is undermined by some regrettable comments that criticise the public authority for its approach 'which clearly favoured "gay rights" over fundamental human rights' (ibid at [5]). The dilemma is more accurately described as a conflict between two different fundamental rights.
26 See, most recently, *S.A.S. v France* (App. 43835), 1 July 2014 [GC].

References

Ahdar, R. (2018). Is Freedom of Conscience Superior to Freedom of Religion? *Oxford Journal of Law and Religion*, 7(1), 124–142.

Beyleveld, D., and Brownsword, R. (2001). *Human Dignity in Bioethics and Biolaw*. Oxford: Oxford University Press.

Dupre, C. (2009). Unlocking Human Dignity: Towards a Theory for the 21st Century. *European Human Rights Law Review, 2*, 190–205.

Dworkin, R. (1993). *Life's Dominion: An Argument about Abortion and Euthanasia*. London: HarperCollins.

Evans, C. (2001). *Freedom of Religion under the European Convention on Human Rights*. Oxford: Oxford University Press.

Evans, M. D. (1997). *Religious Liberty and International Law in Europe*. Cambridge: Cambridge University Press.

Maher, J. (2014). Eweida and Others: A New Era for Article 9? *International & Comparative Law Quarterly, 63*(1), 213–233.

McCrudden, C. (2008). Human Dignity and Judicial Interpretation of Human Rights. *European Journal of International Law, 19*(4), 655–724.

Nehushtan, Y. (2008). Secular and Religious Conscientious Exemptions: Between Tolerance and Equality. In P. Cane et al. (eds) *Law and Religion in Theoretical and Historical Context* (243–267). Cambridge: Cambridge University Press.

Previn, M. P. (1995). Assisted Suicide and Religion: Conflicting Conceptions of the Sanctity of Human Life. *Georgetown Law Journal, 84*, 589.

Smith, S. W. (2015). A Bridge Too Far: Individualised Claims of Conscience. *Medical Law Review, 23*(2), 283–302.

10 Euthanasia, biopolitics, and care of the self

Thomas F. Tierney

Introduction: biopolitics and thanatopolitics

In this chapter, I will interpret the evolution of modern euthanasia discourse through a cluster of concepts that Michel Foucault articulated in the second half of the 1970s – biopower, biopolitics, governmentality. Foucault developed this conceptual framework primarily in three of his posthumously published courses at the Collège de France: *Society Must be Defended* in 1975–1976 (2003); *Security, Territory, Population* in 1977–1978 (2007); and *The Birth of Biopolitics* in 1978–1979 (2008). But the concepts of biopower and biopolitics first appeared in print in 1976, in the final section of the first volume of *The History of Sexuality* (1980). He introduced these concepts to describe a fundamental shift in the way power was exercised, from a repressive form that was ultimately based on "one of the characteristic privileges of sovereign power [which] was the right to decide life and death" (1980, 135) to a modern form of "power that exerts a positive influence on life, that endeavors to administer, optimize, and multiply it, subjecting it to precise controls and comprehensive regulations" (1980, 136–137). In the final lecture of his course from the same year, *Society Must be Defended*, Foucault described this shift as "one of the greatest transformations political right underwent in the nineteenth century," from the sovereign's right to "take life or let live," to the biopolitical right "to make live and to let die" (2003, 241; also 1980, 138).

The following year, in his course *Security, Territory, Population*, Foucault introduced the concept of "governmentality" to describe a specific form of biopolitical rationality that emerged under the more general shift from sovereignty to biopower. Mercantilism had been the dominant form of political rationality throughout Europe in the seventeenth and eighteenth centuries (Foucault, 2007, 32), and was primarily concerned with augmenting the wealth and power of the sovereign, and treated subjects in the sovereign's territory as a resource to be used toward those ends (Foucault, 2007, 68–69, 337–339). Toward the end of the eighteenth century, an alternative form of political rationality – governmentality – emerged, which was concerned with promoting the interests, health, and longevity of the population in a given territory for the sake of that population, rather than that of the sovereign.

DOI: 10.4324/9780429329739-10

Absolutely crucial to this shift in focus from the sovereign's interests to those of the population was the discipline of statistics, which we will later see also indirectly impacted the status of euthanasia.

While Foucault emphasized the life administering and optimizing nature of biopower and governmentality, he did acknowledge that this positive form of power also greatly expanded the capacity to take life. "[W]ars were never as bloody as they have been since the nineteenth century, and … never before did regimes visit such holocausts on their own populations," Foucault wrote in *The History of Sexuality* (1980, 136–137). And in the final lecture of *Society Must be Defended*, he claimed, "Nazism was in fact the paroxysmal development of the new power mechanisms that had been established since the eighteenth century" (2003, 259, 260). Foucault seemed to offer these remarks as a cautionary tale about biopower, not as a condemnation of this form of power altogether. However, Giorgio Agamben took up this "thanatopolitical" dimension of biopower in his 1995 book, *Homo Sacer*, where he argued that biopolitics necessarily culminated in the Nazi death camps, which were "the pure, absolute, and impassable biopolitical space … of modernity" (1998, 123). For Agamben, the crucial step in this process was the 1920 publication of a book by legal scholar Karl Binding and medical professor Alfred Hoche, titled *Authorization for the Annihilation of Life Unworthy of Being Lived*, which argued for the legalization of euthanasia. "Euthanasia signals the point at which biopolitics necessarily turns into thanatopolitics," Agamben proclaimed, "… This is why the problem of euthanasia is an absolutely modern problem, which Nazism, as the first radically biopolitical state, could not fail to pose" (1998, 142–143).

While Agamben may be right that Binding and Hoche's book marks the point when "the concept [of euthanasia] makes its first appearance on the European juridical scene" (1998, 137), the concept was actually discussed throughout the modern period, although not primarily in a juridical sense. In fact, euthanasia was framed in terms that correspond with the long development of biopower and governmentality that Foucault presented in his late-1970s courses, and by tracing this co-evolution of euthanasia and biopower I hope to provide an "affirmative biopolitical" alternative to Agamben's thanatopolitical perspective on euthanasia.

The crisis of the pastorate and spiritual euthanasia: More, Bacon, and Marx

About a third of the way through *Security, Territory, Population* Foucault claimed that a more accurate title for this course would have been "the history of 'governmentality'" (2007, 108). But Foucault actually spent the largest part of this course – four of the thirteen lectures – discussing the history of pastoral techniques, which suggests that the course might also have been called "the history of the pastorate." He traced the origins of the pastorate to the shepherd-flock model of leadership that was "frequently found throughout the Mediterranean East" (2007, 123), but emphasized that "the real history of the pastorate as the source of a specific type of power over men, as a model and matrix of procedures for the government of men, really only begins with Christianity" (2007, 147–148). Foucault discussed the development of the Christian pastorate in great detail (2007, 163–185), but stressed that throughout its history it was challenged by "counter-conducts," such as gnosticism, mysticism, and various forms of extreme asceticism (2007, 196, 201–216). The Reformation was, of course, "the greatest revolt of conduct the Christian West has known" (2007, 196), and afterward "the pastorate opened up … burst open, broke up," creating a "crisis of the pastorate" (2007, 193). It was in this crisis period of the Christian pastorate that the early-modern discussion of euthanasia began.

Euthanasia was widely practiced in ancient Greece and Rome, and the Hippocratic Oath's injunction against physicians giving deadly drugs to patients, even on request, was an attempt to curb a common practice (Battin, 1994, 16, 59, 128 n. 42). The Christian tradition condemned euthanasia, of course, but the first early-modern figure to endorse the intentional hastening of death for the dying was, ironically, the martyr Thomas More. In 1516, the year before Luther nailed his 95 theses to the door of the Wittenberg cathedral, More published *Utopia*, introducing another form of counter-conduct that would challenge existing social arrangements by contrasting them with an idealized, fictional society discovered by a traveler. Among the features recounted by More's traveler, Rafael Hythloday, was the unusual treatment of the dying on the island of Utopia:

> [T]hey treat the sick with great kindness and leave nothing undone to restore their health, whether it is by drugs or by dieting. If anyone is suffering from an incurable disease, they console him by sitting with him, talking to him and supplying all the comforts they can. But if a disease is not merely beyond treatment, but also a constant source of pain and agony, the priests and magistrates remind him that he is not up to all the tasks of life, is troublesome to others and a burden to himself, and is now outliving his own death. Then they advise him not to resolve to feed that pestilence and sickness any longer, nor to hesitate to die, since life is a torment to him. They bid him to take good hope and release himself from that bitter life, as if from a prison or torture rack, or at least give his permission for others to remove him. They tell him that since he is going to put an end not to pleasure but to punishment, he would be well advised to do it; and since in that matter he is going to take the advice of priests, the interpreters of God, his action will also be pious and holy. Those who are persuaded by this either end their own lives by abstinence from food, or else are released from it while they are asleep, without any sensation of death. But they never remove anyone against his will, nor are they any the less considerate to him. It is considered honorable to yield to persuasion and die like this.
>
> More (1965, 88)

The Utopians clearly took a pastoral stance toward the dying, and it important to note that this authority was exercised by primarily by priests and secondarily by magistrates, but not by physicians, who are not mentioned in Hythloday's account. And the end-of-life practices of the Utopians combined two distinct forms of euthanasia that W. Bruce Fye would later distinguish as "spiritual euthanasia," which refers to the comfort and consolation offered to the dying, and "active euthanasia," which is the intentional hastening of death (1979, 492). But even though the Utopians endorsed both spiritual and active euthanasia for the dying, they condemned those who took their own life without authorization from the priests and magistrates, and "flung unburied into some bog" the disgraced bodies of suicides (More, 1965, 88).

It was not until the seventeenth century that physicians were charged with taking responsibility for the death of dying individuals, and one of the first to articulate this duty was Francis Bacon, who is actually credited with coining the English term "euthanasia" in *The Advancement of Learning* (1605) (Emanuel, 1994, 793–794; Vanderpool, 1995, 554 and 1997, 59, n. 18). Bacon was critical of the reluctance of physicians to attend to the dying, and encouraged them to assist with what he called *euthanasia exteriori*, or external euthanasia, which provided physical comfort, in distinction from spiritual euthanasia which helps a person prepare for the departure of their soul from the body.

> I esteem it the office of a physician not only to restore health, but to mitigate pain, and dolours; and not only when such mitigation may conduce to recovery, but when it may serve to make a fair and easy passage. For it is no small felicity which Augustus Caesar was wont to wish to himself, that same *Euthanasia*; and which was specially noted in the death of Antoninus Pius, whose death was after the fashion and semblance of a kindly and pleasant sleep. … But the physicians, contrariwise, do make a kind of scruple and religion to stay with the patient after the disease is deplored; whereas, in my judgment, they ought both to inquire the skill, and to give the attendances, for the facilitating and assuaging of the pains and agonies of death.
>
> Bacon (1857, I, 204)

What Bacon meant by *euthanasia exteriori*, therefore, was a death that was eased and facilitated, but not hastened or caused, by physicians; he did not advocate "active euthanasia," in Fye's terminology. Nevertheless, he was condemned as a heretic for these views, and placed on the *Index Librorum Prohibitorum* in 1688 (Fattori, 2016, 115–118).

Bacon's idea that physicians should take a primary role in providing comfort and solace to the dying was not seriously discussed in the medical profession until the early-nineteenth century, when more than a dozen German dissertations on the topic were written between 1820 and 1840 (Fye, 1979, 494 n. 9). The most influential of these treatises was the essay "Medical Euthanasia" by the physician Carl Friedrich Heinrich Marx (1796–1877), which appeared in 1826, nearly a century before Binding and Hoche's treatise. Marx complained that his colleagues had not yet heeded Bacon's advice, and still abandoned their patients once it became clear that health could not be restored. Though he lamented that there were not more of them, he praised "[t]hose very few" physicians who "with no shining ray of hope remaining, consider it their more lofty duty to lay to peaceful rest a life they can no longer save" (1952, 405). But Marx, like Bacon, did not countenance the intentional hastening of death, and only endorsed "that science, called euthanasia, which checks oppressing features of illness, relieves pain, and renders the supreme and inescapable hour a most peaceful one" (1952, 405). Indeed, he was greatly disturbed by the idea that the physician "should ... be permitted, prompted either by other people's requests or by his own sense of mercy, to end the patient's pitiful condition by purposely and deliberately hastening death." "How can it be permitted," he asked, "that he who is by law required to preserve life be the originator of, or partner in, its destruction?" (1952, 413).

Marx did go beyond Bacon, however, by combining *euthanasia exteriori* with the spiritual euthanasia that had been the pastoral responsibility of priests and clerics. He described in detail the physical comfort that physicians ought to provide to the dying (1952, 406–409), but was also convinced that physicians were much better suited to providing "higher comfort" to the dying than were members of the clergy, and encouraged them to embrace this traditional pastoral responsibility. "Whoever refuses his part in this duty and assigns it solely to priests deprives himself of the most noble and rewarding aspect of his work," he wrote. "Where the priest, administering the sacraments, comes to the bedside to soothe the longing soul with the last solace of religion and of comfort, who will not see the patient's deep shock when he faces this quasi-harbinger of death?" (1952, 410). The physician, in contrast, is a familiar presence to the dying person, and is therefore best suited to bring cheer and hope to the patient's desperate circumstances, but once it was clear that death was indeed at hand, Marx argued that the physician take on the deathbed role formerly reserved for the clergy: "[f]inally, as a truthful interpreter of nature, [the physician] will relieve the troubled from his fear of complete extinction by giving him hope of immortality and of everlasting life of the souls" (1952, 411; see also Tierney, 2004).

As Harold Y. Vanderpool commented, the conception of euthanasia developed by early-nineteenth-century physicians like Marx first "reformulated, then assumed control over, the centuries-old *Ars moriendi* [the art of dying well] tradition of the West's religious heritages" (1995, 558). According to epidemiologist Abdel Omran's theory of "epidemiologic transition," this medicalization of the spiritual form of euthanasia occurred near the end of the long period he described as the "the Age of Pestilence and Famine," in which the major causes of death were infectious diseases, malnutrition, and complications attendant on childbirth. Women and children were particularly susceptible to these causes of mortality, and overall life expectancy hovered between 20 and 40 years (Omran, 1971, 516–517, 520–521; Olshansky and

Ault, 1987, 13–14). All this would change in the second half of the nineteenth century, however, when euthanasia became focused on the active hastening of death under the form of political rationality Foucault described as governmentality.

Governmentality and the active euthanasia debate

The shift from spiritual to active euthanasia was partly due to the development of those statistical techniques for studying populations that contributed to the corresponding transformation from a mercantilist concern with the strength of the sovereign to a governmental interest in the condition of the population. As Foucault described the medical implications of these new techniques, "statistics, which had hitherto functioned within administrative frameworks … of sovereignty now discovers and gradually reveals that the population possesses its own regularities: its death rate, its incidence of disease, its regularities of accidents" (2007, 104). One of the primary responses to this statistical revelation of the population was "the development of, if not sciences, then at least practices and types of intervention," which,

> will include, for example, social medicine, or what at the time was called public hygiene, and it will involve problems of demography, in short, everything that brings to light the state's new function of responsibility for the population in its naturalness; the population as a collection of subjects is replaced by the population as a set of natural phenomena.
>
> 2007, 352

The introduction of public hygiene practices under governmental rationality led to a significant increase in life expectancy, and a change in the leading causes of death, and ushered in a new epidemiological period that Omran dubbed "the Age of Receding Pandemics." During this period, which began in the 1850s and lasted through the 1920s, life expectancy increased to around 50 years in medically advanced nations, as growing numbers of people escaped epidemics and died of degenerative illnesses such as cancer, heart disease, and stroke (Omran, 1971, 516–517; Olshansky and Ault, 1987, 14).

Alongside the public health improvements which increased longevity, the mid-nineteenth century also saw several medical developments that changed the way physicians approached the dying. The introduction of statistical analysis into medicine, which began with Pierre Louis (1787–1872) in Paris and quickly spread to other nations in the first half of the nineteenth century, greatly improved the accuracy of diagnoses and prognoses and allowed physicians to much more confidently determine when a patient was indeed terminally ill. New techniques for treating pain also emerged in this period. In 1846, chloroform was discovered, and while it was initially used as an anesthetic in surgery, it was soon used to control pain in non-surgical situations such as childbirth, and would eventually be suggested as a means of controlling pain for the terminally ill. The development of the hypodermic syringe in the 1850s allowed the injection of morphine (which had been isolated in 1816) directly into the bloodstream (Fye, 1979, 496–498; also see Porter, 1997, 312–315, 365–368, and 663). The increase in the number of deaths caused by chronic degenerative diseases in the second half of the nineteenth century, along with the improved techniques for diagnosing and treating terminally ill patients, rendered the primarily spiritual euthanasia advocated by Bacon and Marx inadequate as a strategy for dealing with death. By the 1870s, conditions were ripe for a public discussion of More's idea of hastening death for the terminally ill, although the responsibility for performing this merciful task was now seen as falling on physicians, rather than priests and magistrates, as in *Utopia*.

One of the first to publicly advocate this active form of medical euthanasia was the English schoolmaster Samuel D. Williams, who contributed an article on euthanasia to a series of essays published in 1870 by members of Birmingham's "Speculative Club." Williams criticized those who claimed that a painful death was "the appointed lot of man," and argued that just as the initial religious opposition to the use of chloroform in childbirth had been overcome, so too should any reluctance to use new medical techniques to relieve the suffering of those who were dying in pain. He suggested,

> [t]hat in all cases of hopeless and painful illness it should be the recognized duty of the medical attendant, whenever so desired by the patient, to administer chloroform, or such other anaesthetic as may by-and-by supersede chloroform, so as to destroy consciousness at once, and put the sufferer at once to a quick and painless death; all needful precautions being adopted to prevent any possible abuse of such duty; and means being taken to establish, beyond the possibility of doubt or question, that the remedy was applied at the express wish of the patient.
>
> Anonymous (1873, 90–91)

In 1873, Lionel A. Tollemache published an essay in the *Fortnightly Review* under the title "A New Cure for Incurables," in which he endorsed Williams's arguments for euthanasia (Fye, 1979, 498–499).

Williams and Tollemache's essays elicited strong condemnations in British journals, such as the *Saturday Review* and *The Spectator*, and the arguments against euthanasia prefigured those that are currently directed against euthanasia and physician-assisted suicide (PAS), such as the impossibility of implementing safeguards that would prevent voluntary medical euthanasia from degenerating into the murder of the hopeless and vulnerable (Anonymous, 1873, 94–95). The American journal *Popular Science Monthly* published an anonymous review of the English euthanasia debate in 1873, which sparked a heated discussion in which American physicians' organizations took a central role (Fye, 1979, 499; Emanuel, 1994, 794–795; Vanderpool, 1997, 38). For instance, the *Medical and Surgical Reporter* published an editorial in 1873 which criticized physicians for "dodging the responsibility" of directly responding to the euthanasia requests of terminally ill patients (Fye, 1979), while the American Medical Association condemned Williams's proposal as a "ghastly" idea in an 1885 editorial in its *Journal of the American Medical Association (JAMA)*.

> [E]even though every member of the Birmingham Club should endorse this horrible principle, though every physician should declare his willingness to be a scientific assassin in these cases, and though every legislative body in the world should elevate this principle to a legal standard,

the JAMA editorialized, "it would still remain, and always will be murder" (JAMA Editorial, 1885, 383).

The thanatopolitical turn

While Agamben identified Binding and Hoche's arguments for euthanizing "lives not worth living" as the point when biopolitics reached its thanatopolitical denouement, other nations besides Germany began to embrace active medical euthanasia around the same time, but not as part of a state-sponsored social hygiene project. Rather, both medical and popular opinion were reconsidering euthanasia largely because of the success of the biopolitical administration of life in staving off death. In fact, Omran identified a third stage in the epidemiologic development of medically advanced nations that began in the 1920s and lasted through the 1960s, which he called the "Age of Degenerative and Man-Made Disease." The major causes of death in this epidemiologic period remained chronic degenerative diseases, but the mortality rates for all ages declined as deaths from heart disease, cancer, and stroke occurred much later in life. According to S. Jay Olshansky and A. Brian Ault, biodemographers who built on Omran's work, death in this period occurred for many people "near what was believed to be the end of the life span. The effect on longevity [was] a life expectancy for the population that reache[d] into seven decades of life and was expected to change little in the future" (Olshansky and Ault, 1987, 14; also see Omran, 1971, 517).

As increasing numbers of people were dying at what was thought to be the end of the "natural" life span, the idea of hastening the death of those who were suffering from a terminal illness became less disturbing, and many in the medical community began to reconsider their traditional hostility to euthanasia. This change became evident as early as 1917, when the American Association of Progressive Medicine (AAPM) overwhelmingly endorsed the legalization of active euthanasia at its sixth annual convention, and passed a resolution that would submit such a recommendation to all state legislatures (New York Times, 1917, 8, col. 2). Indeed, the legalization of active euthanasia became such a common topic in the medical community and the popular press that a 1926 *JAMA* discussion of letters from foreign correspondents was titled "Euthanasia Again," and began by pointing out that euthanasia was "[l]ike a recurring decimal" that regularly appeared as a controversy in the media (Anonymous, 1926, 1491).

By the 1930s, prominent physicians and medical associations in both England and the United States became much more actively involved in the legalization effort. In 1932, Dr. C. Killick Millard used the occasion of his address as President of the British Society of Medical Officers of Health to introduce a model statute for the legalization of euthanasia, and in response to his proposal the English Voluntary Euthanasia Legislation Society was formed in 1935 (Williams, 1974, 330–331; Emanuel, 1994, 796; McInerney, 1999, 140). The United States followed England's lead, and in 1938, the formation of the Euthanasia Society of America was announced by Dr. Charles Francis Potter, head of the First Humanist Society. Many prominent physicians and academics, as well as clergy, served on the board of directors, along with some board members from the British Voluntary Euthanasia Society (New York Times, 1938). Although both of these groups' attempts to legalize euthanasia were unsuccessful, there was substantial public support for euthanasia by the late 1930s. A 1939 American Institute of Public Opinion poll asked, "Do you favor mercy deaths under government supervision for hopeless invalids?" and 46% of Americans responded affirmatively, while 54% were opposed. A simultaneous poll conducted by the British Institute of Public Opinion revealed even greater popular support in England, where 69% favored government-regulated euthanasia (New York Times, 1939a, 1939b; also see Williams, 1974, 331–332).

Support for the legalization of active euthanasia plummeted when the enormity of the crimes committed by Nazi physicians was revealed, and euthanasia came to be seen by many as a treacherous first step on a slippery slope to genocide. This perspective was developed most forcefully by Leo Alexander, an American psychiatrist who served as a consultant to the Nuremberg Counsel for War Crimes in 1946–1947, and published an article in *The New England Journal of Medicine* in 1949 titled "Medical Science Under Dictatorship." Alexander described in great detail the various experiments German physicians conducted on living, conscious prisoners, and explained these physicians' mindset in terms that prefigured Agamben's thanatopolitical charge against biopolitics:

> [i]t started with the acceptance of the attitude, basic in the euthanasia movement, that there is such a thing as life not worthy to be lived. This attitude in its early stages concerned itself merely with the severely and chronically sick. Gradually the sphere of those to be included in this category was enlarged to encompass the socially unproductive, the ideologically unwanted, the racially unwanted and finally all non-Germans. But it is important to realize that the infinitely small wedged-in lever from which this entire trend of mind received its impetus was the attitude toward the nonrehabilitable sick.
>
> Alexander (1949, 44; also see 39–41)

The right to die movement and the return of the pastorate?

Olshansky and Ault identify the current epidemiological stage as "The Age of Delayed Degenerative Disease," which appeared in the last decades of the twentieth century, as "advances in medical technology and public health measures that favored the old over the young" led to the conviction that "life expectancy for some developed nations will reach well into the eighth decade" (Olshansky and Ault, 1987, 16). Additionally, advanced techniques for artificially maintaining respiration, feeding, and hydration made it possible to generate what Olshansky and Bruce A. Carnes call *manufactured time*, which describes "the additional days lived as a result of a successful medical intervention for a life-threatening condition" (2001, 123–124, also 119–136). Expectedly, these developments led to a resurgence of popular support for efforts to legalize "the right to die," which encompasses the non-controversial right to refuse or withdraw life-saving medical treatment, and the use of "living wills" that allow individuals to exercise that right in circumstances where they cannot speak for themselves, as well as the still controversial rights to PAS and medically administered euthanasia. Some countries, such as Germany, Switzerland, Austria, and Finland, as well as eight American states, have legalized PAS, while others, such as the Netherlands, Belgium, and Luxembourg, have legalized both PAS and euthanasia. It is indeed ironic that in 1973, Holland became the first nation to cease enforcing its law prohibiting PAS, and then legalized both PAS and active euthanasia in 2002, since in 1949 Alexander praised Dutch physicians for not following their German colleagues, and voluntarily surrendering their medical licenses to avoid association with the Nazi euthanasia program (1949, 44). While Dutch PAS and euthanasia practices initially involved patients who were terminally ill and suffering, there is currently concern in Holland about the growing number of euthanasia cases involving dementia and other psychiatric disorders (de Bellaigue, 2019).

As other biopolitically advanced nations seem likely to follow the Dutch lead as they progress into the age of delayed degenerative disease and manufactured time, there is a danger that the discussion of the right to die may be limited to that "recurring decimal" of a debate that pits the consensual ending of one's life when it is no longer worth living, against protecting the lives of the vulnerable and dependent. While it is certainly necessary to consider these competing views, from a Foucauldian perspective the rising right to die movement also provides an opportunity to reconsider those questions that were posed by the traditional pastorate, about how one ought to live one's life. Indeed, Foucault himself turned to the classical Greek concept of *epimeleia heautoui*, or "the care of the self," immediately after completing his courses on biopolitics in the late 1970s, and remained immersed in the study of those ancient "techniques of the self" for the remainder of his career. Though he did not focus on suicide or euthanasia in his study of ancient sources, when the right to die is viewed from a Foucauldian perspective on the pastorate and the care of the self, it does raise questions about medical authority's dominance regarding traditional pastoral concerns, particularly the concern about *the end of life*, understood both in the sense of a terminus, but more importantly, as a telos as well.

Although I am certainly not suggesting that religious authority ought to return to a position of prominence regarding euthanasia, one of the more intriguing perspectives on the issue was raised by a religious leader in the immediate aftermath of the Nazi atrocities. Unsurprisingly, most religious figures at this point condemned euthanasia as an affront to the "reverence for life" (e.g., Sperry, 1948), but Joseph Fletcher, an ordained Episcopalian priest who is considered by some to be the "esteemed patriarch of bioethics" (Jonsen, 1996, 50), offered a response that is surprisingly close to what I consider a Foucauldian perspective on euthanasia. In 1949, he delivered the Lowell Lectures at Harvard University, which were published in 1954 as a collection of essays, *Morals and Medicine.* One essay focused on euthanasia, and in it Fletcher recognized that this issue involved more than the humane treatment of the suffering, or the social problems caused by advanced medical techniques, or the influence of a pernicious political ideology; he realized that the public discussion of euthanasia exposed for critical reflection the underlying value of biopolitics – that is, the preservation of life (see Tierney, 1999, 2006). He conceded that under "the present moral philosophy of the law … physical existence is the *summum bonum* …," but nevertheless argued that "it is important to recognize that there is no ground, in a rational or Christian outlook, for regarding life itself as the *summum bonum*" (1979, 184, 191). In a later essay, Fletcher argued even more forcefully that "[t]o subordinate every other consideration to bare sentience is to make biological life, as such, an idol. It is the vitalistic error" (Fletcher, 1968, 145).

This vitalistic error is the reduction of the "life" or the "self" that is to be preserved to its corporeal, or bodily, dimensions, and the central role that medical authority has come to play in the modern biopolitical order has contributed greatly to this reduction. As Foucault put it in an interview conducted in 1976, when he first began developing his concept of biopolitics, "Medicine has taken on a general social function: it infiltrates law, it plugs into it, it makes it work. A sort of juridico-medical complex is presently being constituted, which is the major form of power" (1996, 197). To the extent that the current right to die movement requires that a person who is able to exercise such a right must be seen primarily as a "patient" who is determined by a physician to be terminally ill, and by a mental health professional to be of sound mind, this movement maintains this juridico-medical complex. But Fletcher, unlike other participants on both sides of the post-war euthanasia debate, took the opportunity this controversial issue provided to shift the focus of the discussion from the biopolitical question of how long a person should be kept alive, to the traditional pastoral question that Foucault would later try to recover, of how one ought to live *throughout one's life*:

> [W]e can and must call into question any such pure vitalism. We must deny that "life" is adequately understood as mere vital existence or breathing! For the [person] of moral integrity and spiritual purpose, the mere fact of being alive is not as important as the terms of the living. As every hero and every martyr knows, there are some conditions without which a [person] refuses to continue living. Surely among these conditions, along with loyalty to justice and brotherhood, we can include self-possession and personal integrity.
>
> Fletcher (1979, 186–187)

Of course, Fletcher and Foucault would not likely concur on the answer to the question of how one ought to live, with Fletcher's emphasis on a life that is spiritually integrated and self-possessed, and Foucault's on a life that is aesthetically beautiful and a "dispossessive" conception of the self (see Raulff, 2004, 613). Nevertheless, I think they would agree that even though the care of the self certainly includes a corporeal dimension, it cannot be limited to that, and must also involve reflection on the direction and quality of one's life. And I think that they would further agree that the right to die movement can further such self-reflection, but only if it is not approached out of fear, either of a premature death or a medically prolonged death. While Fletcher's faith would help dispel such fear, Foucault learned a similar lesson from his study of ancient Greek sources:

> [I]f you take proper care of yourself, that is, if you know ontologically what you are, if you know what you are capable of, … if you know what things you should and should not fear, if you know what you can reasonably hope for and on the other hand what things should not matter to you, if you know, finally, that you should not be afraid of death – if you know all this, … there is no danger.
>
> 1997, 288

To the extent that the right to die movement generates critical reflection on what it is about an individual's life or self that is worth preserving, beyond corporeal existence, it has the potential to disrupt the pattern traced in this essay of medicine's ascension to a hegemonic position in modern biopolitical societies. As we have seen, each extension of the life span accomplished by medicine has led to a corresponding development in the conception of euthanasia, as it shifted from spiritual comfort provided by religious authorities to an active hastening of death by physicians. Despite the rhetoric of individual control over death that characterizes much of the current discussion of the right to die, if approached unreflectively this movement poses the risk of further solidifying medicine's authority over life and death. To avoid Agamben's thanatopolitical nightmare, and foster an affirmative biopolitics that is, to borrow Roberto Esposito's phrase, "[n]o longer over life but of life" (2008, 157), we need to take advantage of the current right to die movement's potential for raising pastoral questions about the care of the self, and generating an array of non-medical answers to those questions.

References

Agamben, G. (1998) *Homo Sacer: Sovereign Power and Bare Life*, trans. Daniel Heller-Roazen. Stanford, CA: Stanford University Press.

Anonymous (1873) Euthanasia. *Popular Science Monthly*, 3, 90–96.

Anonymous (1926) Euthanasia Again. *Journal of the American Medical Association*, 87(18), 1491.

Bacon, F. (1857) *The Works of Francis Bacon*, 3 vols. Philadelphia: Parry and McMillan.

Battin, M.P. (1994) *The Least Worst Death: Essays in Bioethics on the End of Life*. New York, NY: Oxford University Press.

de Bellaigue, C. (2019) Death on Demand: Has Euthanasia Gone Too Far? *The Guardian*, Jan. 18, 2019. https://www.theguardian.com/news/2019/jan/18/death-on-demand-has-euthanasia-gone-too-far-netherlands-assisted-dying (Accessed Oct. 9, 2019)

Emanuel, E.J. (1994) The History of Euthanasia Debates in the United States and Britain. *Annals of Internal Medicine*, 121(10), 793–802.

Esposito, R. (2008) *Bíos: Biopolitics and Philosophy*, trans. Timothy Campbell. Minneapolis: University of Minnesota Press.

Fattori, M. (2016) Prolongation Vitae and Euthanasia in Francis Bacon, trans. Mattia Bilardello. In G. Giglioni, J.A.T. Lancaster, S. Corneanu & D. Jalobeanu (eds) *Francis Bacon on Motion and Power*, vol. 218, *International Archives of the History of Ideas* (115–132). Switzerland: Springer International.

Fletcher, J. (1968) Elective Death. In E.F. Torrey (ed) *Ethical Issues in Medicine: The Role of the Physician in Today's Society* (139–157). Boston, MA: Little, Brown & Company.

Fletcher, J. (1979) *Morals and Medicine*. Princeton, NJ: Princeton University Press.

Foucault, M. (1980) *The History of Sexuality: Volume 1: An Introduction*, trans. Robert Hurley. New York: Vintage Books.

Foucault, M. (1996) The Social Extension of the Norm. In M. Foucault and S. Lotringer (ed) *Foucault Live: Collected Interviews, 1961–1984* (196–199). New York: Semiotext(e).

Foucault, M. (1997) The Ethics of the Concern for Self as a Practice of Freedom. In M. Foucault and P. Rabinow (ed) *Ethics: Subjectivity and Truth*, Vol. 1 of *The Essential Works of Michel Foucault: 1954–1984* (281–302). New York: The New Press.

Foucault, M. (2003) *Society Must be Defended: Lectures at the Collège De France 1975–76*, ed. Arnold I. Davidson, trans. David Macey. New York: Picador.

Foucault, M. (2007) *Security, Territory, Population: Lectures from the Collège de France, 1977–78*, ed. Michel Senellart, trans. Graham Burchell. London: Palgrave Macmillan.

Fye, W.B. (1979) Active Euthanasia: An Historical Survey of Its Conceptual Origins and Introduction into Medical Thought. *Bulletin of the History of Medicine*, 52(4), 492–502.

JAMA Editorial (1885) The Moral Side of Euthanasia. *Journal of the American Medical Association*, 87, 382–383.

Marx, C.F.H. (1952) Marx's 'Medical Euthanasia,' trans. Walter Cane. *Journal of the History of Medicine and Allied Sciences*, 7, 401–416.

McInerney, F. (2000) 'Requested Death': A New Social Movement. *Social Science & Medicine*, 50, 137–154.

More, T. (1965) *Utopia*, trans. Peter K. Marshall. New York: Pocket Books.

New York Times (1917) *Urges Legal Killing of Hopeless Invalids: Dr. Guild Wins a Favorable Vote from the 'Progressive Medicine' Convention*, September 25, 8, col. 2.

New York Times (1938) Sanction is Sought for 'Mercy Deaths': New Group Formed to Fight for Legalization of Ending Agony of Incurably Ill January 17, 21, col. 8.

New York Times (1939a) Public Is Divided on Mercy Deaths. April 23, III, 4, col. 1.

New York Times (1939b) Mercy Death Law Proposed in State: Euthanasia Society Drafts Bill to Legalize Painless Killing of Incurables, January 27, 21, col. 7.Olshansky, S.J. and Ault, A.B. (1986) The Fourth Stage of the Epidemiologic Transition: The Age of Delayed Degenerative Diseases. *The Milbank Quarterly*, 64(3), 355–391.

Olshansky, S.J. and Carnes, B.A. (2001) *The Quest for Immortality: Science at the Frontiers of Aging*. New York: W. W. Norton.

Omran, A. (1971) The Epidemiologic Transition: A Theory of the Epidemiology of Population Change. *Milbank Quarterly*, 49(4), 509–538.

Porter, R. (1997) *The Greatest Benefit to Mankind: A Medical History of Humanity*. New York, NY: W. W. Norton.

Raulff, U. (2004) Interview with Giorgio Agamben. *German Law Journal*, 5(5), 609–614.

Sperry, W.L. (1948) Moral Problems in the Practice of Medicine, with Analogies Drawn from the Profession of the Ministry. *The New England Journal of Medicine*, 239(26), 985–990.

Tierney, T.F. (1999) The Preservation and Ownership of the Body. In H. Haber and G. Weiss (eds) *Perspectives on Embodiment: Intersections of Nature and Culture* (233–261). New York: Routledge.

Tierney, T.F. (2004) Foucault on the Case: The Pastoral and Juridical Foundation of Medical Power. *The Journal of the Medical Humanities*, 25(4), 271–290.

Tierney, T.F. (2006) Suicidal Thoughts: Hobbes, Foucault, and the Right to Die. *Philosophy & Social Criticism*, 32(5), 601–638.

Vanderpool, H.Y. (1995) Death and Dying: Euthanasia and Sustaining Life – Historical Aspects. In W.T. Reich (ed) *Encyclopedia of Bioethics*, rev. ed. (Vol. 1, 554–563). New York: Simon & Schuster Macmillan.

Vanderpool, H.Y. (1997) Doctors and the Dying of Patients in American History. In R.F. Weir (ed) *Physician-Assisted Suicide* (33–66). Bloomington: Indiana University Press.

Part IV

Transgressions

11 Laughing to death

Necrosocialities and 'right to die' activism

Ari Gandsman

Introduction

Even seated in the back corner of the crowded auditorium, I am conspicuous among the people gathered in the neighbourhood community centre. I stand out because the approximate average age of the packed hall is 75, and I appear roughly two decades younger than the next youngest person in attendance. A rule of the organization is that nobody under the age of 50 is allowed to attend events or become a member without special permission based on circumstance, a pragmatic exigency resulting from both media controversy and legal scrutiny that includes criminal investigations, police raids, and arrests. This is because, despite the drab and innocuous community centre setting and the kind of PowerPoint projected presentation complete that exudes the aura of a bland lecture, we in the audience will be learning how to kill ourselves using the most 'peaceful' and 'reliable' methods advocated for and developed by Exit International.[1] Exit is one of the most radical 'right to die' organizations, advocating for Do-It-Yourself (DIY) methods outside of all legal or medical constraints and safeguards that include a general advocacy of 'rational suicide' (Richards 2017). This lies outside of medical criteria that form the basis of most assisted dying legislation across the world. Like everyone else present, I am required to fill out an indemnity waiver in which I swear not to use any of the life-ending methods discussed in the presentation today to actually end my life.

A secret society

Signing a legally unenforceable legal document to attend the presentation is an entry into a secret society, a world of hidden knowledge. It is the kind of secret society, as Georg Simmel (1950) described them, in which membership is confidential even if societal presence, as documented by media coverage and online presence, is known. It is the kind of society that, as Simmel also pointed out, inspires both feelings of confidence and being protected in its members. Secrecy comprises an important organizational value. Members are instructed how to encrypt electronic communications and hide their

DOI: 10.4324/9780429329739-11

internet presence behind VPNs (virtual private networks), which, during a small technical meeting I observed with Exit members at one of their informal gatherings, constitute a daunting task. During interviews and conversations, members frequently allude to their possession of illicit life-ending substances using code words, resorting to nebulous phrases like 'action plan' or 'information', while refusing to speak specifically or directly about them, even within the confines of a confidential and anonymous interview. For example, Cath, a woman with late-stage cancers who insisted on me using her real name, told me unprompted immediately after I went through the typical ethical script about protecting anonymity,

> The only thing I won't be talking about today is whether or not I've got anything, alright? Because I'll have the federal police on my doorstep wanting to search the house to prevent me from killing myself even though I've got two cancers.

She obviously 'had something' since she specifically told me of her intention to end her life ('sooner rather than later') when her cancers took a turn for the worse and she was otherwise open and candid about everything. Giving out this information to a non-member was taboo. Others were mortified at the idea of their children knowing they belonged to an organization like Exit. I heard discussion and debate over how or even whether to broach the topic with one's children. At a more informal gathering of the group, I hear a new member nervously giggle to the woman next to her: 'if my children knew I were here.' When my presence as a researcher is introduced to a small group, some worry about protecting their anonymity: 'no photos.' They are assured that no photographs will be taken. This particular workshop is held in Adelaide, Australia, but is one of several I attended as part of a larger ethnographic research project on 'right to die' activism in three countries.[2]

In the workshop we will learn the information that 'they' do not want you to have: how to 'peacefully' and 'reliably' (used counter-intuitively in terms of 'safely') end one's life. The presentation by Exit founder Philip Nitschke is framed humorously but also antagonistically against 'them': whether the state, the police, other medical professionals, religious authorities, or well-meaning but paternalistic family members that infantilize elder parents. Although he gives versions of this presentation around the world, this particular workshop marks Nitschke's triumphant return. The controversial and flamboyant Australian founder went into self-imposed European exile after losing his medical license because of his 'right to die' activism, a license that he would later burn at a press conference in protest. As a former medical doctor, Nitschke assisted several deaths while working in the Northern Territories when assisted dying was briefly legal between 1996 and 1997.[3]

A provocateur known for wearing colourful Hawaiian shirts, Nitschke's presentation is, given the morbid subject matter, lively and humorous, a performance style he perfected at the Edinburgh Fringe Festival in 2015; a one-hour, one-man show filed under 'true life comedy' called 'Dicing with Dr Death'. Complete with audience participation, the show aimed to teach 'the funny side of the "right to die" debate'.[4] The show's best publicity occurred in advance of its premiere when it was threatened with closure as police showed up to investigate whether the show would use compressed gas in Nitschke's simulation of his death deliverance machine (Ellis-Peterson 2015). Embracing the pejorative and accusatory moniker of 'Dr Death' that his opponents have long accused him of being – claiming to be the ninth known holder of the title – he posed for the show's publicity with sickle in hand.[5]

During the workshop, Nitschke explains to the gathered crowd 'why it makes sense how to learn to end one's life' (fieldnotes) and systematically goes through different options for ending one's life before settling on two primary recommendations. First, he advocates securing a life-ending pentobarbital narcotic named Nembutal, once a commonly prescribed sedative that has become illegal. He recommends two dominant sources for its acquisition. First, members are directed to veterinary supply stores in Mexico. This is because, besides being used for executions in the United States, its primary contemporary use is for pet euthanasia. Nitschke advises against buying the brand that is green-dyed for safety because it leaves a tell-tale green moustache on one's corpse. Second, he describes ordering it online from China in a powder form. This is seen as risky since many online scams exist (Exit's message boards for members will direct people to more reliable sources). Also, since it is illegally synthesized, the quality may be suspect, so that Nitschke had in the past gone around in a van purity-testing it. Nitschke's advocacy of Nembutal is commercial jingle catchy, 'You're only going to die once, you may as well have the best drug. Why settle for second best?' The other method involves a nitrogen canister that his side company Max Dog Brewing sells that is in theory used to dispense 'nitro' beer but that can, via instructions his organization provides, be converted through several easy-to-follow steps into a self-administered death deliverance system.[6] The company even has comedic YouTube videos advertising it (as well as being covered in *Vice Magazine* [Vice Staff 2014], thus reaching a younger demographic). Nitschke's most recent provocation has been a 3D-printed futuristic looking suicide machine called the Sarco death pod that, according to its publicity materials when it appeared at the 2019 Venice Biennale, allows one to 'die in style' and asks: 'What if we dared to imagine that our last day might also be one of our most exciting?'[7]

Nitschke himself has been investigated numerous times by the Australian police for 'assisting' suicides, having had his home searched and his computer and phone confiscated.[8] His presentation thus treads carefully but also, as a knowing provocateur, indelicately and even jokingly over what the law will and will not allow him to say, skirting the boundaries over what could be loosely interpreted as legal trespass onto the crime of 'aiding or assisting someone to end their life'.[9] Although Nitschke does not advocate illegal acts, he responds to questions like what is the best method to illegally smuggle Nembutal from Mexico (whether better to bring it as carry-on or checked luggage).

In such a way, despite the mundane surroundings, the event is knowingly subversive, underground, and deliberately broaches taboos – and therein lies part of its appeal. In my interviews with members who have attended these presentations and are part of Exit's organizational activities which include weekly informal 'Coffee and Chat' gatherings, the 'outlaw' image of the organization was a recurring theme and a knowing point of attraction. One person even marvelled at how she had been such an upstanding law-abiding citizen for her entire life only now to be part of a transgressive group at the margins of the law. Another gleefully recounts her thwarted effort to buy cyanide from Thailand when the package ended up being intercepted by customs. She feigned incredulity after police appeared at her door asking her about the package and inquiring into her mental state. Several others speak of assisting other people to die in order to help their deaths escape detection and thwart medical investigation. For example, one tells me of sneaking into a friend's assisted living facility in order to help him set up his nitrogen tank and then, after he finished, sneaking off with the evidence. When the death was marked suspicious, he was brought in several times for questioning by the police.

'A death cult?'

Someone risking criminal charges in order to help a friend end their life is indicative of the deep ties and intimacy that the organization can forge between members, especially those who become part of an inner circle. An oft-repeated motif in my interviews with members was how an organization like Exit becomes a surrogate family, incubators of close friendships, where members could engage with issues that they could not even speak about with their own closest family members. This social aspect can be seen as ironic because an organization like Exit is avowedly DIY, premised on libertarian and individualistic values. After all, Exit opposes the idea of medical assistance and constructs the issue around a solitary individual act outside of social networks and medical control, even if in practice members speak of helping and aiding each other in a variety of ways. The research participants told me this was truer of radical 'right to die' organizations like Exit, with its advocacy of methods outside of the law than more reform-oriented organizations like Dying With Dignity committed to limited changes in the law. This suggested that the underground, illicit, and secretive nature of Exit thickened ties between its members. According to Nitschke, medical assistance and legal reform is unnecessary when individuals are empowered to take action themselves. In his interview with me, Nitschke denounces the medical gatekeeping of the issue, what he sees as a medicalization of a social issue that keeps in place what he sees to be the 'medical paternalism' involved in legal regimes permitting assisted dying. In its organizational discourse, Exit does not claim to provide its members with assistance to die but rather, in a language of self-empowerment, 'information'. Members of the organization tell me how that fear over prosecution of its members for 'assisting a suicide', which could include just being in the same room as an individual as they end their life, results in individuals ending their lives in solitude away from their homes, often in hotel rooms where they are forced to leave a note to call coroners on discovering the body. The possibility of community and group solidarity that the organization offers for its members contrasts with the individuality of the imagined solitary act.

The polemical stances and hidden network of memberships result in accusations that radical 'right to die' activists like those of Exit comprise a 'death cult' (Fickling 2014) or, as the British tabloid press frequently terms it, 'suicide club' (e.g. Massey 2014) with Nitschke as its charismatic leader. For example, *The Australian*, the country's largest newspaper (owned by Rupert Murdoch) called Nitschke a 'messiah of death' and a 'guru of a bizarre suicide cult' (Shanahan 2014a) who 'heads a suicide cult that must be stopped' after directly blamed his group for 'death coaching' a suicide (Shanahan 2014b) The accusation of Exit being a 'death cult' or 'suicide club' ostensibly places Nitschke's advocacy of Nembutal on par with Jim Jones's cult mass suicide in Guayana by drinking Kool Aid laced with cyanide.[10] Criticisms of Exit and Nitschke are found in publications sympathetic to the question of assisted dying and even many reform-minded individuals within the 'right to die' movement find his flamboyant positions and tactics extreme and alienating and accuse him of being an impediment to institutional legal reform (e.g. Davidson 2016; Syme 2014). For example, the chief executive of the UK organization Dignity in Dying has publicly criticized Nitschke's workshops as 'irresponsible', 'illegal', and 'clearly dangerous' (BBC 2008). The term 'death cult' was even used by a former president of *The World Federation of Right to Die Societies* I interviewed.

'Right to die' as rite of death

Although 'death cult' is intended as a pejorative, the rest of this chapter intends to reclaim the notion of a death cult in its more neutral anthropological connotations in how the concept forges collective belonging, opens up particular rites and ceremonies, and offers a larger existential worldview and outlet focussed on processes of death and dying. As envisaged by membership-based groups like Exit, the research participants take part in a shared ethical vision organized around the planning for and carrying out of their deaths. The 'right to die' allows particular rites of death. In other words, the assertion of a 'right to die' enables rites of death that provide a shared community and a way of meditating on, wrangling with, and preparing for death. A 'right to die' is organized around a temporal reckoning ('choosing the time of one's death') that opens up a liminal space for death.

If Exit is secretive and taboo, the interview participants believe that this is because death is still widely considered a secretive societal taboo. Even in our post-Kübler-Rossian universe proliferated by, for example, popular newfound trends in death cafes (Tucker 2014), my informants point to what they consider a death-denying society surrounding them. At one meeting, one member spoke of old taboos, that 'people think if you don't talk about death, it will be less likely to happen', while criticizing and making fun of euphemisms like 'losing someone' ('where did they go?') and sanitized sayings like 'passed away'. Most speak directly from their experience. Often, a central and recurring issue in my interviews is a strong feeling that they are unable to speak with their children about the subject. They wish to engage with a discussion of their prospective death, but feel resistance on the part of their children, an awkwardness that one member compared to a parent's discussion of sex with their child. If their children rebuke their efforts to broach the topic of their death, some sympathetically acknowledge that they do so because they cannot accept the idea that their parents will one day die.

This willingness to engage in issues around death and dying does not matter whether death is imminent and foreseeable or not. To enter the world of this sector of radical 'right to die' activists is not joining, what Paul Stoller (2004) terms, the 'village of the sick'. Many 'right to die' activists are not sick (the majority of those interviewed for my own study, for example). Furthermore, a frequent point made in interviews was that the vast majority of people would not wish to avail of themselves of such a right even if it were a medically available option (pointing to evidence of low rates of deaths through assisted dying where legal[11]). It is not even to enter a world of sufferers because not all of them are, from a medical perspective, suffering from an illness (even if many are). It is, rather, a temporal passage from a community of the living (one predicated on denying the reality of death) into a community of the dying (one intimately involved in discussing and preparing for it), even if strictly speaking, these are people who are not dying (in the sense of a terminal prognosis that many medically assisted dying laws require). Rather, what I will show in the rest of this chapter is how they see in the process of dying a simultaneous process of living. They are deeply engaged with the question of death, resembling what, as I argue in another work (Gandsman, Herington and Przybylak-Brouillard 2016), Heidegger famously termed 'being-toward-death', a liberating consciousness of one's own mortality. This is a movement from the avoidance of death into a state of death consciousness, to recognise its imminence (Beaman and Steele 2018) as a non-event that lurks permanently on the horizon. For my research participants, who procured life-ending substances and have what they term 'action plans' in place, death is kept ever-present and in reach, possessed in material and symbolic form, often literally stored in the bathroom cupboard. Nitschke's workshop also argues for having nitrogen or keeping Nembutal as a form of emergency preparedness. Nitschke speaks of those who have not planned their deaths and when the moment comes, they find themselves panicking and ill-prepared. As an Exit national coordinator described it to me, many contact the organization wrongly expecting them to provide direct material assistance to end their lives. Those who work with more reform-oriented 'right to die' organizations recounted similar stories and similarly frame their work around a discourse of emergency preparedness, even if, unlike Exit, they work within what the law and medical system allows. For example, I attended several *Dying With Dignity* end-of-life workshops that instruct individuals how, among other topics, to prepare advance medical directives, explaining the right to refuse and withdraw treatment, why rejecting antibiotics for pneumonia in a nursing home might be a good idea, and even how to die 'comfortably' by refusing nutrition and hydration. At one workshop, Rodney Syme, the medical doctor making the presentation, argued that a good or dignified death requires significant planning and preparation (Nitschke's 'homework' and 'thinking in advance') pointing to the difficulty of decision making while in the midst of a medical crisis.

Necrosocialities

Having both the knowledge and means to end one's life transforms individuals into their own sovereign masters with the 'right of death and power over life' (Foucault 1978, 133; see also Tierney, this volume). While they do not have, strictly speaking, control and choice over a death that is, after all, inevitable, they do have a limited and over-determined choice and control over the timing of their death. In the process, death does not simply happen to them but is something they can precipitate through their own actions at a pre-determined moment. What does it mean to have this power, this particular orientation towards death? What I would like to show in what follows is how it induces a death-directed subjectivity that allows for a sense of agency over one's life coupled with an affirmation of a like-minded community. This subjectivity involves a particular kind of disposition that I would like to term necrosociality.[12] This describes a shared set of beliefs united by a way of thinking about death that is not pathological but healthy. It involves an absurdist existential stance by offering the illusion of control over what cannot be controlled in the face of one's inevitable demise that is both certain (in the sense that we all die) and uncertain (in the temporal sense that we generally do not know when it will happen).

When Philippe Ariès (1974) wrote of death in the European past as deeply enmeshed with life, he showed how Christian rituals around death and dying were conducted as preparation for the world to come and as a final test for the Last Judgement, an issue that is absent within 'right to die' activism which tends towards the secular, namely, atheistic and agnostic. In that sense, the key to necrosocial disposition is a focus on how to experience the end of life; it is a temporal concern in which the recognition of the 'right to die' offers individuals the possibility of working out how to die in rhythm with or in counterpoint to how they lives. Rather than see death as a moment in time, dying becomes a process over which one can have a sense of control. In this sense, many of my informants spoke of how they wished to die in concordance with how they have lived. Seeing themselves as having had decision-making control over how they lived their lives (e.g. over their professional careers and their personal relationships), they believed they should have decision-making control over their deaths. While this 'choice' may be illusory since it takes place in an overdetermined context of inevitable death (Gandsman 2018), it is a rejection of biomedical technologies and medical interventions. These interventions are, as Sharon Kaufman (2015) illustrates, structured to extend life at all costs, part of a death-denying culture that celebrates rising longevity and life expectancies as values in and of themselves, often devoid of any consideration of content. As self-defined sovereign masters of their own lives and deaths (with the power of death in their hands), 'right to die' advocates reject prolonging life at all costs as an inherent good or goal of medical practice.

Not waiting around to die

In 2018, the story David Goodall generated international media coverage. Goodall, a prominent Australian scientist, travelled to Switzerland at the age of 104 to end his life with the help of Exit International, of which he was a member, and a Swiss 'right to die' organization called Life Circle.[13] Goodall was not suffering from a degenerative condition or terminal illness. His mobility was limited after suffering a fall, and he claimed his failing eyesight and hearing were diminishing his quality of life (McKenzie et al. 2018). Faced with requiring 24-hour home care or going to a nursing home, he refused both. In publicly announcing his decision, saying he was 'happy' to end his life, he declared, 'At my age, and even rather less than my age, one wants to be free to choose the death and when the death is the appropriate time' (Guardian Australia 2018). News coverage was largely sympathetic, reporting on his last meal of fish and chips and cheesecake with family members and friends, that he was singing and laughing, and how he chose Beethoven's Ode to Joy to soundtrack the end of his life (Guardian Australia 2018; Oltermann 2018).

Rather than waiting to die of 'natural' causes, Goodall's death becomes a synchronized moment in time orchestrated through his ability to control the timing of his death. In choosing the 'appropriate time' of death, however, Goodall hints that this moment has already passed and that he has lived longer than he desired ('even rather less than my age'). Even as he signed the paperwork required for his death, he hinted at frustration, telling them, 'What are we waiting for?' (The Guardian 2018) For all of my informants planning on organizing their deaths, how to locate the 'appropriate time' of death was the central question, even if unanswerable. Between 'hanging around too long' or 'waiting too late', temporal considerations dominated, especially with the prospect of biomedical technologies that prolong life but allow for 'lingering' deaths. It is in this context that the manifestation of a desire to die, as in the case of Goodall, becomes a controversy and a problem. This apparent disavowal or rejection of life is less a nihilistic demand but a struggle to find meaning in the face of impending death. For my ethnographic subjects contemplating their deaths, their decision was as much an affirmation of living as a rejection of life.

Although I did not interview Goodall for my research, I did interview others who were similarly planning, preparing for, and trying to locate an 'appropriate time' to die. These activists ranged from those suffering from terminal and degenerative illnesses to those with no major medical condition and encompass what is called 'rational suicide' (Humphrey 1992) a distinction that, as I have argued elsewhere (Gandsman 2018), is not a very clear or easy one. The range of my informants included a woman in her late fifties with advanced leukaemia and breast cancer[14] to a 79-year-old woman with no medical problems who wanted to die at the age of 80 because she felt this would be 'long enough'. At the same time, she acknowledged that she could change her mind at any time. For all of those I interviewed who were contemplating ending their lives, 'dying at the right time' was the crucial ethical dilemma and ultimate paradox.

For example, Cath, the woman with late-stage leukaemia and breast cancer, believes she might 'hold on too long' because she is 'a fighter' and has been fighting cancer for decades: 'They say you'll know when the right time comes, but I'm not sure.' She fears waiting too long, being in hospital at a point where she can no longer self-administer the illicit pharmaceutical substance she has procured to end her life and thus having the agonizing death she wishes to avoid. Brian, an 80-year-old man suffering from what he believes could be early stages of Alzheimer's foresees a similar problem. Having witnessed and cared for his mother who had a long and lingering death from the same disease, he believes he will have to take measures to end his life before he gets to the point where he would no longer have the capacity to self-administer. 'You need to most of all act early. It's sad to need to do that', he tells me while speaking of his fears of 'putting it off' too long. Assisted dying for dementia raises numerous complex ethical questions (Tomlinson and Scott 2014) and was a vexing concern for my informants.

A coordinator of Exit International who consults individuals in such situations told me of a case of a woman in later stages of Alzheimer's who wanted to end her life and had procured the means of doing so, which she wanted to do before she would have to go into a long-term care facility. He recalls visiting her several times. She had got her plan together but waiting for the 'right moment'. He said he visited her frequently and saw at one point that she was 'beginning to fade'. He gently raised the idea that this might be a good time. She told him, next time, that she was not ready to die. The next time he visited her, it was too late. She had forgotten where she had put her stash of life-ending 'medicine' (resembling the plot of the novel and film *Still Alice*) and she ended up being put in a home, the exact fate she dreaded more than any other and was fighting to avoid. This example shows the difficulties of dementia, alongside other degenerative conditions, in terms of the problematic of timing death, because by the time the individual reaches the point where their life according to their professed desire is no longer worth living, they no longer possess the capacity to end their lives.

In such a way, 'right to die' activists use a particular language to speak of working out the timing of death. They speak of a dilemma between having to 'leave the station a stop early' on one hand for those who might be forced to act pre-emptively and thus earlier than they would like and those who 'miss the train or bus' who have waited too long and no longer can self-administer at the point they wish. This is true of those not eligible for a medically assisted death because medical-aid-in-dying is not available or they do not fall into eligibility criteria, like suffering from dementia and other degenerative conditions. However, the problem of time also exists where assisted dying is legal because medical safeguards exist that require a bureaucratic approval process (National Academies of Sciences, Engineering, and Medicine 2018). This includes 'waiting times' between first and second requests in order to document what is considered a 'persistent' desire for death.[15] Many wait too long to file a request, many may be refused for a variety of reasons (such as a previous diagnosis of mental illness), and many die after filling their prescriptions but without using them. For example, in Oregon, during the two decades following the implementation of the Death with Dignity Act, more than one-third of individuals who went through the entire process and received a lethal prescription did not, in the end, use it (Oregon Health Authority 2018). The implication is the individuals either changed their minds, died before self-administration was possible, their disease progressed to the point where they lacked the capacity to self-administer, or they only wanted the prescription as a form of comfort or backup plan. In other words, the demand for a right to die does not necessarily entail using it.

Even if timing death poses a difficult demand and challenging dilemma, the knowledge/power of having the hypothetical ability to control the time of their death has, for many, an indescribable palliative value. All of my informants spoke of the relief that they felt when they were able to procure life-ending substances. Having the choice, the sense of control it afforded, was enough to relieve the toxic anxiety of uncertainty of the dying process. In other words, they believed that they were able to better live in the present moment and better appreciate the time they have. This could also be seen as a way of resisting a symbolic and structural violence of waiting (Jeffrey 2008) – a temporality of passivity in which people are forced into, like in the Townes Van Zandt song 'Waitin' Around To Die'.[16] Having secured the means to die gave them a feeling of agency not only over their deaths but over their lives.[17] My interlocutors felt they were no longer living out of compulsory force; they became moral agents who were alive out of deliberate choice. As Nitschke told me during our interview, the whole problem with the state's restriction of assisted dying is that it assumes 'the only reason you're alive is that you haven't quite worked out how to die.' This is consistent with much of the literature that examines the complex question of 'agency' that, as Anita Hannig (2019) argues, becomes, even where medical aid-in-dying is legal, diffused onto the disease, medical technologies, the medical system, and the state.

Conclusion: laughing to death

In the context of a 'slow death', Lauren Berlant (2007) argues for a way of speaking about human agency in ordinary life that allows individuals to endure under conditions of perpetual mortal threat. In this way, the kind of 'gallows humour' that I discussed at the onset of this article is central to the agency and subjectivity of the participants in my research, in that it captures what I have termed a 'necrosocial' disposition. Humour expresses both the agency and subjectivity of individuals as well as a vehicle for expressing their own ambivalences and moral concerns (Kuiper 2016). Waiting before the start of the Dying With Dignity workshop, a well-known member walks in and is asked by the coordinator, 'How are you doing?' He laughs, 'Do you really want me to tell you?' 'Oh, is that why you came?' she says and they both start laughing. As Woodruff (1997, 319) writes, 'the paradox of comedy is that it must attract and repel at the same time.' In particular, dark comedy, as La Farge (2011) writes, deals with shattering taboos and status quos, confronting anxiety and fears, and an attraction to destruction as well as a desire for 'happy closure' (285).

This can explain why rather than being dour and depressing, the meetings and gatherings I attend during my fieldwork are, like Nitschke's presentation, lively and fun, filled with gallows humour. For example, at an annual local chapter meeting in an affluent suburb, I witness a festive atmosphere that includes raffle prizes, jokes, and laughter. The host of the event tells me that this is typical: 'We have a fun time.' This meeting features a presentation on eco funerals by a funeral director. Participants are disappointed to discover that it ends up being more about a sales pitch than an environmental philosophy and being far more conventional than expected. Several members laugh as they request to 'try out' the coffin. They joke about 'early bird' cremation specials, vertical burials, and fluid leakage during cremation. They grill the mortician on issues ranging from why make up makes dead people look like Barbie and the Joker from Batman to what happens to medical prosthetics and implants during the cremation process (answer: anything electronic needs to be removed because of chance of explosion but everything else is smelted down and recycled, but not for profit). Most of my research participants tell me that they do not care or worry what happens to them after death when the topic arises, and overtly reject the pieties, formalities, and seriousness of contemporary death rituals, focussing their mental energies more on the process itself. What comes after death is less a focus of action than the events that will lead up to death itself. While this casual response to the seriousness of death can be dismissed as a kind of deflection or false bravado, whether performative or not, I argue that it reveals an idealized ethical stance, a means of laughing in the face of death that provides reassurance to one's self and others and captures the necrosocial sense of belonging and absurdist existential stance.

As a concrete example of this disposition in dying, I cite the death of Michèle Causse, a well-known French radical lesbian theorist. At the age of 74, with a litany of non-life-threatening ailments – from compressed vertebrae to osteoporosis to losing a kidney to being asthmatic – 'My illness is invisible; it's nothing spectacular', she declares as she chooses to die at the Dignitas clinic in Switzerland (Menoud 2010). Accompanied by a film crew, her death was eventually broadcast on Swiss television in a documentary (ibid). Her death scene depicts her smiling, making jokes, laughing about how bad the medication tastes, about how much she will need to drink to end her life, about whether she will drool as she dies, and about chasing down the bad taste with chocolate. At a coffee and chat meeting I attend in Melbourne, a coordinator speaks of hearing about the death of Exit members that they have known: 'You'll be sad that they're gone. But you won't be sad. You'll feel happy that they went out on their own terms.' The audience smiles in approval. Laughter has long been considered in the psychological literature as a means of 'ageing well' (Solomon 1996) and as a measure of general quality of life (Thorson et al. 1997) but can equally be considered as an important component of 'dying well'. While laughing in the face of death is often seen as a defence or coping mechanism, it can also be seen, as Thorson (1985, 206) writes, as an 'offense mechanism'. Like Nembutal in the cupboard, it offers a measure and illusion of control over the uncontrollable, sense over senselessness, meaning over meaninglessness, and the last hope for the hopeless.

Notes

1 https://exitinternational.net.

2 This ethnographic research project examined the lifeworlds and experiences of 'right to die' activists in North America, Europe, and Australia, including a four-month research stint in Melbourne. Research was funded by an Insight Development Grant from the Social Sciences and Humanities Research Council (SSHRC) of Canada and approved by the Social Sciences and Humanities Research Ethics Board at the University of Ottawa. The purpose of the study was to better understand how this issue has emerged as a major political concern of the twenty-first century and, in particular, how 'right to die' activists made their appeals through the use of personal narratives and how individuals understood their political activism in relation to their life histories and personal relationships. Research included observations at legislative inquiries and participant-observation fieldwork at various institutional activities of several 'right to die' organizations, including board meetings, member events, informal discussion groups, and the attendance of workshops instructing people how to end their lives. Newsletters, publications, websites, legislative inquiries, newspaper articles, and publicly available testimonies were also consulted in order to analyse public rhetoric and arguments. Sixty semi-structured interviews were conducted with a broad array of activists and advocates, including doctors, nurses, lawyers, political figures, and other individuals affiliated with the movement. This included both presidents of organizations as well as board members and coordinators as well as more general members. Many informants who are public figures, like Philip Nitschke, chose to forego anonymity and pseudonyms. In terms of organizations, research was conducted with more mainstream reformist organizations dedicated to legal

reform as well as more radical organizations that advocate Do-It-Yourself (DIY) approaches that inform members how to end their lives at the time of their choice.

3 While the law was passed by the territory's Legislative Assembly, it was voided shortly after by the federal government (see Fleming 2000).

4 https://www.theguardian.com/australia-news/2015/aug/06/dr-death-philip-nitschke-euthanasia-comedy-edinburgh-fringe-threatened-closure.

5 Edinburgh Festival, https://edinburghfestival.list.co.uk/event/507117-dicing-with-dr-death/.

6 Max Dog Brewing, https://maxdogbrewing.com.

7 https://www.exitinternational.net/sarco/.

8 https://www.theguardian.com/world/2014/aug/01/philip-nitschke-to-speak-to-police-over-suicide-death-of-terminally-ill-man.

9 Although suicide has large been decriminalized in much of the world throughout the twentieth century, assisting someone to die remained crime, except where 'right to die' legislation subsequently changed the law to enable a physician-assisted death. In Australia, assisting someone to die is still a criminal act everywhere except in the state of Victoria, although their Voluntary Assisted Dying Act of 2017 has very narrowly defined and restrictive eligibility criteria that organizations like Exit oppose.

10 Such a comparison between Nitschke and Jones is made directly in the 'anti-euthanasia' movement. https://www.noeuthanasia.org.au/triple_suicide_in_qld_why_aren_t_we_celebrating.

11 As stated in a recent *CBC News* article,

> Using data from Statistics Canada, the report shows medically assisted deaths accounted for 1.07 per cent of all deaths in the country over those six months. That is consistent with reports from other countries that have assisted death regimes, where the figure ranges from 0.3 to four per cent.
>
> Harris (2018)

12 A term I misguidedly believed I was clever enough to coin but turns out has already been taken by a *Journal of the Royal Anthropological Institute* article (Kim 2016), but in any event I use it in an altogether different sense.

13 Foundation of lifecircle – https://www.lifecircle.ch/en/about-us/foundation-of-lifecircle/.

14 Who would fall into category allowed in the most restrictive states where medically assisted deaths are available in California, Oregon, Washington and Vermont under the condition of having a prognosis of six months or less to live.

15 For example, in the Canadian law, there is a ten-day minimum 'reflection period' between the written request and when the service can be provided (https://www.canada.ca/en/health-canada/services/medical-assistance-dying.html).

16 https://americansongwriter.com/behind-the-song-townes-van-zandt-waitin-around-to-die/.

17 This is connected to a key issue in the assisted dying literature in which who is granted over the agency of the individual's death (the medical condition or the patient) is a central concern that is often distinguished between measures that involve the 'passive' and 'active' hastening of death (see Meisel 2005).

References

Ariès, P. (1974). *Western Attitudes Toward Death*. Baltimore: The Johns Hopkins University Press.

BBC News (2008). Doctor defends suicide workshops, *BBC News* [Online] 10 October. http://news.bbc.co.uk/2/hi/health/7662928.stm (Accessed 19 August 2019).

BBC News (2018). David Goodall: Scientist, 104, ends his life in Switzerland, *BBC News* [Online] 10 May. https://www.bbc.com/news/world-europe-44069885 (Accessed 10 April 2019).

Beaman, L. G., & Steele, C. (2018). Transcendence/religion to immanence/nonreligion in assisted dying. *International Journal of Human Rights in Healthcare*, 11(2), 129–143.

Berlant, L. (2007). Slow death (sovereignty, obesity, lateral agency). *Critical Inquiry*, 33(4), 754–780.

Davidson, H. (2016). Philip Nitschke: How the face of the voluntary euthanasia campaign became its outcast. *The Guardian* [Online] 22 September. https://www.theguardian.com/australia-news/2016/sep/22/philip-nitschke-how-the-face-of-the-voluntary-euthanasia-campaign-became-its-outcast (Accessed 20 April 2019).

Ellis-Petersen, H. (2015). Dr Death euthanasia play to go ahead at Edinburgh fringe after closure threat. *The Guardian* [Online] 6 August. https://www.theguardian.com/australia-news/2015/aug/06/dr-death-philip-nitschke-euthanasia-comedy-edinburgh-fringe-threatened-closure (Accessed 20 April 2019).

Fickling, D. (2004). A happy ending? *The Lancet*, 364, 831–832.

Fleming, J. (2000). Death, dying, and euthanasia: Australia versus the Northern Territory. *Issues in Law & Medicine*, 15(3), 291–305.

Foucault, M. (1978). *The History of Sexuality*. New York: Pantheon Books.

Gandsman, A. (2018). Paradox of choice and the illusion of autonomy: The construction of ethical subjects in right-to-die activism. *Death Studies*, 42(5), 329–335.

Gandsman, A., Herington, T., & Przybylak-Brouillard, A. (2016). Mourir comme mode de vie: être vers la mort et phénoménologie de l'activisme du droit de mourir. *Anthropologie et Sociétés*, 40(3), 59–84.

Guardian Australia (2018). David Goodall singing and laughing the day before his death (YouTube video) 10 May. https://www.youtube.com/watch?v=PrJ2dt-nmSVg (Accessed 6 January 2021).

Hannig, A. (2019). AUTHOR(IZ)ING DEATH: Medical aid-in-dying and the morality of suicide. *Cultural Anthropology*, 34(1), 53–77.

Harris, K. (2018). Number of Canadians choosing medically assisted death jumps 30%. *CBC* [Online] 21 June. https://www.cbc.ca/news/politics/maid-assisted-death-increase-1.4715944 (Accessed 20 April 2019).

Humphrey, D. (1992). Rational suicide among the elderly. *Suicide and Life Threatening Behavior*, 22(1), 125–129.

Jeffrey, C. (2008). Waiting. *Society and Space*, 26, 954–958.

Kaufman, S. (2015). *Ordinary Medicine*. Durham: Duke University Press.

Kim, J. (2016). Necrosociality: Isolated death and unclaimed cremains in Japan. *Journal of the Royal Anthropological Institute*, 22(4), 843–863.

Kuiper, G. (2016). Follow the joke: Humour and ethnography. *Etnofoor*, 28(2), 125–129.

La Farge, B. (2011). Comic anxiety and kafka's black comedy. *Philosophy and Literature*, 35(2), 282–302.

Massey, N. (2014). Controversial doctor dubbed 'Dr Death' launches 'suicide club' in Britain. *The Mirror* [Online] 28 September. https://www.mirror.co.uk/news/uk-news/controversial-doctor-dubbed-dr-death-4337430 (Accessed 20 April 2019).

McKenzie, S., Bell, M., Vandoorne S., & Westcott, B. (2018). 104-year-old scientist David Goodall 'welcomes death' at Swiss clinic. *CNN* [Online] 9 May 2018. https://edition.cnn.com/2018/05/08/health/david-goodall-australia-switzerland-interview-intl/index.html (Accessed 6 January 2021).

Meisel, A. (2005). Ethics and law: Physician-assisted dying. *Journal of Palliative Medicine*, 8(3), 609–623.

Menoud, J-B. (2010). *Dignitas – La mort sur ordonnance* (film). Radio Télévision Suisse.

National Academies of Sciences, Engineering, and Medicine. (2018). *Physician-assisted Death: Scanning the Landscape: Proceedings of a Workshop*. National Academies Press. Available at https://www.ncbi.nlm.nih.gov/books/NBK525938/.

Oltermann, P. (2018). David Goodall, Australia's oldest scientist, ends his own life aged 104. *The Guardian* [Online] 10 May. https://www.theguardian.com/society/2018/may/10/david-goodall-australias-oldest-scientist-ends-his-own-life-at-104 (Accessed 29 September 2019).

Oregon Health Authority (2018). *Death with Dignity Act Annual Reports*. Available at: https://www.oregon.gov/oha/PH/PROVIDERPARTNERRESOURCES/EVALUATIONRESEARCH/DEATHWITHDIGNITYACT/Documents/year21.pdf.

Richards, N. (2017). Old age rational suicide. *Sociology Compass*, 11(3), e12456.

Shanahan, A. (2014a). Police appear paralysed as 'messiah of death' Philip Nitschke expands his euthanasia organisation. *The Australian* [Online] 2 August. https://www.theaustralian.com.au/commentary/opinion/police-appear-paralysed-as-messiah-of-death-philip-nitschke-expands-his-euthanasia-organisation/news-story/36bcc53d041713c49a961b8aeec26e65 (Accessed 6 January 2021).

Shanahan, A. (2014b). Nitschke heads a suicide cult that must be stopped. *The Australian*, [Online] 25 July. https://www.theaustralian.com.au/commentary/opinion/nitschke-heads-a-suicide-cult-that-must-be-stopped/news-story/a1c78c02938485b2bbc7ed45c47b07cd (Accessed 6 January 2021).

Simmel, G. (1950). *Sociology of Georg Simmel*. Translated and edited by Kurt H Wolff. New York: The Free Press.

Solomon, J. C. (1996). Humor and aging well: A laughing matter or a matter of laughing? *American Behavioral Scientist*, 39(3), 249–271.

Stoller, P. (2004). *Stranger in the Village of the Sick*. Boston: Beacon Press.

Syme, R. (2014). Philip Nitschke should not be the sole face of the euthanasia movement. *The Guardian* [Online] 24 July. https://www.theguardian.com/commentisfree/2014/jul/24/philip-nitschke-should-not-be-the-sole-face-of-the-euthanasia-movement (Accessed 6 January 2021).

Thorson, J. A. (1985). A funny thing happened on the way to the morgue: Some thoughts on humor and death, and a taxonomy of the humor associated with death. *Death Studies*, 9(3–4), 201–216.

Thorson, J. A., Powell, F. C., Sarmany-Schuller, I., & Hampes, W. P. (1997). Psychological health and sense of humor. *Journal of Clinical Psychology*, 53(6), 605–619.

Tomlinson, E., & Stott, J. (2015). Assisted dying in dementia: A systematic review of the international literature on the attitudes of health professionals, patients, carers and the public, and the factors associated with these. *International Journal of Geriatric Psychiatry*, 30(1), 10–20.

Tucker, E. (2014). What on earth is a death cafe? *The Guardian* [Online] 27 March. https://www.theguardian.com/lifeandstyle/2014/mar/22/death-cafe-talk-about-dying (Accessed 20 April 2019).

Vice Staff (2014). Death in a can: Australia's euthanasia loophole. *Vice Magazine* [Online] 2 July 2014. https://www.vice.com/en_au/article/qbe3g3/death-in-a-can-australias-euthanasia-loophole (Accessed 20 April 2019).

Woodruff, P. (1997). The paradox of comedy. *Philosophical Topics*, 25(1), 319–335.

12 Choosing death in anticipation of older age-related suffering

Reflections based on a Dutch study

Els van Wijngaarden

Introduction

In late modern society, social-cultural ideas about living towards the end of life are challenged by what is called 'a new demography of death' (Leeson 2014, 1–2). Life expectancy has significantly increased at individual and population levels, with more and more people reaching advanced old age. Additionally, new medical technologies and the growing science of ageing aspire to push back ageing and lengthen our lifespan even more. These ongoing developments do have fundamental consequences for the way in which we view our extending lives, life course (planning), family dynamics, the distribution of resources, and our relationship towards deep old age and death.

Although high quality of life and a good state of well-being can be enjoyed even in great old age, the question is now raised: How long a life is enough life? (Callahan and Gaylin 2017). Indeed, a growing fear of living too long can be noticed, especially among older people. Fuelled by the fear of disabled life-expectancy, the frailty and abjection of the 'fourth age' (Higgs and Gilleard 2017), the prospect of a disappearing identity and eventually an undignified death, people may wish for setting limits and exercising control on the time and manner of death and dying (Callahan 1995, Davis 2014, McCue and Balasubramaniam 2017).

In the Netherlands – one of the few countries in the world that has legalized euthanasia and assisted suicide[1] under strict criteria[2] – there are some remarkable developments regarding the growing tendency to regulate death in old age. In recent years, the social acceptance of assisted dying is altering: gradually growing numbers of people are now dying on request without having a life-threatening physical disease, but because they suffer from dementia or multiple age-related (not immediately life-threatening) physical diseases (Onwuteaka-Philipsen et al. 2017). In addition, there is considerable debate about whether older people who consider their lives to be 'completed' and no longer worth living – while being relatively healthy – should have a legal option to ask for assisted dying. Despite considerable reluctance present in the Dutch population (Schnabel et al. 2016), growing numbers of people are convinced that even the suffering from an expected, feared future situation should be an argument in favour of legal dying assistance (van Rein 2013).

DOI: 10.4324/9780429329739-12

In this chapter, these current developments are examined. The question whether older people who consider life no longer worth living should have legal options to request for euthanasia falls outside of the scope of this chapter. Instead the focus is on a question that – in my view – precedes the former one, namely, how we should understand the nature of these death wishes: What are the driving concerns of older people who request assisted dying while being relatively healthy? When 'older people' are referred to in this chapter, I mean people aged 70 years and over. It is not intended to suggest older people are a homogeneous group facing common problems. On the contrary, the argument here is limited to those older people who – by their own standards and based on their own experiences – explicitly relate their wish to die[3] to late life and age-related losses and concerns. Also, within this specific group, I acknowledge the diversity of social positions, life course factors, life views, and personal circumstances that shape the experience of later life and old age.

This chapter is composed of three themed sections. First, drawing on Dutch empirical data, there is a detailed description of lived experiences, needs and concerns of older people who wish to die because in their view, their quality of life has diminished to such an extent that they prefer death over life. Second, some of the wider societal developments related to this specific wish to die are considered. Then, drawing on these insights, the final section highlights some issues that in my view need careful consideration in relation to the current debate about a self-chosen death in old age.

The chapter is based on a critical review of existing literature, supplemented by both empirical-phenomenological research on this topic (see below) and exchanges, conversations, discussions with leading professionals (scholars and practitioners) between 2012 and 2019. The two main sources, namely, conceptual and empirical research, are used in a dialectical relation with each other (Rehmann-Sutter, Porz, and Scully 2012).

Summary of empirical research methodology

The empirical work underlying this chapter consists of a qualitative, phenomenological interview study conducted in the Netherlands (Van Wijngaarden, Leget, and Goossensen 2015, 2016). A phenomenological approach was chosen because of its primary focus on the lifeworld: the world of lived experience. Rather than giving causal, behavioural explanations and using external theories and interpretive frameworks, the focus is on giving a description of the phenomenon as it is experienced by those who are studied (Dahlberg, Dahlberg, and Nystrom 2008, Finlay 2011). The two main research questions were:

1. What is the lived experience of older people who consider their lives to be completed and no longer worth living?
2. What does it mean to live in-between the intention to end life at a self-directed moment and actually choosing a self-directed death (or not)?

The project started in 2013 with 25 white Dutch older people, who had mental capacity to consent, and were without evidence of a terminal or mental illness. The sample comprised 11 male and 14 female participants, 67–99, with a mean age of 82 years. People were recruited between April and September 2013. Advertisements were placed in four Dutch magazines and on three Dutch websites all targeting older people. Sample criteria were: having an actual wish to die; ideating on a self-chosen death; richness of experiences; differences in (physical) health; different ideological and demographic backgrounds; and nationwide coverage. Eighteen participants had no partner (widowed, divorced or single for life). Fourteen participants with children had contact with their children, two did not; nine participants did not have children. Most participants lived independent or semi-dependent. Only two participants lived in care institution. Twenty-three participants had had a paid job; only two female participants were engaged full time in home-based household and voluntary work. Ten participants reported having no serious illness. The other 15 mentioned several physical problems (such as sensory disorders, serious itchiness, chronic fatigue, arthritis, diabetes, or valvular heart disease). The first interviews took place in 2013, with follow-up interviews with surviving participants in 2017 (n = 11) and 2019 (n = 6).

Research findings: the lived experience of older people ideating on a self-chosen death

Lived experience is an important source of knowledge for understanding what it means for older people to be ideating on a self-chosen death. What is happening in their lives so that they come to prefer death over life while not being terminally ill? What are their concerns? In this chapter, I therefore take our point of departure in the lived experience of the older people in question. Drawing on our ongoing research, a vignette is now presented to provide an initial impression of the older people concerned.

> Linda (79) had had important political jobs during her life and held influential board positions, also after retirement. But that has stopped a few years ago. She finds it encouraging, but also very difficult to see others taking over her work. She told: "I still have the expertise, but I no longer play a role on stage. Actually, I'm useless."
>
> Her husband died a year ago after a short but severe illness: "You know, it's a combination, there's nothing more to expect. What remains are diversions; welcome but worthless. Currently, the only meaningful thing left is that I want to write farewell letters to my children and grandchildren."
>
> Although Linda has warm relationships with family, loneliness fills her days. "I have sweet children. I can always call or visit them. I just have to squeak and they come around. But deep down, I feel very alone.

> Actually, my children don't need me anymore. Whether or not I organize a Christmas lunch or dinner, it doesn't really matter."
>
> In anticipation of what she perceives as a "limited and frightening future", Linda is seriously contemplating a self-chosen death: "Really, I feel that I'm done. My life's completed. It can only get worse. Strolling with a walker, panting on a sidewalk, stumbling over curbs…, I want to safeguard myself from such misery". She speaks about her intention to pre-emptively ending her life as "a solution", "a rational consideration". "It's an ultimate choice, sure, but why not? I just don't think my life is worth it anymore."
>
> van Wijngaarden (2016, 53–56)

The vignette above briefly describes Linda's struggle with life. She – as well as many of the other research participants – suffered from feelings of loss and loneliness,[4] the pain of feeling like she did not matter to others, the growing inability to find meaningful pathways to self-expression, intense existential fatigue, and aversion of (feared) anticipated dependence and loss of control (van Wijngaarden, Leget, and Goossensen 2015, 260–262). Such a string of existential concerns can create a sense of 'disconnectedness to one's actual life' (van Wijngaarden, Leget, and Goossensen 2019, 3), permeating the way people experience their identities, their bodies, their social relations, as well as how they relate to the surrounding world (van Wijngaarden, Leget, and Goossensen 2019).

Reading the vignette, some might suggest that Linda was still lost in grief and might have found new purpose and meaning when her grief was less severe. Others might say she was lonely, and helping her to make new friends might reduce her loneliness and make life feel more like living. Others that she needed anti-depressant medication, counselling, a hobby, some charity work, or to be more involved by her children in their family life. In other words, they may jump to the conclusion that Linda's loss of interest in life was merely situational and mutable. Although this might be the case in some situations, in this chapter I make a plea for a phenomenologically inspired approach, first trying to slow down and understand the lifeworld of people like Linda on a deeper level, and approaching this experience as a legitimate experience that first needs to be and recognized rather than explained, categorized or 'solved'.

The fear of losing one's personal identity

The older people in the study who were ideating on a self-chosen death for anticipatory reasons tended to characterize themselves as being 'pro-active' and 'independent' people (van Wijngaarden, Leget, and Goossensen 2015, 262). Often they viewed themselves as reflective individuals, being quite self-aware, able to define their personal priorities and what they considered to be the essence their existence, as the case of Linda illustrates. The whole process of ageing causes considerable distress to these individuals, one of the main concerns appearing to be connected with the fear of losing one's identity. Drawing on MacIntyre (1977), Prado uses the notion of an 'epistemological crisis' to refer to such issues (Prado 1998, 23). He describes how the self-identity of the ageing individuals can be severely threatened by interpretative difficulties. This corresponds with the people under research: they were at a complete loss because they realized that the deterioration process was destroying essential traits that made up who they thought themselves to be. Not only was ageing seen as threatening their ability to continue certain activities, but the process of ageing was also diminishing their sense of identity. Despite biologically living on, in their view, biographically they no longer existed as the people they once were. This often created a deep existential crisis: the participants felt like 'reduced' individuals. They felt forced to redefine themselves, but they resisted as they felt not only unable but also unwilling to do so. In their view, life could continue only in what they considered to be an 'unacceptably' reduced way; they had 'outlived' themselves (van Wijngaarden, Leget, and Goossensen 2015, 262).

This process shows resemblance with Freeman's notion of 'narrative foreclosure' (Freeman 2000, 81, 83). This is the conviction that even though one's life as such continues, in one's mind, one's life story has already ended. Regardless of whether one continues to get up every morning, no new chapters are apt to be added to one's story: life is not over, but the perception is that the life story is. Again, there is close correspondence with the people we investigated. They felt unable to identify with their current life stories: life seemed to be too alienating, too meaningless and incoherent, too shameful or frightening, too constrained and/or dominated by others. Having no pleasant future expectations, the participants were afraid of a new narrative opening, as they expected only unwanted ones. However, despite expressing an outspoken wish to die, the older research participants also – implicitly and explicitly – expressed a desire to be visible, recognized, wanted, needed, valued, depended on, or attended to by others (van Wijngaarden, Leget, and Goossensen 2015, 262). This shows that in some cases the wish to die and the wish to rediscover meaning coexist.

Tiredness of life

Next to the struggle with self-identity, the research participants all mentioned (often intertwined) varying forms of physical, mental and existential tiredness (van Wijngaarden, Leget, and Goossensen 2015, 261). Some people explicitly related their sense of tiredness to physical deterioration, diseases and pain. Others mainly linked it to mental pain such grief or past trauma that had come to the foreground in the silences of older age. Most, however, primarily related their sense of tiredness to a lack of meaningful daytime activities resulting in feelings of boredom. Debilitated by the slowness, the monotony and the emptiness of their lives, they not only lacked an invitation to participate by others but also experienced a lack of interests and listlessness in themselves. Often the hope that the emptiness could be filled again seemed gone. Life had become 'an aching void that cannot be filled anymore' (van Wijngaarden et al. 2017, 254). Consequently, for many of our participants the sense of time had changed considerably. Time was more and more experienced as an enemy; it stagnated, slowed down and kept them 'imprisoned' (van Wijngaarden et al. 2017, 258). Frightening thoughts about the future and – in some cases – wistful thoughts about the past deprived the lust for life.

While our research has shown that 'tiredness of life' – understood in a multidimensional way beyond the physical – is an important constituent of the experience that life is no longer worth living, I would argue that it should not be understood as a synonym as is sometimes done (Dijkhuis et al. 2004). Indeed, in my view, the term 'tiredness of life' too strongly suggests that the associated wish to die is merely an individual issue, a matter of person lack of interest and purpose. As will be described in the following part, our research has also shown that the wish to die in old age has a distinct social dimension as well. I would argue that the term 'tiredness of life' gives too little account of these social drivers.

Distancing and internalizing

More or less, the group under investigation also lacked the feeling of mattering and being needed within their communities (van Wijngaarden, Leget, and Goossensen 2015). Striving to establish and preserve their membership of society as long as possible, the majority of older people explicitly sought to distance themselves from the category 'old' and the accompanying ageist stereotypes in the ways they expressed themselves. Simultaneously, though, they seemed to have internalized monolithic stereotypes of old age, having a considerable negative impact on their self-esteem (van Wijngaarden et al. 2017). When the older people with a wish to die referred to old age in general, or when they referred to themselves as undergoing this later stage of life, they often used language indicating a sense of redundancy, indignity and burdensomeness (van Wijngaarden et al. 2017, 253, 258). Sometimes explicit comparisons were made between themselves increasingly burdening the health care or pension system and alleged ancient traditions about the self-chosen death in old age, such as putting an unproductive older family member 'on an ice floe' (van Wijngaarden, Leget, and Goossensen 2016, 8). Some even supposed the self-chosen death to be a way to take responsibility and stop burdening one's family or society.

Social needs, concerns and vulnerabilities

To some extent, the reported sense of indignity and unworthiness in the research participants appeared to be rooted in concrete experiences of societal ignorance, marginalization and exclusion (van Wijngaarden, Leget, and Goossensen 2015). In other words, the wish to die was partly driven by unmet societal needs. Not only were everyday life experiences of ageing affected by physical aspects such as the loss of mobility, (the fear of) declining health and fatigue or by psychological realities of bereavement and coping with age-related losses, but for a significant part, they were also constituted by social practices.

To illustrate, while there are many situations in which older people receive good – or even excellent – older age care in the Netherlands, most of the older people in the study had quite negative expectations of and bad experiences with homecare or institutionalized care. One complained, for example, that for her daily dinner (brought to her by homecare meals services), she was allowed to choose from three meals only, but in her view, all three of them were not tasty and much too salty while she had a low-salt diet. Another person said that the homecare nurses regularly put the wrong ointment on her wound 'because they are in too much of a hurry …' And several times it was mentioned that older people often had to 'wait endlessly' for assistance, because of a shortage of staff … Most people can cope with such circumstances if they are "one-offs", but if things pile up, a sense of worthlessness may be strengthened. In our studies, 13 older people explicitly made a link between their wish to die and their lack of trust in sufficiency of care. Hence, they envisioned a self-chosen death as a way to pre-emptively safeguard oneself from such practices.

The concept of vulnerability has been criticized for its negative and stereotyping connotation with weakness, dependency and lack of agency. It is also widely disputed for its fixed understanding, while in reality the experience of vulnerabilities may differ and change over time. Moreover, it is contested as a harmful label attached to someone given certain conditions, a psychological trait or an individual problem, thereby neglecting the multiple contextual sources of vulnerabilities (Luna 2009). The concept can nonetheless be helpful if used in a nuanced way, following Luna's argument who understands vulnerability as a flexible concept – connoting situational vulnerabilities operating on different layers (Luna 2009, 2019). Using the concept as such goes beyond fixed thinking that older people "are" vulnerable, and may help us considering particular situations that can make or render someone vulnerable.

Notwithstanding the particularity of each person in our sample, all participants suffered from diverse overlapping layers of vulnerabilities such as ill-health; age-related losses; bereavements; loneliness; isolation; burdensomeness on the family; having a low social status associated with retirement; poor economic situation due to a limited pension; lack of available meaningful projects; and/or the uncertainty about the adequacy of welfare services and care arrangements. Indeed, these are all examples of situational vulnerabilities that partly shaped the negative experiences of the research participants (van Wijngaarden, Leget, and Goossensen 2015). Such vulnerabilities, however, depend for a great deal on social norms, policies and institutions that perhaps could be changed for the better, if prioritized (Mackenzie, Rogers, and Dodds 2014). Identifying the layered vulnerabilities in those with a wish to die allows us to unfold how these vulnerabilities interact not only with personal (emotional, cognitive and physical) but also social, economic and political contexts (Luna 2009, 2019).

The ambiguity of choosing death

In the rational suicide literature, a pre-emptive death is regularly described as a rational and autonomous decision to release oneself from suffering. To be considered 'rational', the decision should be made by a person who has mental capacity. The decision should also follow validly from true premises, be based on a proper motivation and sound reasoning, in line with one's values, and made in full awareness of the consequences and free of undue pressure (Lester 2006, Prado 1998, 2008). This cognitive conception of 'rationality' is reflected in Cantor's argument for a legal possibility to organize a timely death to avoid dementia. He states, 'I care mightily about posthumous recollections of my personality, and I strive to shape my life trajectory, including a dying process, consistently with my personal vision of dignity' (Cantor 2018, 16).

The majority of the older people we interviewed over the years underscore Cantor's position. For them, the principles of individual choice and (prospective) autonomy were their bedrock. They claimed that choosing death in anticipation of what is perceived as age-related suffering is their self-determined decision giving them a sense of reassurance, certainty and of (maintaining or regaining) autonomy. Most of them talked about making a reasoned assessment of their situation, in consonance with their fundamental interests and values (van Wijngaarden, Leget, and Goossensen 2016, 9). Simultaneously, though, most of them also felt driven by uncontrolled inner compulsions, referred to as 'obsessions', a state of 'panic' or 'despair' (van Wijngaarden, Leget, and Goossensen 2016, 6). They disclosed deep uncertainty about their own considerations and the consequences for their loved ones, reflected in questions such as: How, when, where and with whom do I prefer to die? And what do my choices mean for my relatives? Despite all efforts taken to 'organise' a good death, their accounts were permeated by worries realising the impossibility to control death (van Wijngaarden, Leget, and Goossensen 2016).

Moreover, most of the research participants felt ready to give up on life urgently and yet also tended to postpone hastening death due to certain (emotional and bodily) attachments to life such as vitality, a healthy appetite or responsibilities and duties towards themselves and others. Not exceptionally, parallel to a wish to die, they reported a sense of some lust for life or a 'forlorn hope' that things may change a bit for the good. Indeed, they kept doing exercises or keep going to the doctors for help and ideas to improve their physical situation, for example by opting for medication or treatment like a hip replacement or cataract surgery (van Wijngaarden, Leget, and Goossensen 2016).

Although still in its infancy, the current body of empirical research has shown that living towards the ultimate choice regarding a pre-emptive death is often quite messy and murky process, and experienced as an inner conflict. Indeed, ideating on a self-chosen death is characterized by ambivalent feelings of being torn (van Wijngaarden, Leget, and Goossensen 2016). Research has thus shown the inadequacy of considering this decision-making process merely as a matter of rational calculation and choice. Indeed, these existential choices cannot be captured in logical constructions without considering the sense perception.

Thus far, this section has described the lived experience of the older people who consider their life to be no longer worth living and consequently wish for a self-chosen death. As the short vignette of Linda shows, such a wish to die is associated with a tangle of intertwined physical, psychological, existential, relational and socio-cultural dimensions. The integrity of the person is deeply threatened. Ideating on a self-chosen death seems to be a way to escape from this threat. The section also provided a description of the complexity and the ambiguity of choosing death. The related decision-making process appears to be an existential conundrum characterized by a mix of rational (including both cognition and emotions), a-rational and irrational drivers. Indeed, it is driven by the great value people attach to their independence, autonomy and authenticity (and thus to their own life view), as well as strongly influenced by a sense of loneliness, social isolation, burdensomeness and ageing anxieties. The section that now follows moves on to consider the wider social-cultural horizon of these death wishes.

The new old ages and the self-chosen death

De Beauvoir (1996), among others, reminds us that we should not view the situation and meaning of old age solely through a biological or psychological lens, but take into consideration its social, cultural, political and ideological embeddedness. Ageing always takes place within a community. The image of old age is strongly related to the nature of that community and depends on the goals pursued by a society (de Beauvoir 1996, 86). It is thus against a socio-cultural background that we can better comprehend how general features influence the ways we view and experience finitude and death. This section therefore further theorizes and contextualizes the described experiences by depicting the wider socio-cultural horizon. It specifically examines the implications of the new old ages and the new demography of death and link these to late modern notions the self, old age and death and dying. Doing this, the aim is to show that the wish to choose death partly originates from other late modern core norms such as reflexivity, authenticity and narrativity.

Ageing and dying in times of advanced medicine

Ageing anxieties and the wish for a pre-emptive self-chosen death are far from new phenomena. Contemplating on old age and a self-chosen death, the Stoic philosopher Seneca wrote,

> [if old age] begins to shake my mind, if it destroys its faculties one by one, if it leaves me not life but breath, I will depart from the putrid or tottering edifice. (…) if I must suffer without hope or relief, I will depart, not through fear of the pain itself, but because it prevents all for which I would live.
>
> Seneca, quoted in Werth Jr (1996, 13)

There is a degree of similarity between the current wish for a pre-emptive death and Seneca's wish, but there are also considerable differences and new challenges. Under the influence of medical-technological progress, increasing welfare, individualization, democratisation and secularization, the way we age and die has radically changed in the last decades. Due to a major worldwide demographic evolution in the late nineteenth and twentieth centuries, large-scale longevity is a new phenomenon in human history (Harper 2014, Leeson 2014). Since long life-expectancy comes with the rise of chronic illness and disability as well as subjective concerns among older people about losing their homes and gardens, their circle of friends, their privacy and autonomy, it is certainly not experienced as a blessing by anyone. Especially the gradual decline in functioning and the memory and identity loss associated with dementia that many experience as they age, raise new and urgent questions about the meaning of living towards the end of life. Through the dominance of women in epidemiological numbers of oldest old (Gilleard and Higgs 2018), women are even at greater risk for dementia, and live longer with greater age-related disabilities, ill-health and care needs. Consequently, the challenges seem even greater for older woman.

With the advance of medicine, the cause of dying has changed considerably. Most deaths among older people are now associated with frailty, organ failure, general deterioration, and an assortment of serious, disabling and chronic diseases. Instead of sudden deaths, long dying trajectories have become more common in recent years, producing more journeys of dying that can be very difficult, tiresome, unsettling, testing or even stigmatizing not only for the dying, but also for the loved ones of the dying person. Kellehear coined these deaths as 'shameful deaths' referring to the 'tragedy' of dying with loss of awareness and identity, far beyond the social death (Kellehear 2007, 213–233). In other words, both the fear of dying a tragic death is powerful, but also the fear of *not* dying is very powerful (Callahan 2000).

Not only have death trajectories changed, but our knowledge about expected trajectories has also increased enormously. Lay people have more access to medical knowledge and are increasingly familiar with medical prognoses. Moreover, people are caring for friends and family members with age-related health problems and/or disabilities, making them more aware of their own possible futures and wonder if they would face the same fate. Such medical and experiential knowledge creates possibilities for looking forward and anticipate what the future might bring. This in turn involved considering and exercising a certain control by making choices and end-of-life decisions.

While such choices are supposed to be liberating, the increased knowledge and amount of options may also promote different anxieties and, inevitably, bring up a new set of moral challenges (Callahan 2000).

The quest for personal control becomes more vividly present in the fears of a western society that has become terrorized at the prospect of deep old age and long or uncertain dying trajectories. People are concerned about being a burden on one's family for too long (Roest, Trappenburg, and Leget 2019), or living out a life of 'pointless' suffering. For many modern citizens, suffering and dying are no longer viewed as givens, but rather as problems we should solve as a society, thus requiring human acts, including both medical-technological possibilities as well as personal choice to anticipate and set limits. It follows that dying is increasingly experienced as a huge individual responsibility, rather than a natural occurrence.

In the context of these medical-technological developments, a self-chosen death may be seen as a decisive step to resist the medical imperative and prevent the invasive medicalisation of ageing and dying. It can be interpreted as an effort to safeguard oneself from being kept alive too long and enable a timely and peaceful death. Paradoxically, though, this 'solution' also depends on medical-technical means and can consequently also be seen as another way of medicalising death. While there are, of course, significant differences between people with different worldviews, for a growing group of Western people, medicine is increasingly supposed to provide a solution to the problem of human suffering and meaninglessness.

The self-chosen death as a means to maintain one's integrity

To understand the wish to control the manner and timing of death among some older people, we also need to take a closer look at two related tendencies, namely, secularisation and individualisation. Among others, Giddens (1991) has clearly described how these tendencies have influenced late modern society. With the rise of secularisation, and the marginalization of religious institutions, people become separated from tradition (including its communal understanding of life and death, shared language, rituals and practices).

For many people, this is experienced as a liberation, but the dis-embedding of traditions also creates new challenges, uncertainties and anxieties (Giddens 1991). In previous times, suffering and death were integral parts of religious life views, but many late modern western people have lost a collective cosmology to support their understanding of life and death. Consequently, they have to personally reformulate their life views and find new answers to existential questions about the nature of being, relations, self-identity and the finitude of life.

Closely related to secularisation is the process of individualisation, as this rests on the right of individuals to seek for themselves that which – in their private judgement – can be seen as good (Callahan 2000, 58). Realizing the self – and its goals – has become an individual project of which fundamental components are choice, control and personal responsibility (Giddens 1991, 80). A related, powerful Western social ideal is that of the self-disciplined, independent and productive agent as the cornerstone of society (Taylor 2004, 150–151) resulting in high valuation of personal (work) projects: one's public contribution to society is viewed as one of the most important goals in life. Drawing on Giddens, the following are further features of late modern individualism:

- First, the self is seen a reflexive project for which the individual is responsible, requiring constant self-formation and reorganisation of the self towards a rewarding sense of the self (the malleability of life and the self);
- Second, the self forms a trajectory of development from the past to the anticipated future, requiring awareness of the various phases of the lifespan and constant self-monitoring to stay 'in charge' of its trajectory (colonisation of the future).
- Third, the active process of self-construction and self-actualisation presumes the building of a personal narrative that sustains an integrated sense of the self. An important moral thread is one of authenticity (being true to oneself).
- Fourth, self-development and self-actualisation are internally referential and seen as a personal achievement (or a personal failure in case one is not successful; Giddens 1991, 75–77).

Applied to ageing, these general features of late modern societies can help us to better understand the impact of negative views of increasing deterioration of health and capabilities as well as other age-related vulnerabilities. They immediately threaten the ideal of the malleability of life and the self. Moreover, they may even compromise a sense of full citizenship.

With regard to death and dying, it may clarify how dying has increasingly become an expression of one's own lifestyle. To manage and design a 'good death' has first and foremost become a personal journey, rather than a social or interpersonal one, that the individual seeks to accomplish in consultation with (medical and funeral) professionals (Kehl 2006, Kellehear 2007). The fear of what Kellehear (2007) terms a 'shameful death' should be understood in relation to the impeding threat of integrity of the self, the coherence of one's narrative and eventually as personal insufficiency (Giddens 1991). Since for many Western people, death is more often perceived as the very end (mainly a '*this-world* experience' rather than an '*other-world* journey'), a socially intact goodbye becomes even more important (Kellehear 2007, 81). To be in charge over the last phase of life means being able to actualize the final chapter of one's narrative. Dying on your own terms gradually seems to become an imperative. In a sense, it can be seen as a last manner of self-expression and a very personal way of 'leaving an immaterial legacy' (Kehl 2006, 262) moulding the way one is remembered. In the context of late modern society, this is not only an issue of preference, but it is also understood as another responsibility.

The challenge of choosing death

As mentioned in the introduction, in the Netherlands physician-assisted dying has been legalized since 2002. Currently, increasing numbers of Dutch citizens are in favour of a more relaxed interpretation of the law (Onwuteaka-Philipsen et al. 2017). Mainly based on an ethos of self-determination and autonomy, there is a strong political lobby for the legal right to assisted dying when life is considered to be completed and no longer worth living (van Rein 2013). Against the socio-cultural backgrounds of late modern times, it may be fairly understandable that more and more dying people – as well as their loved ones – are eager to find ways to control their deaths in order to avoid a shameful death and bring the biological death in consonance with the social death. However, the descriptions in this chapter also shed light on many complex challenges and ambivalences. Having described these existential and societal challenges, this final section of this chapter applies these insights to the debate on assisted dying in old age and formulates some important comments that – in my view – need careful consideration both in academia and in public.

The multi-dimensional nature of the wish to die

First, we have seen that the wish to die is associated with a tangle of intertwined physical, psychological, existential, relational and socio-cultural dimensions. Moreover, research has illuminated diverse overlapping layers of vulnerabilities such as age-related deterioration and losses, bereavements, loneliness, perceived burdensomeness, low social-economic status of retirement, or a lack of trust in the sufficiency of welfare and care services. Naming and classifying the different layers of vulnerability helps to better understand the complex nature of these death wishes, and also allows to target differences or variations among people. Part of the vulnerabilities point to political-ethical dimension of the wishes to die, thus showing that we should not perceive these wishes as merely a subjective, individual issue. Indeed, some of the needs and concerns that drive the wish to die seem to depend partly on customs and policies that supposedly could be changed for the better, for example by putting effort in reducing the level of public distrust in care; improving tailored care especially for people who attach great importance to their independence; and enhancing a meaningful place and role for older people (especially the oldest old) in society (Schnabel et al. 2016).

The interplay of personal and public images of old age

As indicated previously, the wish to die is associated with profound negative discourse about old age. The older people with a wish to die seemed to distance themselves from 'old age' and label it as a socially subordinate phase of life. Simultaneously, they had internalized deeply pessimistic images, negatively shaping their self-esteem. For a proper understanding of how people talk and think about the wish to die in old age, it is important to also acknowledge the interplay between societal images and personal experiences. Experiences of 'completed life' and of meaninglessness in old age may be very personal, but they do not arise in a social vacuum. Sociocultural ideals, images and assumptions may influence and shape how older people privately assess their lives. This means that the assessment that 'life is no longer worth living' or that someone 'has lived past his times' cannot be completely separated from societal value judgements. In fact, such assessments indicate certain social, economic and political values and expectations about a person's worth to others or society (Kellehear 2007, 240–241) that at least in part arise from a high valuation of certain dimensions of human life, such as capacities, cognition and participation (van Wijngaarden et al. 2017).

Given demographic changes, it is no wonder that social ideas regarding old age are being renegotiated in society. Especially when these conceptions are in flux, more in-depth research is needed on the interplay between the wide spectrum of public and personal images about the meaning of old age (including those of people of different socio-economic, religious and cultural backgrounds) and how these images influence the lived experiences of older people and structure how people orient themselves.

Towards an understanding of the self-chosen death that recognizes complexity

Finally, as described above, empirical research nuances and qualifies the conception of a rational pre-emptive self-chosen death. In many cases, people feel torn between their cognitive-rational considerations and their much more ambiguous and multivoiced experiences. Moreover, looking closely at these experiences, it becomes clear that choice is not only liberating but also deeply frightening. One has to make assessments about the course of life and death. Such timing is extremely complicated, as timing is not just an abstract, neutral decision of duration. In contrast, time gives human experience its storied nature; it indicates feelings of possibility, but also limited possibilities and anxieties about future closing down. Consequently, choosing the time and manner of death involves a highly complex synchronizing of biological, psychological, social and spiritual/existential aspects of life. To facilitate deep understanding of those with a wish for a self-chosen death, we should acknowledge of the complexity of choosing death: it not only a rational-choice-narrative, existential-crisis-narrative, a tragedy-narrative, a failure-in-care narrative nor a stereotype-embodiment-narrative only. In contrast, research has shown that these narratives are often complementary. Such an integral understanding may help us to recognize these different aspects as part of a complex whole.

To conclude, this chapter started with the vignette of Linda's wish to die. Political, medical and public commitment all is needed to preserve dignity and address and relief suffering of fellow human beings, such as hers. Acknowledging their wishes, concerns and suffering, including their outspoken wish to set limits as well as the deep anxieties and doubts, is of utmost importance. Concrete actions, decisions and policies that follow from these commitments can have several possible forms, and do not automatically lead to endorsing the plea for assisted dying. Before rushing into solutions, what is required is careful debate and further empirical inquiries addressing the complexity of the wish to choose death.

Notes

1 In the Dutch context, euthanasia means that the physician administers a lethal substance to the patient. In the case of assisted suicide, the physician supplies a lethal substance that the patient takes in the physician's presence. For the purpose of this chapter, we mainly use the term 'assisted dying' to include both practices.

2 These requirements of due care stipulate that the physician:

a Is convinced that the patient's request is voluntary and well-considered;
b Is convinced that the patient's suffering is unbearable and that there is no prospect of improvement;
c Has informed the patient about the situation he/she is in and about his/her prospects;
d Is convinced, together with the patient, that there is no other reasonable solution for the patient's situation;
e Has consulted with at least one other independent physician who has seen the patient and has provided a written opinion on the due care requirements referred to in (a)–(d); and
f Shall terminate a life or assist in a suicide with due care

(Adapted from de Jong, van Dijk, 2017).

See also: https://english.euthanasiecommissie.nl/due-care-criteria.

3 A 'wish to die' (WTD) is defined here as a wish or a desire for death to come, understood against the backdrop of various forms of consciousness: a range of conscious thoughts, perceptions, emotions, memories as well as more elusive bodily experiences, tactile sensations and bodily movements (Dainton 2008). NB: this should *not* be confused with the particular psychoanalytical meaning of death wishes.

4 Loneliness is understood here as not merely a quantitative lack of social relations, but rather a qualitative change in one's relations; a lack of close companionship with people to whom they can really relate, and sense a form of sameness, recognition and reciprocity (van Wijngaarden et al. 2015).

References

Callahan, D. (1987). *Setting limits: Medical goals in an ageing society*. New York: Simon and Schuster.

Callahan, D. (2000). *The troubled dream of life: In search of a peaceful death*. Washington: Georgetown University Press.

Callahan, D., & Gaylin, W. (2017). How long a life is enough life? *Hastings Center Report*, *47*(4), 16–18.

Cantor, N. L. (2018). On avoiding deep dementia. *Hastings Center Report, 48*(4), 15–24.

Dahlberg, K., Dahlberg, H., & Nyström, M. (2008). *Reflective lifeworld research*. Lund: Studentlitteratur.

Dainton, B. (2008). *The phenomenal self.* Oxford: Oxford University Press.

Davis, D. S. (2014). Alzheimer disease and pre-emptive suicide. *Journal of Medical Ethics, 40*(8), 543–549.

De Beauvoir, S. (1996). *The coming of age*. New York: WW Norton & Company.

de Jong, A., & van Dijk. (2017). Euthanasia in the Netherlands: Balancing autonomy and compassion. *World Medical Journal, 63*, 10–15.

Dijkhuis, C. (2004). *Op zoek naar normen voor het handelen van artsen bij vragen om hulp bij levensbeëindiging in geval van lijden aan het leven*. Utrecht: KNMG.

Finlay, L. (2011). *Phenomenology for therapists: Researching the lived world.* West Sussex: Wiley-Blackwell.

Freeman, M. (2002). When the story's over: Narrative foreclosure and the possibility of self-renewal. In M. Andrews, D.S. Sclater, C. Squire and A. Treacher (eds) *Lines of narrative*, 95–105. Abingdon: Routledge.

Giddens, A. (1991). *Modernity and self-identity: Self and society in the late modern age*. Palo Alto, CA: Stanford University Press.

Gilleard, C., & Higgs, P. (2018). Gender and the social imaginary of the fourth age. In S. Westwood (ed) *Ageing, diversity and equality: Social justice perspectives*, 48–65. Abingdon: Routledge.

Harper, S. (2014). Economic and social implications of aging societies. *Science, 346*(6209), 587–591.

Higgs, P., & Gilleard, C. (2017). The nature of the fourth age as a challenge to ageing societies. In M. Schweda et al. (eds) *Planning later life*, 57–71. Abingdon: Routledge.

Kehl, K. A. (2006). Moving toward peace: An analysis of the concept of a good death. *American Journal of Hospice and Palliative Medicine, 23*(4), 277–286.

Kellehear, A. (2007). *A social history of dying*. Cambridge: Cambridge University Press.

Leeson, G. W. (2014). Increasing longevity and the new demography of death. *International Journal of Population Research*, http://dx.doi.org/10.1155/2014/521523.

Lester, D. (2006). Can suicide be a good death? *Death Studies, 30*(6), 511–527.

Luna, F. (2009). Elucidating the concept of vulnerability: Layers not labels. *IJFAB: International Journal of Feminist Approaches to Bioethics, 2*(1), 121–139.

Luna, F. (2019). Identifying and evaluating layers of vulnerability–a way forward. *Developing World Bioethics, 19*(2), 86–95.

MacIntyre, A. (1977). Epistemological crises, dramatic narrative and the philosophy of science. *The Monist, 60*(4), 453–472.

Mackenzie, C., Rogers, W., & Dodds, S. (eds.). (2014). *Vulnerability: New essays in ethics and feminist philosophy*. Oxford: Oxford University Press.

McCue, R. E., & Balasubramaniam, M. (eds.). (2016). *Rational suicide in the elderly: Clinical, ethical, and sociocultural aspects.* New York: Springer.

Onwuteaka-Philipsen, B. D., Legemaate, J., Evenblij, K., & Pasman, H. R. W. (2017). *Derde evaluatie Wet toetsing levensbeëindiging op verzoek en hulp bij zelfdoding.* Den Haag: ZonMW.

Prado, C. G. (1998). *The last choice: Preemptive suicide in advanced age* (No. 63). Westport CN: Greenwood Publishing Group.

Prado, C. G. (2008). *Choosing to die: Elective death and multiculturalism*. Cambridge: Cambridge University Press.

Rehmann-Sutter, C., Porz, R., & Scully, J. L. (2012). How to relate the empirical to the normative: Toward a phenomenologically informed hermeneutic approach to bioethics. *Cambridge Quarterly of Healthcare Ethics, 21*(4), 436–447.

Roest, B., Trappenburg, M., & Leget, C. (2019). The involvement of family in the Dutch practice of euthanasia and physician assisted suicide: A systematic mixed studies review. *BMC Medical Ethics, 20*(1), 23.

Schnabel, P., Meyboom-de Jong, B., Schudel, W. J., Cleiren, C. P. M., Mevis, P. A. M., Verkerk, M. J., van der Heide, A., Hesselmann, G., & Stultiëns, L. F. (2016). *Voltooid leven: Over hulp bij zelfdoding aan mensen die hun leven voltooid achten*. Den Haag: Adviescommissie voltooid leven.

Taylor, C. (2004). *Modern social imaginaries*. Durham, NC: Duke University Press.

van Rein, P. S. (2013). *Petitioning for completed life: A thematic content analysis*. Doctoral dissertation, Walden University.

van Wijngaarden, E., Leget, C., & Goossensen, A. (2015). Ready to give up on life: The lived experience of elderly people who feel life is completed and no longer worth living. *Social Science & Medicine, 138*, 257–264.

van Wijngaarden, E. (2016). *Voltooid leven: over leven en willen sterven* [Completed life: about living and the wish to die], Amsterdam/Antwerpen: Atlas Contact.

van Wijngaarden, E., Leget, C., & Goossensen, A. (2016). Caught between intending and doing: Older people ideating on a self-chosen death. *BMJ open, 6*(1), e009895.

van Wijngaarden, E., Leget, C., Goossensen, A., Pool, R., & The, A. M. (2019). A captive, a wreck, a piece of dirt: Aging anxieties embodied in older people with a death wish. *OMEGA-Journal of Death and Dying, 80*(2), 245–265.

13 Dying alone

Exercising a right or transgressing the rules?

Glenys Caswell

Introduction

This chapter argues that individuals who live and die alone, appearing to breach the socially imposed limits on acceptable choices about dying, should be able to do so without their deaths being reframed as stories of tragedy and blame. When a lone death takes place, the aftermath of the death is managed by state agencies and reported by the media, particularly when the individual's body is undiscovered for an extended period of time (Caswell, 2013). Such management is likely to result in the rewriting of the individual's identity, as well as in criticism of their life and death choices. A lone death is defined here as when individual who lives on their own dies alone at home, their body is not found immediately and they lack family and friends to take care of post-death processes and rituals (Caswell and O'Connor, 2015).

In a social setting that emphasises a need for individuals to live a life of their own choosing, individuals are expected to create and recreate their own identities (Giddens, 1991). Individuals are subjected to pressure to make choices and be the controllers of their own lives, but there are always constraints which limit the options available to them. What is possible in terms of individuals' life choices is bounded by what is deemed socially acceptable, and those boundaries are embedded in stratifying factors such as disability, age, sexuality, class, ethnicity, education, gender, as well as by individuals' self-conceptions (Giddens, 1991; Thalos, 2016).

Individuals are expected to live in a way that demonstrates the uniqueness of their identity, yet paradoxically they are required to do so in a manner that reflects social norms so that other members of society can recognise their uniqueness (Bauman, 2005). Individuals, that is, '… must follow the same life strategy and use shared – commonly recognizable and legible – tokens to convince others they are doing so' (Bauman, 2005, p. 16). Such an approach to life does not suit everyone, but failure to conform does have consequences (Craib, 1994). A UK funeral, for example, which does not reference the character of the person who died and tell the story of their life may be regarded by those attending as strange and inappropriate (Caswell, 2011–2012).

DOI: 10.4324/9780429329739-13

Death is a topic that people sometimes find difficult to contemplate, and there have long been debates about the level of fear that death inspires and the extent to which it is a taboo topic that must not be discussed (Sayer, 2010). However, death has emerged from the shadows for some groups in the population, making it increasingly acceptable to talk about death as well as to make plans for one's own, authentic death (Walter, 1994). It is possible, that is, for people to create their own death and ensure that it reflects their own unique identity.

Linked to this greater openness is the promise made in English healthcare policy that all adults are entitled to a good death which includes choice about the manner and place of their death (Department of Health, 2008; Borgstrom, 2015; Pollock, 2015; The Choice in End of Life Care Programme Board, 2015). The ongoing development of palliative care as a specialist healthcare discipline and the encouragement for people with life limiting illnesses to engage in a process of advance care planning has increased the number of people who make choices about their end of life care and deaths while they are still well enough to do so (National Palliative and End of Life Care Partnership, nd). Advance care planning of this kind is assumed to contribute to individuals' being enabled to plan for their own good death.

Despite greater talk about it, death is still a threat to society and there is a collective need to manage death and find ways to control it (Berger, 1969; Howarth, 2007). So while English health care policy emphasises the right to a good death and choice, there are boundaries to what is acceptable. Some possibilities are precluded by law, while others are subject to the rules of social acceptability, but in all cases breaking the rules may lead to sanctions. End of life care policy helps to maintain the boundaries by laying out what the approved choices are and healthcare practitioners play their part by offering those in their care choices from the approved range of options.

There are also legal and social processes which come into play once a person has died, and which help to maintain the status quo with regard to death. Each death is recorded and statistics are compiled on behalf of the state, while for the family and friends of the person who died there will usually be a funeral. These processes, both the regulatory procedures and the funeral, have the capacity to help repair any damage caused by deaths which did not meet approved social criteria. This is necessary because despite increasing openness in some sectors of the population with regard to death and dying, death remains a threat to society and requires to be controlled (Berger, 1969; Howarth, 2007).

Deaths which break the boundaries of approved social criteria and which need repair can occur in a number of ways, such as through violence or by accident. This chapter, however, is concerned with one category of such deaths, lone deaths, which occur when an individual lives alone and dies alone at home, their body is undiscovered for extended period of time, and they lack family and friends who can take charge of the post-death processes and rituals (Caswell and O'Connor, 2015).

The chapter begins by discussing the pressures which individuals face to create their own identities, before considering the notion of the self-styled death and the socially approved choices that are available for people to make. It goes on to describe briefly the empirical work which underpins the subsequent sections on lone deaths and the case study presented there of the repair work carried out through the application of regulatory processes. The chapter will round off with a discussion of the implications of the empirical findings for our understanding of how far individuals have a genuine right to die in the manner of their own choosing without being subjected to the judgements of others.

Self-styled life

The requirement for an individual to create their own identity is a feature of the period that has been termed late, or high, modernity. The concept of modernity refers to an era characterised by factors such as industrialisation, rational belief systems and extensive social institutions. Late modernity, the term preferred in this chapter, describes a time which has both continuities and discontinuities with modernity and it is characterised, among other things, by an emphasis on both institutional and individual reflexivity (Giddens, 1990, p. 4, 1991, p. 3).

Reflexivity is a key component of identity creation for individuals, who must reflect continuously on their lives so that they can make decisions about how to live in order to achieve their goals (Giddens, 1991, pp. 75–80). The idea that individuals should think about their lives, decide what kind of person they wish to be and then make choices as to how they might achieve this is not original to those living in a period of late modernity, but the pressure on individuals to make reflexive choices about their lives is new. The hold of traditional institutions such as churches and families is weaker and the range of options apparently open to people is wider (Giddens, 1991, pp. 206–207; Caswell, 2011). In late modernity, people have no choice but to choose and they are often thrown on their own resources when making those choices (Giddens, 1991, p. 81).

Despite the apparent plethora of choices available and the sense of freedom and anxiety this may create for individuals there are a range of constraints that serve to limit the options practicable for individuals. A person's self-conception is important, as how individuals view themselves impacts their behaviour and choices; thus, someone who sees themselves as bad at science will not view a career in medicine as a viable option (Thalos, 2016). Individuals' choices are also constrained by a range of factors outside their control. An individual's social positioning or personal characteristics may, for example, expose them to forces of prejudice, discrimination and stigma, thus limiting the choices available to them. People with access to capital, whether social or financial, have a wider range of options to call on than those who lack such access (Giddens, 1991; Carpiano, 2006). It is also the case that life choices which are not recognised as valid by other members of society are subject to social sanctions (Bauman, 2005). People who hoard possessions to such an extent that their home becomes difficult to access and navigate, for example, are not considered to be harmless eccentrics, but are perceived as odd and may be subjected to media parody (Salkovskis and Lambe, 2015).

Living a self-styled life is not something that all members of UK society aspire to, but for those who make the attempt it is not straightforward, and opting to make decisions about death is even more complex. There are, however, a number of ways in which individuals can take charge of their deaths and some of these are considered below.

Self-styled death

Some people in the UK plan their own funerals. This may be when an older person, or a terminally ill person, decides to plan and pay for their own funeral in order to save their family the work, stress and cost involved (Marie Curie, 2018; Money Advice Service, 2019).

Planning ahead is not only possible with reference to funerals. Advance care planning (ACP) is a way of forward planning for healthcare so that a person's choices will be known to those providing their care as they become increasingly ill (Marie Curie, 2018). For those who are dying, there is a range of options available in the ACP menu, although some choices are not legally available in England. Assisted dying, for example, is illegal although some individuals do opt for assisted dying either by travelling to Switzerland to utilise the resources of Dignitas or by enlisting covert assistance (see Huxtable; Ward and Kennedy, this volume).

The policy focus on the right to a good death in England has led to the adoption of certain assumptions about what is considered to be a good death, which includes dying at home, being accompanied by family, being free of pain and being treated with respect (Borgstrom, 2015; Pollock and Seymour, 2018).

Empirical work

The data used in this chapter come from a sociological pilot study which I conducted in the Midlands of England. The study explored how best to approach research examining perspectives on dying alone. There were two elements to the study, the first of which consisted of 11 semi-structured interviews with older people living alone about their views on the possibility of dying alone. Participants were all white, UK nationals, and eight were female and three male, with ages ranging from 64 to 83; they were recruited through advertisements and self-identified as older. Two group interviews were also carried out with seven Hospice at Home nurses, who care for dying patients in their own homes, about their views and experiences of caring for dying people who lived alone. These findings have been reported elsewhere (Caswell and O'Connor, 2019).

This chapter focusses on the second part of the project which comprised a study of four lone deaths using the sociological autopsy as methodology, which involves taking an ethnographic approach to the study of documents, approaching them as both sources of data and the objects of study (Fincham *et al.*, 2011). Data collection began with the study of the coroner file held on the particular case. In England, Wales and Northern Ireland, the coroner is a judicial office holder who is simultaneously an independent practitioner and an agent of the state, with a responsibility to investigate suspicious deaths to ensure that they were not caused by the actions of either the person who died or others (Dorries, 2014). Independence means the office holder is not expected to be subject to influence from state agencies or individuals, while being part of the state system for managing deaths suggests that coroners have a role in supporting collective approaches to death (Prior, 1989).

Deaths are described in this chapter as lone deaths when the individual concerned lived alone and died alone at home, when they had no family or friends who could take on the handling of post-death processes, and when their body was undiscovered until sometime later. It was not possible to specify a time period for this as there was insufficient prior research on such deaths to enable a judgement to be made (Caswell and O'Connor, 2015). The coroner file on the case was a key data source in the study of these lone deaths, and this has been extensively drawn on in the case study of Paul Carter below.

Before beginning data collection ethical approval was obtained from the University of Nottingham's Faculty of Medicine and Health Sciences Research Ethics Committee. Conducting research exploring aspects of death and dying involves a range of ethical issues and in this project, in addition to protecting the rights of living participants I was also concerned about involving people who were already dead. Views differ on whether the dead can be harmed (Wilkinson, 2002), so I made the decision to protect the identities of both the living and the dead, and to this end names have been changed in reporting findings. The study methods have been discussed in greater detail elsewhere, but it is important to note that this is a qualitative, exploratory study which is intended to be neither generalisable nor representative (Caswell and O'Connor, 2015, 2019).

Lone deaths

People die alone in various locations, including care homes (Thompson *et al.*, 2018), in hospitals (Puchalski, 2002) and at home (Kellehear, 2009). There are instances where an individual who lives on their own dies alone at home, their body is not found immediately and they lack family to take care of post-death arrangements (Caswell, 2013). Such a death is described here as a lone death, to distinguish it from the kind of dying alone which takes place with other people nearby such as occurs in an institutional setting, or in a shared domestic setting and where it may be expected that the individual's body will be found and cared for soon after death. Undergoing a lone death is often seen as indicative of a failure of care (Kellehear, 2009), and the idea of dying alone in this way and having their body undiscovered is frightening for some people who live alone (Lloyd-Williams *et al.*, 2007). When such a death occurs and there is no one to take charge of the necessary post-death processes such as registering the death and organising the funeral local authorities in England and Wales have a legal duty to ensure that the body of the deceased is appropriately dealt with (UK Government, 1984).

There is some evidence to suggest that for some people in this situation a lone death is a matter of choice (Kellehear, 2009; Caswell and O'Connor, 2015), and that for others it is a matter of no consequence (Howse, 1997). The fact that their bodies are not found until much later may be unimportant to them (Bradshaw *et al.*, 1978; Howse, 1997; Caswell and O'Connor, 2019). When a person's body is found after an extended period of time it increases the likelihood of the death being reported in the local news media, and when years have passed it is likely to be reported in the national press (Caswell, 2013). A media review conducted by Seale (2004) of a week's Anglophone press reports in 1999 found that reports made judgements which were often negative; about the person who died, about their families and communities, and about wider society (Seale, 2004). A similar review conducted during January 2019 of UK press reports found that such a death tended still to be cast as a bad death, however, there was also an acknowledgement in some cases that dying alone may have been a choice made by the individual (Turner and Caswell, 2019).

A case study will now be presented, in order to illustrate a number of the issues discussed above. Case studies are a useful way of drawing together different data sources around one instance of the phenomenon under consideration (Yin, 2014). In this chapter, the case of Paul Carter is drawn on.

The death of Paul Carter

In England, when there is doubt about the cause of death or identity of a deceased person, the case will be reported to the coroner (Dorries, 2014). This happened in the case of the death of Paul Carter, and what follows below is taken from an analysis of the coroner documents and media reports in the case of Paul Carter. All names have been changed, as noted above, and the location has been omitted in order to protect the identity of Mr Carter and any living relatives or friends he had. The documents which form the basis of the analysis presented here are the post-mortem report, a witness statement from Cathy Traynor (family friend), a witness statement from Brendan Chivers (neighbour), a witness statement from the police officer who found Mr Carter's body, a series of email exchanges between the police officer and the coroner's officer and four reports in the local news media.[1]

Background

Paul Carter was in his mid-seventies when he died. He had never married and had always lived alone. He came from a small family and had just one sibling, his younger sister Janice. Paul Carter lived in a housing association flat in a city suburb, having lived there a number of years. He had worked as a carpenter until his retirement. He and Janice had been close until her death five years previously, but he had lost contact with her adult children.

When his death was reported in the local press an old family friend, Cathy Traynor, came forward. In media interviews, Ms Traynor described Paul Carter as a private man who was considerate of others and who had been fiercely independent. She said that she had visited Paul about a year before his death and that he appeared to be in good health. The flat in which he was living seemed rather untidy and grubby, and Ms Traynor offered to help Paul clear up, but he had turned her offer down. Cathy Traynor believed that Paul had depended quite heavily on his sister Janice after the death of their parents, and that after Janice's death Paul had become very much alone. She felt, however, that this did not distress him as he was a man who was contented with his own company (WS1).

In late July 2014, Paul Carter's next door neighbour, Brendan Chivers, contacted his landlord to say that he had not seen his neighbour for several weeks, whereas previously he had seen him two or three times a week as he came and went from his flat. Mr Chivers was not aware of the landlord taking any steps to check on his neighbour whose name he did not know. In the middle of August, Mr Chivers contacted the police to say that a nasty smell was coming from his neighbour's flat and that he still had not seen the neighbour. In his written statement to the coroner's inquest Brendan Chivers said, '… although I did not know the male by name (that) he was the only male living in the flat … I have never seen anyone else visiting him' (WS2).

When police officers broke into the flat they found a body in a state of advanced decomposition. It was not possible to tell visually whose body it was, even if they had been able to find someone who knew the deceased man well enough to carry out a visual identification. In addition, DNA was not a viable route to identifying the body given that the flat's occupant, Paul Carter, had no direct relatives still living; his sister's children were not genetically close enough. The coroner made the decision that, given that the body was found in Mr Carter's flat and that his neighbour said that he had never seen or heard anyone else staying there, then the assumption could be made that the body was that of Paul Carter (EX1). The police officers checked the flat for signs of a disturbance but found none. They did not find an address book, nor any sign of contact details for family members in the flat, nor were they able to find such contact details through Mr Carter's GP, landlord or neighbours. They did, however, find a loaf of bread in the flat with a 'use by' date of about six weeks prior to the finding of his body (WS3).

The coroner requested that a post-mortem be carried out in an effort to discover the cause of death. According to the written post-mortem report there was '… no evidence of significant trauma or injury', supporting the police view that there had been no break in nor violence involved in the death. The pathologist concluded that the cause of death was 'unascertainable', as, given the '... advanced state of decomposition more precise assessment is not possible' (PM).

The inquest returned an open conclusion, as it was not possible to assign a cause of death and therefore no conclusion could be reached as to whether the cause was natural, accidental or caused by human intervention (Dorries, 2014). The identity of the deceased man was presumed to be Paul Carter, the cause of death was recorded as indeterminate and the date of death was recorded as the date on which Mr Carter's body was found by the police officers who broke into the flat (EM1; MR1, 2 &3).

One local newspaper covered the story of Paul Carter's death, reporting on the developing story on four occasions in its print and online editions. It wrote that the case of Paul Carter 'highlighted the tragedy of people dying alone ...', particularly given that in this case his neighbours did not know his name. The coverage included a quote from a representative of the organisation Age UK, who remarked on how sad it was and asked people to look out for older people living near them who might be lonely (MR1,2,3,4). Mr Carter's funeral was a public health funeral, organised and paid for by the local authority and attended by Cathy Traynor as an old family friend (MR4; UK Government, 1984).

Documents as research data

The documentary data used in the description of Paul Carter's death and its aftermath were the coroner file on his death, consisting of the post-mortem report, witness statements and email exchanges between police and coroner's officers, plus local news media reports. Each source can be approached in two ways as a research resource; firstly, as a source of data about the death of Paul Carter and secondly as an object of study in its own right (Prior, 2003). The account above offers a summary of the data about the death of Mr Carter, while this section concentrates on the documents as objects of study. All the documents were written from a particular perspective and with a specific purpose in mind, and these need to be explored in order to assess the utility of the data they present about the death of Paul Carter (Prior, 2003; Fincham *et al.*, 2011; Caswell and O'Connor, 2015).

When someone dies in England and Wales, there is a requirement for a medical practitioner to sign a certificate detailing cause of death which the responsible person, who is often a relative, takes to a registrar in order to register the death. This procedure must take place before the funeral and disposal of the body can occur (UK Government, nd). There are deaths, however, which must be reported to the coroner. Mr Carter's death was reported to the coroner because there was doubt as to the identity of the deceased person, the date and time of death were unknown, and the cause of death was unknown (Dorries, 2014).

Through an examination of events the coroner and their team are able to categorise deaths which at first sight seem to have taken place outside the bounds of what is acceptable. Categorising deaths in this way makes them both comprehensible and also susceptible to being incorporated into statistical data sets (Prior, 1989). In the case of Paul Carter, we do not know what he would have wanted in terms of his death, but there is no evidence to suggest that he wanted to die differently to how he did. It is not against the law to die in the way that Mr Carter did. Despite this, however, this chapter suggests that efforts were made on behalf of the state during post-death processes to rewrite his death in such a way that it fitted within a socially acceptable script. The news media, however, were influenced by the need to maintain and increase their readership and therefore took a more emotive approach to the death of Mr Carter (Hanusch, 2010).

The documents from the coroner file were all written in a professional and impersonal style, suggesting that they were presenting facts without interpretation. For example, the post-mortem report was presented on a template with various headings which guided the pathologist to comment on specific aspects of the deceased body. The pathologist did not add extraneous comments nor did they write anything which hinted at their own view about the man who was Paul Carter. The focus was on the state of the body, which was in 'an advanced state of decomposition' and the state of internal organs, although decomposition made their assessment difficult and ultimately meant that the cause of death was 'unascertainable' (PM). While Paul Carter's date of birth was known, his date of death was stated as the day that the police officers broke into his home and discovered his body. There was no comment in any of the documents which acknowledged that this was not the date on which he died (EX1; PM; WS3).

The witness statement written by the police officer who broke into Mr Carter's home and found his body was short and, unlike the other statements, it was handwritten. The officer stated that she and a colleague were called to a sudden death and that it was necessary to break into the flat, where they discovered a body that was clearly deceased as decomposition was fairly advanced. They checked the flat for signs of forced entry or disturbance, but although the flat was rather untidy and not very clean, the police officer did not think that anyone had broken in. She noted that there was no address book, nor any computer or phone on which contact details might be stored. Despite the informal appearance of the handwritten statement, the language used was formal. The statement comments on the lack of tidiness and cleanliness in the flat and remarks on an air of mustiness. This appears to offer a comment on Mr Carter and the way in which he lived, but must be considered alongside the need to assess whether anyone else had been in the flat and had been implicated in Paul Carter's death (WS3).

The witness statement from the neighbour, Brendan Chivers, was taken by a police officer and typed up before signing. The language used was not professional in the same manner as that of the pathologist, but neither was it the colloquial language of a member of the general public. It is not clear whether the choice of words was made by Mr Chivers, or whether he answered questions posed by the police officer and responded using similar language, but the language is formal and rather stilted. For example, after saying that the landlord had been informed that he had not seen his neighbour for several weeks, Mr Chivers's written statement goes on to say that 'they (landlords) stated to me that they would look into this', and once the police arrived, 'I passed to them all the details in relation to the last time that I had seen the occupant of the flat'. The use of such formal language again suggests that the statement is simply presenting the facts to which only Brendan Chivers has access (WS2).

Professional, scientific and formal language is used in this context to convey a sense of reliability and trustworthiness. This is important, as the neighbour's evidence to the effect that he had never seen anyone other than the occupant of the neighbouring flat was a key factor in the decision that the deceased person was Paul Carter. These documents were written with the purpose of answering the questions as to who had died, and when, where and how this had occurred (Dorries, 2014). The answers to these questions enable the categorisation of each individual death and its inclusion in the nation's statistical data sets, thus containing unruly and socially dangerous deaths (Prior, 1989).

The media reports of Paul Carter's death purported to deal in the facts of the case and inform their readership of the circumstances of the death and the subsequent inquest. However, the reports used emotive language and presented value judgements as facts, such as the tragic nature of Mr Carter's death. This is a common feature of news media which combines telling their readership a story with shaping people's views on a subject about which they are likely to know little (Tuchman, 1978). Lone deaths fall into this category, in that most people will know only what they read in the news about the people who undergo such a death.

Discussion

It seemed probable that Paul Carter had died approximately six weeks before police broke into his flat and found his body. According to the statement from a friend of his family, he had been an independent man who had been close to his sister who had predeceased him, but he had lost touch with her children. There is no way of knowing precisely when or how Mr Carter died, and a reasonable assumption was made that the body was his, given the lack of a suitable DNA comparator.

The coroner, as representative of the state, caused enquiries to be made to answer questions about identity and cause of death, and an inquest was held. The result of this was that Paul Carter's death could be appropriately categorised, despite the lack of certainty about the body and the death. The coroner's work meant that a death certificate could be issued and a funeral could be held for Paul Carter. His death could also be entered into the appropriate statistical data sets; it was just one among the half a million or so that take place in England and Wales each year (Office for National Statistics, 2018). The manner of Paul Carter's death was rewritten such that it fitted the confines of the regulatory system (Prior, 1989).

There was no way of knowing what Paul Carter thought about the situation in which he lived and died. He may have been one of the individuals who feared dying alone, but may as easily have been someone who preferred to be alone and was unworried about the consequences of this. The media reports about his death, however, assumed that his death was a bad one and took an emotional tone which would alert other people to the dangers inherent in a life lived alone, without family or friends, and the bad death which awaits someone in that position.

It is acceptable for an individual to plan for their own death, by mapping out the care they wish to receive when dying or by planning for their own funeral (Marie Curie, 2018). When such planning is carried out under the guidance of experts, such as palliative healthcare professionals or funeral directors, the choices made are likely to be recognised by others and accepted as valid ways of showing self-styled identity (Bauman, 2005). When the choices an individual makes with regard to their death stray too far outside the social boundaries the choices are not recognised as signs of unique identity and there are consequences for that individual (Bauman, 2005). People like Paul Carter are subjected to the judgements of others regarding the manner of their deaths. They are re-categorised by the state, and they are held up by the media as a warning to the rest of us.

Conclusion

We have no way of knowing whether Paul Carter was lonely and wished for company, and we cannot know whether his death alone was a tragedy. It is possible that he chose to live alone and that dying alone was the inevitable consequence of this; for him, perhaps, it was a good death despite the aftermath (Bradshaw *et al.*, 1978; Howse, 1997; Caswell and O'Connor, 2019).

The right of people in Paul Carter's situation to die in the manner of their own choosing is compromised, not by legal regulation but by social rules placed on how people should die. Whether Mr Carter wanted to die alone or not, his right to do so without being judged for it was taken away from him by the application of rules that sought to neutralise the perceived harm that such dying does. It appears therefore that individuals do not have the right to make choices which result in a lone death without also laying themselves open to the negative judgements of others.

Note

1 Documentary research data (available from the author on reasonable request):

WS1: Statement from Cathy Traynor, family friend
WS2: Statement from neighbour, Brendan Chivers

WS3: Statement from police officer
EX1: email exchanges between police officer and coroner's officer
PM: post-mortem report
MR1: local newspaper report, 11/1/2014
MR2: local newspaper report, 13/1/2014
MR3: local newspaper report, 14/1/2014
MR4: local newspaper report, 25/4/2014

References

Bauman, Z. (2005) *Liquid Life*. Polity Press, Cambridge.

Berger, P. (1969) *The Sacred Canopy*. Anchor Books, New York.

Borgstrom, E. (2015) Planning for an (un)certain future: Choice within English end-of-life care. *Current Sociology Monograph, 63*(5), 700–713. doi: 10.1177/0011392115590084

Bradshaw, J., Clifton, M. and Kennedy, J. (1978) *Found Dead a Study of Old People Found Dead*. Age Concern, London.

Carpiano, R.M. (2016) Toward a neighborhood resource-based theory of social capital for health: Can Bourdieu and sociology help? *Social Science & Medicine, 62*, 165–175. doi: 10.1016/j.socscimed.2005.05.020

Caswell, G. (2011) Death as a fateful moment? The reflexive individual and Scottish funeral practices. *Sociological Research Online, 16*(3), 22. Available from: http://www.socresonline.org.uk/16/3/22.html

Caswell, G. (2011–2012) Beyond words: Some uses of music in the funeral setting. *Omega: Journal of Death & Dying, 64*(4), 319–334. doi: 10.2190/OM.64.4.c

Caswell, G. (2013) Managing death in twenty-first century Scotland. In N. Hinerman, and L. Steffen (eds) *New Perspectives on the End of Life: Essays on Care and the Intimacy of Dying*, 109–128. Inter-Disciplinary Press, Oxford.

Caswell, G. and O'Connor, M. (2015) Agency in the context of social death: Dying alone at home. *Contemporary Social Science, 10*(3). doi:10.1080/21582041.2015.1006806

Caswell, G. and O'Connor, M. (2019) 'I've no fear of dying alone': Exploring perspectives on living and dying alone. *Mortality, 24*(1), 17–31. doi: 10.1080/13576275.2017.1413542

Craib, I. (1994) *The Importance of Disappointment*. Routledge, London.

Department of Health. (2008) *End of Life Care Strategy: Promoting High Quality Care for All Adults at the End of Life*. Available from: https://www.gov.uk/government/publications/end-of-life-care-strategy-promoting-high-quality-care-for-adults-at-the-end-of-their-life [Accessed 9th April 2019].

Dorries, C.P. (2014) *Coroners' Courts: A Guide to Law and Practice* (3rd ed.). Oxford University Press, Oxford.

Fincham, B., Langer, S., Scourfield, J. and Shiner, M. (2011) *Understanding Suicide: A Sociological Autopsy*. Palgrave Macmillan, Basingstoke.

Giddens, A. (1990) *The Consequences of Modernity*. Polity Press, Cambridge.

Giddens, A. (1991) *Modernity and Self-Identity*. Stanford University Press, Stanford, CA.

Hanusch, F. (2010) *Representing Death in the News: Journalism, Media and Mortality*. Palgrave Macmillan, Basingstoke.

Howarth, H. (2007) *Death & Dying*. Polity Press, Cambridge.

Howse, K. (1997) *Deaths of People Alone*. Centre for Policy of Ageing, London.

Kellehear, A. (2009) Dying old – and *preferably* alone? Agency, resistance and dissent at the end of life. *International Journal of Ageing and Later Life, 4*(1), 5–21.

Lloyd-Williams, L., Kennedy, V., Sixsmith, A. and Sixsmith, J. (2007) Perceptions of people over the age of 80 on issues surrounding death and dying. *Journal of Pain and Symptom Management, 34*(1), 60–66.

Marie Curie. (2018) *Planning Ahead.* Available from: https://www.mariecurie.org.uk/help/support/publications/all/planning-ahead [Accessed 20th March 2019].

Money Advice Service. (2019) *Funeral Plans and Funeral Insurance.* Available from: https://www.moneyadviceservice.org.uk/en/articles/funeral-plans [Accessed 21st March 2019].

National Palliative and End of Life Care Partnership. (nd) *Ambitions for Palliative and End of Life Care: A National Framework for Local Action 2015–2020.* Available from: http://endoflifecareambitions.org.uk/ [Accessed 21st March 2019].

Office for National Statistics. (2018) *Deaths Registered in England and Wales: 2017.* Available from: https://www.ons.gov.uk/peoplepopulationandcommunity/birthsdeathsandmarriages/deaths/bulletins/deathsregistrationsummarytables/2017 [Accessed 11th April 2019].

Pollock, K. (2015) Is home always the best and preferred place of death? *British Medical Journal, 351.* doi: 10.1136/bmj.h4855

Pollock, K. and Seymour, J. (2018) Reappraising 'the good death' for populations in the age of ageing. *Age and Ageing, 47*, 328–330. doi: 10.1093/ageing/afy008

Prior, L. (1989) *The Social Organization of Death.* Macmillan, Basingstoke.

Prior, L. (2003) *Using Documents in Social Research.* Sage, London.

Puchalski, C.M. (2002) Spirituality and end-of-life care: A time for listening and caring. *Journal of Palliative Medicine, 5*(2), 289–294.

Salkovskis, P. and Lambe, S. (2015) We are all hoarders but for some it spirals out of control, *The Conversation*, 8th January 2015. Available from: https://theconversation.com/we-are-all-hoarders-but-for-some-it-spirals-out-of-control-35967 [Accessed 9th April 2019].

Sayer, D. (2010) Who's afraid of the dead? Archaeology, modernity and the death taboo. *World Archaeology, 42*(3), 481–491. doi: 10.1080/00438243.2010.498665

Seale, C. (2004) Media constructions of dying alone: A form of 'bad death'. *Social Science & Medicine, 58*, 967–974.

Thalos, M. (2016) *A Social Theory of Freedom.* Routledge, Abingdon.

The Choice in End of Life Care Programme Board. (2015) *What's Important to Me. A Review of Choice in End of Life Care.* Available from: https://www.gov.uk/government/publications/choice-in-end-of-life-care [Accessed 21st March 2019].

Thompson, G., Shindruk, C., Wickson-Griffiths, A., Sussman, T., Hunter, P., McClement, S., Chochinov, H., McCleary, L., Kaasalainen, S. and Venturato, L. (2018) "Who would want to die like that?" Perspectives on dying alone in a long-term care setting. *Death Studies, 43*(8), 509–520. doi: 10.1080/07481187.2018.1491484

Tuchman, G. (1978) *Making News: A Study in the Construction of Reality.* The Free Press, New York.

Turner, N. and Caswell, G. (2019) Moral Ambiguity in Media Reports of Dying Alone. *Mortality.* doi: 10.1080/13576275.2019.1657388 (online first).

UK Government. (1984) *Public Health (Control of Disease) Act 1984.* Crown copyright. Available from: https://www.legislation.gov.uk/ukpga/1984/22/section/46?view=extent [Accessed 11th April 2019].

UK Government. (nd) *What to Do When Someone Dies: Step by Step*. Crown Copyright. Available from: https://www.gov.uk/when-someone-dies [Accessed 11th April 2019].

Walter, T. (1994) *The Revival of Death*. Routledge, London.

Wilkinson, T.M. (2002) Last rights: The ethics of research on the dead. *Journal of Applied Philosophy, 19*(1), 31–41.

Yin, R.K. (2014) *Case Study Research*. 5th ed. Sage, London.

14 Embodiment, choice and control at the beginning and ending of life

Paradoxes and contradictions. A provocation

Sue Westwood[1]

Introduction

Imagine an alien comes to planet Earth and writes a report for their home planet about how humans in a land called 'England' organise the beginnings and endings of human life. The alien being notes that in this land:

1 It is lawful for a human being to end their life. However, it is unlawful for another human being to be present with them at the time and/or to assist them with this lawful act.
2 Humans are lawfully provided with medical assistance to choose when and how lives begin through contraception and reproductive technologies and, under specific circumstances, end the beginnings of human life by state controlled 'abortion'. However, humans are prohibited by law to receive medical assistance to control when and how their lives end once they have been born.
3 Humans can lawfully choose when and how to end the lives of companion animals who are suffering unbearably at the end of life. This is regarded as a 'good' thing, while not ending an animal's life when they have no quality of life and/or are experiencing unbearable suffering is seen as a 'bad' thing. However, humans cannot lawfully be assisted in choosing when and how to end their own lives when they are suffering unbearably at the end of life. To do so is seen as a 'bad' thing, while not ending a human being's life when they have no quality of life and/or are experiencing unbearable suffering is seen (by many) as a 'good' thing.
4 Laws protect the rights of humans to be free from cruel and inhuman treatment. However, many humans with debilitating physical conditions experience protracted, painful, undignified deaths – which some of them consider to be cruel and inhuman treatment – because they are not allowed to be helped to die according to their own choosing.
5 Humans have rules which protect the right to life. However, there are no rules which protect the right to death, even in very old age when someone has no quality of life and wants their life to end. The default

DOI: 10.4324/9780429329739-14

position is that humans wait passively for death irrespective of how long, unpleasant and unwanted that wait is.

This alien, and the alien readers of their report, might think that this is a strange state of affairs. This chapter considers each of these apparent paradoxes and contradictions in turn. The aim of using the 'alien' lens is to help to cut through some of the more abstract and convoluted arguments in relation to assisted dying, stripping bare exactly what is at stake, in terms of lived experience.

Context

In its global context, at the time of writing, some form of assisted dying – facilitating the death of another person at their capacitous behest – is lawful in '… parts of Australia, Belgium, Canada, Colombia, Luxembourg, The Netherlands, Switzerland, and several US States' (My Death, My Decision, 2020).[2] The ways in which it is lawful, for whom, how, what safeguards are involved, and what rationales underpin this, vary widely (see Penney Lewis's analysis in Chapter 2: Lewis, 2021) and have been contested in wide-ranging case law (exemplified by Alex Ruck Keene's chapter, Chapter 3, in this volume, Ruck Keene, 2021). In the vast majority of the countries in the world, including England, assisted dying continues to be against the law.

In the context of the debate about assisted dying, that is, whether it should be lawful and if so under what circumstances, several key ethical and moral principles are engaged (Huxtable, 2007; see also Richard Huxtable's (2021) and Isra Black's (2021) respective chapters, Chapters 5 and 7, in this volume). Those advocating *for* assisted dying in some form or another primarily make claims based on autonomous choice (i.e. that we as individuals should have the right to make the choice about whether we live or die), embodied rights (that we should have the right to decide what happens to our bodies), and relief from suffering (i.e. that we should not have to endure unbearable suffering and/or should not have to die in unpleasant ways which could be avoided). Those arguing *against* assisted dying make claims based on the intrinsic value of human life (previously referred to as the sanctity of life, but less so now due to the term's Christian overtones); a normative trumping of the value of human life's intrinsic worth over other values (autonomy, dignity, etc.); and slippery slope arguments (i.e. that even limited assisted dying will devalue the meaning of human life and/or eventually lead to some form of eugenics). These competing claims have been discussed in several chapters in this volume, most notably in Richard Huxtable's (2021) and Anthony Wrigley's (2021) discussions in Chapters 5 and 6, respectively.

The central argument in this chapter coheres around individual bodily autonomy and capacitous choice, that is, that an individual human being with capacity should have the right to choose when and how their life ends, and to be empowered in making this choice by the assistance of others when they want it. It advocates creating a right to assisted dying and a right to death for *those who wish to exercise that right as long as they have the mental capacity to decide*, to include people with terminal illnesses and severely debilitating conditions as well as 'rational suicide' (Richards, 2017) among people in older age. It is not advocating for imposing 'assisted dying' on those who do not want to be helped to die. To end someone's life when they do not want to die[3] would not be assisted dying at all, but wrongful killing.

Paradoxes and contradictions

Each of the five alien-confusing paradoxes in relation to human living and dying in England will now be considered in turn.

Paradox 1: While it is lawful for a person to end their life, is it unlawful to be with them while they perform this lawful act, or to assist them in doing so.

Excessive state protectionism

It does appear fundamentally illogical that it should be unlawful to help an autonomous adult to commit a lawful act, and even more oddly, to be present while they do so.[4] While in secular law, ending one's own life is no longer illegal in many parts of the world, helping to end someone else's, even by being only peripherally involved, is not. This is fundamentally a protectionist stance: protecting individuals from having their lives ended by someone else against their will. There are two problems with this protectionism. First, it assumes that continued existence is what all individuals value the most. For those who do, protecting them from having their lives ended makes complete sense. It is empowering. It promotes the potential for them to continue living. However, for those people who do not want to live, providing them with a 'protection' they do not want can be paternalistic and over-protective. It can be disempowering, minimising the potential for them to end their lives in the way that they want to, especially those who are physically unable to do so without assistance. This in turn can unreasonably constrain free choice. There are concerns that such free choice may be subject to coercion. This is where regulation comes in. We have regulation for various rites of passage, and various checks and balances in place to make sure they are passed through in safe ways. Regulated assisted dying, where there is a clearly defined death plan (how we want to die, where, and who with), and where proper safeguards are in place, would still provide protection whilst also empowering those who wish to die, and have the capacity to make such a choice. It would ameliorate excessive state intervention for those capacitous individuals who are very clearly expressing a wish to have greater control over their own deaths. Steve Parlanti, writing on the Dignity in Dying website, describes how his mother, being denied access to assisted dying, and unable to travel to Dignitas, felt, during a protracted, painful death she did not want:

> She died very angry, feeling that it was simply unfair that other people should have made her suffer in this way and denied her choice. Every mentally competent individual should be allowed to choose when and how they depart.[5]

Indirect privileging of the able-bodied

Assisting someone to die is constructed quite expansively in English law. Section 2(1) of the Suicide Act 1961 defines unlawful 'encouraging or assisting' as follows:

> If D arranges for a person ("D2") to do an act that is capable of encouraging or assisting the suicide or attempted suicide of another person and D2 does that act, D is also to be treated for the purposes of this Act as having done it.

The indirect outcome of prohibition is that someone who is physically capable of ending their life without someone else being present and/or physically assisting them will be able to do so, if they wish, even if they would prefer not to do so alone. However, someone who is not physically capable of ending their own life (someone who is paralysed for example) and cannot be assisted due to the prohibition, will not be able to die. This privileges those individuals who are able-bodied over those who are not.[6]

Taking the social model of disability – that is, a person is not inherently disabled, it is society's response to their needs that is disabling – then the prohibition on assisted dying further disables someone with disabilities because it disables their ability to end their lives *if they want to,* and in a way they find acceptable (Shakespeare, 2013; Shildrick, 2015; Riddle, 2017). This is not to discount those who are concerned that people with disabilities might be at risk of having their lives ended when it is not their wish (Coleman, 2010; Mullock and Ost, 2011). Properly regulated assisted dying would have safeguards to prevent this, given it 'is about choice, not getting rid of disabled people'.[7] It would ensure people with disabilities have equitable access to suicide [sic] and have the same ability to exercise choice over their own deaths as a non-disabled person.

Legal uncertainty

There is also legal uncertainty for those individuals who need their friends/family members to accompany them in order for them to be able to travel overseas to die, for example to Dignitas in Switzerland (Gauthier et al., 2015). Following Debbie Purdy's successful UK claim[8] which established that the

Crown Prosecution (CPS) guidance at the time was not compatible with Article 8 of the European Convention on Human Rights, the guidance was supplemented by an offence-specific policy (CPS, 2014). While technically it remains unlawful to assist someone in ending their lives under the Suicide Act, CPS guidance now states that individuals who help someone else to end their own lives will only be prosecuted, if, on balance, there are sufficient 'public interest factors' to justify doing so. As of 31 July, 162 cases were referred to the CPS by the police that were recorded as assisted suicide (CPS, 2020). Of these, 107 were not proceeded with by the CPS and 32 cases were subsequently withdrawn by the police. According to the CPS,

> There are currently seven ongoing cases. Three cases of encouraging or assisting suicide have been successfully prosecuted. One case of assisted suicide was charged and acquitted after trial in May 2015 and nine cases were referred onwards for prosecution for homicide or other serious crime.
>
> CPS (2020, no page number)

This has created a grey area where an individual cannot know in advance whether or not they will be prosecuted for helping someone to travel to die, although they do know they will undergo a legal process which could lead to prosecution. One of the foundational principles of law is that of legal certainty (Fenwick, Siems and Wrbka, 2017); in other words, a person is entitled to know where they stand in relation to law. This grey area creates legal uncertainty, which is unacceptable. Creating a regulatory framework which allows for the formal planning of assisted dying, would remove this uncertainty and provide greater legal clarity, both for those who want to do so and those who want to help them in doing so.

Thou shalt end thy life alone?

Next the alien says, observing this place called England, 'Well, even if you can't actively help to end the person's life, why can you not at least sit with them and urge them on in fulfilling their (lawful) aim to end their lives?' This is one of the major objections raised by some of my own research participants who spoke about ending their lives in my study on lesbian, gay and bisexual ageing (Westwood, 2017, 10):

> I mean it's the last taboo, isn't it? I mean that would be ideal, I suppose, to have your loved ones help you at the time that suits you without them getting done over.
>
> Stella, aged 66

> My worry is, of course, the law. Because, if this is to work with the current legislation, you can't involve your friends. What I would like is to have a party, where there's everybody I love around, say 'OK guys, bye'

> [waves], stick the bag over my head, turn the valve on, please. But I have to do it earlier if it's me only. And that really annoys me. That's other people's wanky prejudices, really silly, dictating stupid outcomes. And that means I will die earlier.
>
> Phil, aged 62

As can be seen here, the law prevents these two individuals from being able to end their lives in the ways in which they would prefer. If they choose to end their lives, they will have to do so alone, which they do not want. Some people may want to die alone, as Glenys Caswell (2021) has argued in Chapter 13 of this volume. The point here is that those who do not want to end their lives while they are alone are *forced* to do so under the current rules. In addition, as Phil points out, and as Anthony Wrigley (2021) has so coherently analysed in Chapter 6 of this volume, he will have to die sooner than he would want to, if he is not allowed to receive assistance in ending his life. In other words, the prohibition on helping someone to die can result in someone dying sooner than they might otherwise have done, exemplifying one of the unintended consequences of the prohibition on assisted dying. The solution, again, is a regulatory framework which allows for advance legal planning for an assisted dying arrangement, where a person who wishes to end their life can be supported in doing so.

Three arguments

So, to sum up, three main arguments have been presented here. First, *regulated* assisted dying would remedy the excessive protectionism of current legislation. Second, enabling the death of a person who wants to die but whose disabilities prevents them to do so should not only not be prohibited but be actively permitted in order to empower such individuals and provide them with parity alongside non-disabled individuals. Third, a regulatory framework that creates formal mechanisms for an assisted dying plan would provide legal clarity for those in the liminal place between prosecution/non-prosecution for assistance. It would also enable the person who is choosing to die to not be forced to do so alone.

Paradox 2: While women can be lawfully assisted to exercise control over preventing and ending the new life of others through contraception and abortion, they (and men) cannot be lawfully assisted to exercise control over their own bodies' endings.

Embodied choice and control

Many anti-abortionists and those opposed to assisted dying have in common the privileging of vitality over individual choice (Ross and Kaplan, 1994; Busscher, 2015; Kitzinger, 2015). By contrast many pro-abortion and pro-assisted dying campaigners emphasise the right to exercise choice over our own bodies (Sheldon, 1997; Fletcher, Fox and McCandless, 2008; Ost, 2010). Dena Davis has been a most vocal exponent of the parallels between the embodied rights of contraception, abortion and assisted dying:

> A feminist view of contraception suggests an argument for a feminist view of rational suicide. To use contraception or sterilization is to view one's fertility as contingent rather than given, and to limit one's fertility as a way of maximizing one's interests and goals. To resort to rational suicide when faced with terminal illness or impending dementia is to view one's body's continued ability to pump blood and oxygen as contingent, and no longer a good for one's life but rather a threat to one's values and interests in how the final chapter of that life is written.
>
> Davis (2015, 113)

While Davis limits her argument to those with terminal illnesses and/or 'impending' dementia, it also resonates with wider embodied rights arguments in support of legalised assisted dying. As she observes,

> If we insist that we can and must be trusted with the power to decide whether or not to destroy a potential human life, how can we not insist on the right to be trusted with the decision whether or not to end our own?
>
> Davis (2015, 116)

For feminists, embodied rights can lend both support for and opposition to assisted dying (the right to choose; the right to care/protection, Kitzinger, 2015). For pro-assisted dying feminists, the right to choose what happens to our own bodies (not the right to die, but the right to choose whether one has an elective death *or not*) prevails over all other priorities (Mackenzie, 1992). Those who object to assisted dying are concerned about (a) those with less power (e.g. people with severe disabilities) having their lives ended against their wishes by those with greater power; and (b) the possibility that older women may elect to die in order to avoid being a 'burden' to their families (Wolf, 1996; Callaghan, 2015).

In terms of the need to protect people who may not have the physical and/or mental capacity to exercise free choice, appropriate, strict, regulatory protections would ensure that their lives cannot be ended when it is not their wish for them to end. However, as observed in the previous section, and as argued by the feminist Margrit Shildrick (2015), allowing regulated assisted dying could potentially empower capacitous people with disabilities who presently want to die but cannot because they do not have the physical means to make this happen.

In terms of protecting women who might wish to sacrifice themselves, although this position is claimed by many feminists, it implies that women cannot be trusted to make their own choices about their bodies (Fletcher, Fox and McCandless, 2008). Clearly women can and should be trusted. Indeed if they wish to sacrifice themselves in older age, as long as they are not being coerced, it is their right to do so. Also implied in this argument is that women with the ability to exercise choice over assisted dying should deny themselves that choice in solidarity with those who cannot. As Dina Davis observes, 'That sounds like a very unfeminist call to women to uphold the moral values of society by limiting their own freedom and behavior. We've been there before' (Davis, 2015, 134). Embodied rights concerns can also apply in relation to men as well; however, women's embodied rights arguments throw the issues into heightened contrast.

Key argument

The key argument here is a simple one: we should have the right to make our own capacitous choices about what happens to our bodies. Women do now have reproductive rights over their own bodies. They should also have them over when and how they die. No one else, including the state, should be able to make these choices for us.

Paradox 3: While it is lawful and considered a 'good' to end the life of a suffering, dying animal, it is unlawful and considered 'bad' to help end the life of a suffering, dying human being who wants to die.

'You wouldn't let an animal die this way'

Everyday discourse about end-of-life rights for human beings, often involve analogies being drawn with euthanasia of companion animals.[9] From my own research with older lesbian, gay and bisexual people in the UK, several of the participants who wanted assisted dying to be legalised drew a stark contrast between how animals and humans are treated at the end of their lives.

> You keep people alive for longer, 'Oh we're all living for longer'. It's not necessarily a quality life. My mum was kept alive for god knows how many years, when all she wanted to do was shuffle off this mortal coil. It was bloody cruel. It was ridiculous. Our cat wasn't well and so we had her put down eventually. I don't want to be that skeleton that was lying on my mother's bed.
>
> Daphne, aged 60 (Westwood, 2017, 11)

This theme also came up in Rosie Harding's recent UK research with dementia carers:

> My mother wanted to die … In her words, 'Oh Lord, relieve me from this terrible death'. Clearly, she was going to die. One is allowed to have

> a dog put to sleep but my mother had to go through hell, as did her family seeing and knowing what was going on.
>
> [Quest_157] (Harding, 2017, 186)

The idea that double standards are being unreasonably applied to animals and humans was also echoed in Armstrong and colleagues' research with families of people with dementia in the US:

> She was in so much pain, she asked my sister, you know, the oldest one. One day, she asked her, "Can't you just take me out back and shoot me?", the next night, she said, "Can't you just go in the kitchen and get a knife and stab me?" … We should treat humans as least as well as we treat our animals. (#2, daughter)
>
> Armstrong et al. (2019, 8)

> He would say, "Can you call Dr. Kevorkian?" and that was pretty horrifying to the staff at the nursing home. And even after he completely lost his memory, he'd have them call and say, "Call that doctor for me." … I've become, a pretty strong advocate of death with dignity… We treat our pets better. (#5, wife)
>
> Armstrong et al. (2019, 8)

So, why is it that animal euthanasia and human euthanasia are treated so differently? Well, the first major reason is the core principle that one human being should not take the life of another, whereas the same principle is more conditional in regard to animals. Not all societies see animal suffering in the same way and many see it as justifiable (food; blood sports) and/or necessary (animal testing for human health benefits). Ironically, because there is less value placed on an animal's life than a human's life that an animal's is more likely to be ended with dignity and compassion than a human's.

A further contrast between human euthanasia (and by association, assisted dying) and animal euthanasia is that the latter is justifiable because animals are 'subordinate' to humans, but that human euthanasia is unjustifiable because no one human should be subordinate to another (Cholbi and Varelius, 2016). However, imposing a manner of dying on a person who does not want to die this way *does* subordinate them, to both the state, and to those who are opposed to assisted dying. The only way for such subordination to be avoided is to give individuals choice about how, when and where they die.

Key argument

This chapter is not advocating for human euthanasia (that is for another day). It is arguing for capacitous assisted dying. There should be parity between animals and humans. If the life of a suffering animal can lawfully be ended, so too should that of a capacitous suffering human being who wants their life to end, with assistance, if they so wish.

Paradox 4: The law protects a person from cruel and inhumane treatment, apart from when they are dying.

Cruel and inhuman deaths

When death is imminent, as in the case of someone who has a terminal illness, and is reaching the final stages of life, the issue is not whether one is going to die, but rather when, where and how. The desire to be free from unbearable pain and suffering (actual or anticipated) is the primary motivator amongst those who want to be able to access assisted dying and who advocated for it (Hendry et al., 2013). As one of the campaigners for Dignity in Dying, Heather McQueen has said,

> After I watched my mother suffer a cruel and inhumane death from terminal cancer, I decided I would do everything I can to change the law.[10]

Consider the deaths of three British assisted dying campaigners Debbie Purdy, Dianne Pretty and John Close. Debbie Purdy had severe multiple sclerosis (MS). Denied the right to die in the manner and timing of her own choosing, she spent the final year of her life in a hospice, intermittently starving herself until her death. She said about her condition, 'It's painful and it's uncomfortable and it's frightening.'[11] Dianne Pretty, who had motor neurone disease (MND), wanted 'a quick death without suffering, at home surrounded by my family'.[12] Denied the lawful assistance to do so, she eventually died, also in a hospice, in the manner which she foresaw, most feared, and had wanted to avoid,[13] eventually falling into a coma after ten traumatic days of struggling to breathe.

By contrast, John Close, who also had MND, went to Dignitas to die. His sister, Lesley Close, accompanied him, and described his death as follows:

> Knowing that John would be in control of his death was a tremendous source of comfort for me as well as for John. Indeed at a stage when MND had almost totally eroded his dignity, knowing he would have that control gave some dignity back to him. John's death was sad but my grief at losing him was tempered by the control he had over the way he died.[14]

All three individuals were going to die shortly. Debbie Purdy and Dianne Pretty experienced protracted pain, distress and a lack of dignity that they had unsuccessfully tried to avoid through legal remedy. They both died in ways they did not want to. By contrast, John Close had a peaceful, pain-free, death over which he had control (although he was still not able to die in the place where he wanted to die, i.e. at home).

Compare again their experiences with the planned death of Jil Finnegan in California, US. Jil, 53, had terminal cancer, was in progressive pain, and feared a (likely) agonising death.[15] A supporter of the right to die, Jil allowed her final days to be documented by a journalist, photographed and filmed.[16] Under California's End of Life Option Act 2016, Jil's oncologist had provided her with medication she could take to end her life. On a pre-determined day (her wedding anniversary), she held a party for her close friends, neighbours, co-workers and family who celebrated her life, sang to her, and said their farewells to her. There were tears, and there was also much laughter. In the early afternoon, people left, with just her closest friends and family members remaining. Jil took her anti-nausea medication.

> It began to rain lightly outside. So in a moment of delight, Jil walked out to look up at the sky, feeling the drops of rain splash on her face and her palms. A hospice nurse was on her way to oversee the process and answer questions.

Jill then lay down on her bed, cuddled up with her husband and her dogs, took the fatal medication, lost consciousness and then, slowly and peacefully, died. Her friends and family then held a mini-wake while she was lying dead in the bedroom, intermittently visiting the room to say their farewells. Finally, her body was removed by an undertaker. One of her close friends described the way Jil died as 'a new and more honest way of dealing with death'.[17]

While Jil's death seems the comparably better death to me, the argument I am presenting here is not that all deaths should be like hers, nor that all assisted deaths are 'good' or non-assisted deaths 'bad'. The argument I am making here is that a chosen death such as Jil's should be possible for *those who wish to make that choice.*

Various national and international instruments protect individuals from cruel and inhumane treatment (see the chapters by Sharon Young (2021) and Elizabeth Wicks (2021) in this volume, Chapters 8 and 9, respectively). The UN Convention on the Rights of Persons with Disabilities states, in Article 15 that '[n]o one shall be subjected to torture or to cruel, inhuman or degrading treatment or punishment.' Denying a person the right to die on their own terms and to do so in a way which avoids unnecessary pain and suffering, must constitute cruel and degrading treatment, however repeatedly the courts have failed to agree.

Key argument

The key argument here is that capacitous dying people should be allowed to choose when, where and how they die, and should be able to choose to shorten their lives if they face the prospect of deaths which involve undignified and/or unbearable suffering. As Penney Lewis (2021) has observed in this volume, if the autonomy argument prevails (see Chapter 2 above), then the suffering argument outlined here does not need to be applied. However, as Lewis has also observed, 'autonomy is perhaps not as attractive to litigants and judges as it is to commentators', in which case the suffering/cruel and inhumane treatment arguments may still have a place in progressing assisted dying legislation.

Paradox 5: The right to life is enshrined in law, but the right to death is not.

The growth of medicalisation – the increasing ways in which medicine informs our lives and can control our deaths in particular – is a double-edged sword. It is to be celebrated for enabling humans to live healthier lives for longer. However, it is also problematic in that medicine is now used to keep people alive for longer when they have no quality of life left. This goes beyond the issue of unbearable suffering addressed in the previous section and speaks more to the issue of governmentality of death and dying (Beauchamp, 2006; Tierney, 2010). The primary questions are twofold: Why are we required to die passively, subjected to the vagaries of our bodies and circumstances? Why is the duration of our (now extended) older ages not something over which we can exercise choice and control?

Active versus passive deaths

Consider the living conditions of someone in protracted end stages of dementia, who may experience the following (Ouldred and Bryant, 2008).

- Dependence in activities of daily living requiring the assistance of caregivers to survive
- Severe impairment of expressive and receptive communication often limited to single words or nonsense phrases
- Loss of the ability to walk followed by inability to stand, problems maintaining sitting posture and a subsequent loss of head and neck control
- Development of contractures because of muscle rigidity and de-conditioning
- Loss of ability to recognize food, self-feed and swallow effectively
- Bowel and bladder incontinence
- Inability to recognize self and others

The person is kept alive through 'artificial hydration and nutrition such as percutaneous endoscopic gastrostomy, nasogastric tubes and subcutaneous infusions' (310). They may be in pain, but unable to communicate it. They usually end up in a fixed foetal position, being moved in slings, often crying out whether in pain or fear, or both, when this is happening. They are at risk of 'aspiration pneumonia infections, pressure sores [and] malnutrition' (310). This can go on for *years*.

While there are strong arguments for the need for improved palliative care, especially for older people and people with dementia, this does not resolve the issue of those people who, at the end of their lives do not want such protracted palliative care, no matter how good it is, but want to be helped to die instead, and who want to die before they reach the state(s) described above.

Those who want a protracted passive death (e.g. to take many years to die in the end stages of a debilitating disease) should not be denied one. Legalisation of assisted dying would not do so. They could still be among the thousands and thousands of people who die in the ways described above every year. However, those individuals who want a different kind of death should also be allowed to make that choice, rather than having compulsory passivity imposed on them. This would enable them to live their lives fully in the present, without fear of the future. As Sandy Briden, who died in 2017, said during the run-up to her death, 'I want to live as fully as possible in my remaining time, without the fear of a painful death hanging over me'.[18]

Rational suicide in older age

For older people who want to die when they are ready, not when their bodies finally give in, rational suicide – a reasoned ending of their lives because death is on balance, the best thing for them (see Isra Black's (2021) chapter, Chapter 7, for a more theoretical engagement with this) – takes on growing significance (Richards, 2017; see also Ari Gandsman's (2021) and Els van Wijngaarden's (2021) chapters in this volume, Chapters 11 and 12, respectively). Some older people want to die, often for complex reasons (see Els van Wijngaarden's (2021) chapter in this volume, Chapter 12). For some, it is because they are done, sated with life and want to leave the table rather than sit and wait for death to come and get them. Elizabeth Wicks (2021) has argued in this volume (Chapter 9) that a wish to die 'with dignity' could potentially be protected as a belief in law. It might also be possible to extend this argument to rational suicide in older age.

The oldest man to travel to Dignitas to die was 104-year-old David Goodall from Australia[19] who did not have a terminal illness and asserted shortly before his death "an old person like myself should have full citizenship rights including the right of assisted suicide."[20] This citizenship discourse is also echoed in a recent international systematic review of families' involvement in assisted dying in Switzerland observed that "families perceive assisted dying as a civil right and not a medical act" (Gamondi et al., 2019, 12).

It has been argued that limiting assisted dying to only those in the last six months of life – in those states/countries where assisted dying is permitted at all – is discriminatory, disadvantaging those without a formal prediction of imminent mortality (Sleeman and Chalmers, 2019). It could also be considered age discriminatory, given it is the older members of society who are more likely to want to exercise rational suicide (see Ari Gandsman's (2021) chapter in this volume, Chapter 11). Importantly, the voices of older people are seldom heard in research on assisted dying (van Wijngaarden, Leget and Goossensen, 2018; Deuter et al., 2019), suggesting that the voices of those most affected are being excluded while the voices of more powerful others – for example younger healthcare professionals – are being privileged over theirs.

De-medicalising death

This brings into question whether and to what extent medicine should be involved in death choices at all. One of the key complicators around assisted dying are arguments from medical practitioners who feel intentionally helping someone to die would breach their raison d'être and professional ethics (Smith et al., 2018). There are three simple solutions to this.

a Only healthcare practitioners who approve of assisted dying should be required to participate in it. Those who do not can refer patients who want to be assisted to die on to those practitioners who support assisted dying (Magelssen, Le and Supphellen, 2019).

b Assisted dying, like reproductive medicine and abortion clinics, becomes a specialist service, run by healthcare professionals who do not experience moral unease in relation to assisted dying (Savulescu and Schuklenk, 2017).

c The ending of life is taken out of the hands of healthcare professionals altogether, de-medicalised (Ost, 2010), and regulated within a new non-medical legal framework (Coggon, 2010), with in-house and 'death-at-home' services run by non-medical end-of-life doulas (Fukuzawa and Kondo, 2017; Rawlings et al., 2019).

Key arguments

The first key argument here is that (a) those healthcare professionals opposed to assisted dying should not be required to participate in it, and (b) those in support of assisted dying should be allowed to participate in it, within a regulatory framework which ensures proper checks and balances are employed. The second is that ending one's life should be de-medicalised altogether. This would prevent the opinions of those healthcare professionals who are opposed to assisted dying prevailing over those who support it. It would also, as the *Lancet Commission on the Value of Death* recently observed, promote greater societal engagement with, rather than resisting death, instead focussing on *how to die well* (Smith et al., 2018, 1292).

Conclusion: a vision of the future

Let us imagine now that humans have a universal right to die and – with strict controls – lawfully assisted dying and euthanasia. The alien revisits the Earth and the place called England and produces a new report. This one says:

1 It is lawful for a human being to end their life and it is lawful for another human being to be present with them at the time and/or to assist them with this lawful act, providing both parties fully consent.

2 Humans are lawfully provided with medical assistance to choose when and how they create new life and to determine when and how their lives end. Medical practitioners who do not want to provide this service do

not have to do so and refer patients on to practitioners who are willing to do so and/or /services dedicated to the ending of life.

3 Humans can choose when and how to end the lives of companion animals who are suffering and also their own lives when they are suffering in similar ways.
4 Laws protect the rights of humans to be free from cruel and inhuman treatment, and this includes freedom from dying in ways an individual does not want, when an alternative is available.
5 Humans have rules which protect both the right to life and the right to death. Humans are death-aware, living their finite lives to the full proactively engaging and preparing for the reality and inevitability of death.

Under this hypothetical set of circumstances our alien being, and the alien readers of their new report, might now think that humans have a compassionate, consistent, logical and coherent approach to both the beginnings and endings of human life. It is to be hoped that human society will have achieved this before alien beings are actually among us, that is, if they are not already here, baffled by current inconsistencies towards matters of life and death.

Notes

1 My sincere thanks to Els van Wijngaarden, Anthony Wrigley and Isra Black for their extremely helpful comments on an earlier draft of this chapter.
2 https://www.mydeath-mydecision.org.uk/info/assisted-dying-in-other-countries/.
3 There is also the issue of what it would mean to end the life of someone who lacks mental capacity, and so cannot consent in law. Should their prior capacitous self be able to give consent in advance? This engages with debates about advance directives in general and more specifically in relation to the end of life (Gillett, 2019). They can become red herrings in debates about whether capacitous persons should be assisted to die.
4 According to S1 of the Suicide Act 1961, it is unlawful to commit an act 'capable of encouraging or assisting the suicide or attempted suicide of another person' which 'was intended to encourage or assist suicide or an attempt at suicide.' Simply being present with the purpose of supporting a person while they are in the process of ending their lives could 'constitute encouraging or assisting suicide' (CPS, 2014).
5 https://www.dignityindying.org.uk/story/pam-parlanti/.
6 This also indirectly privileges wealthy disabled people who have the finances to travel to Dignitas, for example. One couple recently paid £20000 for a private air ambulance to fly the wife to Dignitas to die, not an option available to less affluent disabled members of society: https://twitter.com/dignityindying/status/1145271016991678464.
7 https://www.theguardian.com/society/2018/jun/03/assisted-dying-law-is-about-choice-not-getting-rid-of-disabled-people.
8 R (Purdy) v DPP [2009] UKHL 45.
9 https://www.independent.co.uk/life-style/health-and-families/features/euthanasia-for-animals-what-can-it-teach-us-about-assisted-suicide-in-humans-10405840.html.
10 https://www.dignityindying.org.uk/story/heather-mcqueen/.

11 https://www.bbc.co.uk/news/uk-england-leeds-25741005.
12 http://news.bbc.co.uk/1/hi/health/1983941.stm.
13 https://www.dignityindying.org.uk/story/diane-pretty/.
14 https://www.dignityindying.org.uk/story/john-close/.
15 https://www.mercurynews.com/2017/10/01/right-to-die-in-california-the-last-days-of-jil-finnegan/.
16 https://www.youtube.com/watch?v=PnaZa1P69cY&t=134s.
17 https://www.mercurynews.com/2017/10/01/right-to-die-in-california-the-last-days-of-jil-finnegan/.
18 https://features.dignityindying.org.uk/sandy-briden/.
19 https://www.bbc.co.uk/news/world-europe-44069885.
20 https://www.theguardian.com/australia-news/2018/apr/30/david-goodall-australia-oldest-scientist-to-end-own-life-in-switzerland.

References

Armstrong, M. J., Alliance, S., Taylor, A., Corsentino, P., & Galvin, J. E. (2019). End-of-life experiences in dementia with Lewy bodies: Qualitative interviews with former caregivers. *PloS one*, *14*(5), e0217039.

Beauchamp, T. L. (2006). The right to die as the triumph of autonomy. *Journal of Medicine and Philosophy*, *31*(6), 643–654.

Black, I. (2021). A pro tanto moral case for assisted death. In S. Westwood (ed) *Death rights: Regulating the ending of life*. Abingdon: Routledge. Chapter 7.

Busscher, D. (2015). Linking assisted suicide and abortion: Life, death, and choice. *Elder Law Journal*, *23*, 123.

Callahan, S. (2015). III. A feminist case against self-determined dying in assisted suicide and euthanasia. *Feminism & Psychology*, *25*(1), 109–112.

Cavanaugh, T. A. (2016). Dignity, pet-euthanasia and person euthanasia. In J. Mizzoni (ed) *G.E.M. Anscombe and human dignity*, 117–142. Aston, PA: Neumann University Press.

Cholbi, M., & Varelius, J. (Eds.). (2015). Introduction. In M. Cholbi and J. Varelius (eds) *New directions in the ethics of assisted suicide and euthanasia* (Vol. 64). New York: Springer.

Coggon, J. (2006). Could the right to die with dignity represent a new right to die in English law? *Medical Law Review*, *14*(2), 219–237.

Coleman, D. (2010). Assisted suicide laws create discriminatory double standard for who gets suicide prevention and who gets suicide assistance: Not dead yet responds to autonomy, Inc. *Disability and Health Journal*, *3*(1), 39–50.

Crown Prosecution Service (CPS) (2014). *Suicide: Policy for Prosecutors in Respect of Cases of Encouraging or Assisting Suicide. Legal Guidance, Violent crime*. Issued by The Director of Public Prosecutions, February 2010, updated October 2014, https://www.cps.gov.uk/legal-guidance/suicide-policy-prosecutors-respect-cases-encouraging-or-assisting-suicide

Crown Prosecution Service (CPS) (2020). *Assisted Suicide*. https://www.cps.gov.uk/legal-guidance/suicide-policy-prosecutors-respect-cases-encouraging-or-assisting-suicide

Davis, D. S. (2015). VII. Feminism and suicide in the face of dementia. *Feminism & Psychology*, *25*(1), 131–136.

Deuter, K., Procter, N., Evans, D., & Jaworski, K. (2016). Suicide in older people: Revisioning new approaches. *International Journal of Mental Health Nursing*, *25*(2), 144–150.

Fenwick, M., Siems, M., & Wrbka, S. (Eds.). (2017). *The shifting meaning of legal certainty in comparative and transnational law*. London: Bloomsbury Publishing.

Fletcher, R., Fox, M., & McCandless, J. (2008). Legal embodiment: Analysing the body of healthcare law. *Medical Law Review, 16*(3): 321–345.

Fukuzawa, R. K., & Kondo, K. T. (2017). A holistic view from birth to the end of life: End-of-life doulas and new developments in end-of-life care in the West. *International Journal of Palliative Nursing, 23*(12), 612–619.

Gamondi, C., Fusi-Schmidhauser, T., Oriani, A., Payne, S., & Preston, N. (2019). Family members' experiences of assisted dying: A systematic literature review with thematic synthesis. *Palliative Medicine, 33*(8), 1091–1105.

Gandsman, A. (2021). Laughing to death: Necrosocialities and 'right-to-die' activism. In S. Westwood (ed) *Death rights: Regulating the ending of life*. Abingdon: Routledge. Chapter 11.

Gillett, G. (2019). Advance decisions in dementia: When the past conflicts with the present. *Journal of Medical Ethics, 45*(3), 204–208.

Harding, R. (2017). *Duties to care: Dementia, relationality and law*. Cambridge: Cambridge University Press.

Hendry, M., Pasterfield, D., Lewis, R., Carter, B., Hodgson, D., & Wilkinson, C. (2013). Why do we want the right to die? A systematic review of the international literature on the views of patients, carers and the public on assisted dying. *Palliative Medicine, 27*(1), 13–26.

Huxtable, R. (2007). *Euthanasia, ethics and the law: From conflict to compromise*. Abingdon: Routledge.

Huxtable, R. (2021). Assisted dying, ethics and the law: For, against, or somewhere in between? In S. Westwood (ed) *Death rights: Regulating the ending of life*. Abingdon: Routledge. Chapter 5.

Kitzinger, C. (2015). I. Feminism and the 'right to die': Editorial introduction to the special feature. *Feminism & Psychology, 25*(1), 101–104.

Lewis, P. (2021). Legal change on assisted dying. In S. Westwood (ed) *Death rights: Regulating the ending of life*. Abingdon: Routledge. Chapter 2.

Mackenzie, C. (1992). Abortion and embodiment. *Australasian Journal of Philosophy, 70*(2), 136–155.

Magelssen, M., Le, N. Q., & Supphellen, M. (2019). Secularity, abortion, assisted dying and the future of conscientious objection: Modelling the relationship between attitudes. *BMC Medical Ethics, 20*(1), 65.

Mullock, A., & Ost, S. (2011). Pushing the boundaries of lawful assisted dying in the Netherlands? Existential suffering and lay assistance. *European Journal of Health Law, 18*(2), 163–189.

Ost, S. (2010). The de-medicalisation of assisted dying: Is a less medicalised model the way forward?. *Medical Law Review, 18*(4), 497–540.

Rawlings, D., Tieman, J., Miller-Lewis, L., & Swetenham, K. (2019). What role do death doulas play in end-of-life care? A systematic review. *Health & Social Care in the Community, 27*(3), e82–e94.

Richards, N. (2017). Old age rational suicide. *Sociology Compass, 11*(3), e12456.

Riddle, C. A. (2017). Assisted dying & disability. *Bioethics, 31*(6), 484–489.

Ruck Keene, A. (2021). Contesting death rights: Reflections from the courtroom. In S. Westwood (ed) *Death rights: Regulating the ending of life*. Abingdon: Routledge. Chapter 3.

Savulescu, J., & Schuklenk, U. (2017). Doctors have no right to refuse medical assistance in dying, abortion or contraception. *Bioethics, 31*(3), 162–170.

Shakespeare, T. (2013). *Disability rights and wrongs revisited*. Abingdon: Routledge.
Sheldon, S. (2013). *Beyond control: Medical power and abortion law*. London: Pluto Press.
Shildrick, M. (2015). XI. Death, debility and disability. *Feminism & Psychology*, *25*(1), 155–160.
Sleeman, K., & Chalmers, I. (2019). Assisted dying: Restricting access to people with fewer than six months to live is discriminatory. *British Medical Journal*, *367*, l6093.
Smith, R., Blazeby, J., Bleakley, T., Clark, J., Cong, Y., Durie, R., Finkelstein, E., Gafer, N., Gugliani, S., Horton, R., & Johnson, M. (2018). Lancet commission on the value of death. *The Lancet*, *392*(10155), 1291–1293.
Tierney, T. F. (2010). The governmentality of suicide: Peuchet, Marx, Durkheim, and Foucault. *Journal of Classical Sociology*, *10*(4): 357–389.
van Wijngaarden, E. (2021). Choosing death in anticipation of older age-related suffering: Reflections based on a Dutch study. In S. Westwood (ed) *Death rights: Regulating the ending of life*. Abingdon: Routledge. Chapter 12.
van Wijngaarden, E., Leget, C., & Goossensen, A. (2018). Ethical uneasiness and the need for open-ended reflexivity: The case of research into older people with a wish to die. *International Journal of Social Research Methodology*, *21*(3), 317–331.
Westwood, S. (2017). Older lesbians, gay men and the 'right to die' debate: 'I always keep a lethal dose of something, because I don't want to become an elderly isolated person'. *Social & Legal Studies*, *26*(5), 606–628.
Wicks, E. (2021). Dying with conscience: The potential application of article 9 ECHR to assisted dying. In S. Westwood (ed) *Death rights: Regulating the ending of life*. Abingdon: Routledge. Chapter 9.
Wrigley, A. (2021). Euthanasia as life-extension. In S. Westwood (ed) *Death rights: Regulating the ending of life*. Abingdon: Routledge. Chapter 6.
Young, S. (2021). Understanding rights in the context of a "right to die". In S. Westwood (ed) *Death rights: Regulating the ending of life*. Abingdon: Routledge. Chapter 8.

Index

Note: Page numbers followed by "n" refer to notes.

For Product Safety Concerns and Information please contact our EU representative GPSR@taylorandfrancis.com
Taylor & Francis Verlag GmbH, Kaufingerstraße 24, 80331 München, Germany

www.ingramcontent.com/pod-product-compliance
Lightning Source LLC
LaVergne TN
LVHW021123300926
849160LV00010B/837
* 9 7 8 1 0 3 2 0 7 3 2 9 3 *